Sources of Han Décor

Sources of Han Décor

Foreign Influence on the Han Dynasty Chinese Iconography of Paradise (206 BC-AD 220)

Sophia-Karin Psarras

Archaeopress Publishing Ltd
Summertown Pavilion
18-24 Middle Way
Summertown
Oxford OX2 7LG
www.archaeopress.com

ISBN 978-1-78969-325-6
ISBN 978-1-78969-326-3 (e-Pdf)

Cover image: Yanjiacha (Suide, Shaanxi) stone bas relief. Zhongguo meishu 1988: 67, Pl. 79.

This book is available direct from Archaeopress or from our website www.archaeopress.com

Contents

Abbreviations .... **vii**
Chronologies .... **vii**
Early China vii
Egypt viii
Mesopotamia (Key Dates) ix
Greece (art historical) ix
Chinese Vessel Names .... **x**

Introduction **1**

I: Major Iconographies

Chapter 1 Eastern Zhou Context **11**
Chapter 2 The Animal Master **15**
Chapter 3 Developments Related to the Animal Master **25**
Lesser Deities 25
Man-Animal Combat 27
Human Activity 29
Specific Artistic Conventions 30
Kavaem Khvareno 30
Flying Gallop 31
Parthian Shot 32
Three-Quarter View 33
Chapter 4 Tree of Life **37**
Mountainous Landscapes 42
Chapter 5 Animal Predation **45**
The Bird Head 52

II: Decorative Elements

Chapter 6 Fantastic Elements **57**
Chapter 7 Plant Motifs **61**
Conclusion **75**
Maps **77**
Figures **81**
Selected References **121**
Index **137**

List of Maps and Figures

Map 1: Overview of the Mediterranean through China 77
Map 2: Modern Chinese Provinces 78
Map 3: Selected Chinese Cities 79
Map 4: Selected Scythian and Sarmatian Sites 80

Figure 1. Mawangdui (Changsha Municipality, Hunan) M1 black lacquered coffin 81
Figure 2. Northwestern Iran bronze vase, *c.* 10th-8th centuries BC 82
Figure 3. Cyprus, hematite cylinder seal, *c.* 14th century BC 83
Figure 4. Gaozhuang (Huaiyin Municipality, Jiangsu) M1:114-2 incised bronze fragment 83
Figure 5. Jiagezhuang (Tangshan Municipality, Hebei) M5 copper-inlaid bronze *hu* 84
Figure 6. Mancheng (Hebei) M2:3004 partially-silvered bronze *boshanlu* incense burner 84
Figure 7. Gaozhuang (Huaiyin Municipality, Jiangsu) M1:0137 incised bronze fragment 85
Figure 8. Nanyang (Henan) stamped brick 85
Figure 9. Nimrud carved stone (gypsum alabaster), Neo-Assyrian, *c.* 883-859 BC 86
Figure 10. Liulige (Huixian, Henan) *hu* M59:23 (bronze) 87
Figure 11. Hanjiaqu (Yishui, Shandong) stone bas relief 87
Figure 12. Hejiagou (Suide, Shaanxi) stone bas relief 88
Figure 13. Yanjiacha (Suide, Shaanxi) stone bas relief 89
Figure 14. Xindu (Sichuan) stamped brick 90
Figure 15. Songshan (Jiaxiang, Shandong) stone bas relief 90
Figure 16. Yingzhuang (Nanyang Municipality, Henan) stone bas relief 91
Figure 17. Daodunzi (Tongxin, Ningxia) M10:33 Xiongnu bronze plaque 91
Figure 18. Suide (Shaanxi) stone bas relief 91
Figure 19. Maquan (Xianyang Municipality, Shaanxi) lacquered *lian* toiletries box 92
Figure 20. Greek or Boeotian calyx-krater, red figure terra cotta, *c.* early 4th century BC 93
Figure 21. Pingshuo (Shanxi) 6M50:8 gilded bronze plaque 93
Figure 22. Yangzishan (Chengdu Municipality, Sichuan) M1 stone bas relief 94
Figure 23. Jiunüdun (Suining, Xuzhou Municipality, Jiangsu) stone bas relief 94
Figure 24. Xichagou (Xifeng, Liaoning) Xiongnu bronze plaque 94
Figure 25. Erlanhugou 二蘭虎溝 (Qahar [Chaha'er] Right Rear Banner 察哈爾右翼後旗, Inner Mongolia) Xianbei bronze plaque 95
Figure 26. Liulige (Huixian, Henan) M76:85 bronze *hu* 95
Figure 27. Mancheng (Hebei) M1:2250 gilded bronze harness ornament 95
Figure 28. Yaozhuang (Hanjiang, Yangzhou Municipality, Jiangsu) M101:190 lacquered *lian* with silver fittings and carnelian inlay 96

Figure 29. Qinglongshan (Peixian, Xuzhou Municipality, Jiangsu) stone bas relief..................97
Figure 30. Noyon uul (Batsumber, Tuv [Mongolia]) M6:254 silver plaque..................................97
Figure 31. Western Iran bronze beaker, Iron Age II (*c.* 10th-9th centuries BC) 98
Figure 32. Dyrestuj (Burjatija [Russia]) bronze plaque 98
Figure 33. Unprovenanced ("Ordos") Xiongnu bronze plaque..99
Figure 34. Shuihudi (Yunmeng, Hubei) M47:93 carved wood comb 99
Figure 35. Jiawang (Tongshan, Xuzhou Municipality, Jiangsu) stone bas relief 99
Figure 36. Aluchaideng (Hanggin Banner, Inner Mongolia) Xiongnu gold plaque 100
Figure 37. Sanlidun (Lianshui, Jiangsu) gold garment hook 100
Figure 38. Shaogou (Luoyang Municipality, Henan) M1028A:14 earthenware model well....101
Figure 39. Zhangxu (Suining, Xuzhou Municipality, Jiangsu) stone bas relief 102
Figure 40. Luoyang (Henan) hollow brick 103
Figure 41. Aluchaideng (Hanggin Banner, Inner Mongolia) Xiongnu gold plaque, inlaid with turquoise and red stone..103
Figure 42. Thracian silver goblet, *c.* 4th century BC 104
Figure 43. Mancheng (Hebei) M2:3032 gilded bronze double cup stand, inlaid with turquoise, jade rings 105
Figure 44. Shilipu (Xuzhou Municipality, Jiangsu) stone bas relief 105
Figure 45. Tomb of Lord Feng or his consort (Tanghe [Nanyang Municipality, Henan]) stone bas relief...105
Figure 46. Greek situla, South Italian, Apulian, attributed to the Lycurgus Painter; red figure terracotta, *c.* 360-340 BC 106
Figure 47. Pazyryk kurgan 2 copper plaque 107
Figure 48. Aluchaideng (Hanggin Banner, Inner Mongolia) Xiongnu gold headdress 107
Figure 49. Pazyryk kurgan 2 torque, gilded wood and horn on a copper ring (reconstruction). 108
Figure 50. Left Wu Family Shrine (Jiaxiang, Shandong), stone 2 (bas relief) 108
Figure 51. Pazyryk kurgan 1 leather appliqués on a felt saddle blanket 108
Figure 52. Shuanggou (Suining, Xuzhou Municipality, Jiangsu) stone bas relief 108
Figure 53. Taishang (Tongshan, Xuzhou Municipality, Jiangsu) stone bas relief 109
Figure 54. Daodunzi (Tongxin, Ningxia) M19:9 gilded bronze plaque......................................109
Figure 55. Pad' Sudži (Burjatija) bronze appliqué..109
Figure 56. Archaic Greek or Cretan black-figured terracotta hydria (water jar), attributed to the Eagle Painter, *c.* 520-510 BC 110
Figure 57. Zhengzhou (Henan) hollow brick 111
Figure 58. Zengjiabao (Chengdu Municipality, Sichuan) M1 stone bas relief 111
Figure 59. Zhengzhou (Henan) stamped brick 112
Figure 60. Noyon uul (Batsumber, Tuv [Mongolia]) M25:22 bronze fitting.............................112
Figure 61. Stag rhyton, gilded silver inlaid with garnet and glass, inscribed in Aramaic (or Persian?); Near Eastern (Parthian), *c.* 50 BC - AD 50 113

Figure 62. Xiaotianxi (Fuling, Sichuan) M3:23 silver-inlaid bronze, *c.* Middle-Late Warring States 114
Figure 63. Mashan (Jiangling, Jingzhou Municipality, Hubei) M1, N2, embroidered silk......115
Figure 64. Mashan (Jiangling, Jingzhou Municipality, Hubei) M1, N7, embroidered silk......116
Figure 65. Mashan (Jiangling, Jingzhou Municipality, Hubei) M1, N9, embroidered silk......117
Figure 66. Dahuting (Mixian, Henan) M2 painted ceiling......117
Figure 67. Wu family Front shrine (Jiaxiang, Shandong) stone bas relief......118
Figure 68. Jiunüdun (Suining, Xuzhou Municipality, Jiangsu) stone bas relief......118
Figure 69. Ionian (East Greek) terracotta oinochoe, *c.* 625 BC......119

Abbreviations

BMFEA Bulletin of the Museum of Far Eastern Antiquities

KG Kaogu 考古

KGXB Kaogu xuebao 考古學報

KGXJK Kaoguxue jikan 考古學集刊

KGYWW Kaogu yu wenwu 考古與文物

M *mu* 墓 / *mogila* tomb

NMGWWKG Neimenggu wenwu kaogu 內蒙古文物考古

SJ Sima Qian 司馬遷. *Shiji* 史記. Beijing: Zhonghua shuju, 1982.

WW Wenwu 文物

WWZLCK Wenwu ziliao congkan 文物资料丛刊

Chronologies

Early China

Late Shang: *c.* 14th-mid-eleventh centuries BC

Western Zhou: *c.* 1050/1040-772 BC

- Early Western Zhou: *c.* 1050/1040-951 BC
- Middle Western Zhou: *c.* 950-851 BC
- Late Western Zhou: *c.* 850-772 BC

Eastern Zhou: *c.* 771-222 BC

- Springs and Autumns: *c.* 771-476 BC
  - Early Springs and Autumns: *c.* 771-671 BC
  - Middle Springs and Autumns: *c.* 670-571 BC
  - Late Springs and Autumns: *c.* 570-476 BC
- Warring States: *c.* 475-222 BC
  - Early Warring States: *c.* 475-391 BC
  - Middle Warring States: *c.* 390-311 BC
  - Late Warring States: *c.* 310-222 BC

Qin: 221-207 BC

Han: 206 BC-AD 220

Western Han: 206 BC-AD 8

Early[1] Western Han: *c.* 206-134 BC

Middle Western Han: *c.* 134-62 BC

Late Western Han: *c.* 62 BC-8 AD

Wang Mang: AD 9-24

Eastern Han: AD 25-220

Early Eastern Han: *c.* 25-89 AD

Middle Eastern Han: *c.* 90-154 AD

Late Eastern Han: *c.* 155-220 AD

Egypt[2]

Predynastic: prior to *c.* 3100 BC

Early Dynastic (Dynasties 1-2): *c.* 3100-2686 BC

Old Kingdom (Dynasties 3-6): *c.* 2649-2150 BC

First Intermediate Period (Dynasties 7-11 [partial]): *c.* 2150-2030 BC

Middle Kingdom (Dynasties 11 [partial]-13): *c.* 2030-1640 BC

Second Intermediate Period (Dynasties 14-16): *c.* 1640-1550 BC

New Kingdom (Dynasties 17-19): *c.* 1550-1070 BC

Third Intermediate Period (Dynasties 19-24): *c.* 1070-712 BC

Late Period (Kushite Period, Dynasty 25; Saite Period, Dynasty 26; Persian Period, Dynasty 27; assorted, Dynasties 28-30): *c.* 712-332 BC

Ptolemaic Period: *c.* 332-30 BC

Roman Rule: *c.* 30 BC-395 AD

[1] It is more common to divide according to the reigns of emperors. For the present discussion, however, the identity of the emperor is not relevant; I have therefore divided time into approximately equal periods.

[2] Early dates are uncertain and differ according to author. Here, based primarily on the timeline from the University College London, Egyptian Chronology (dated 2000) <https://www.ucl.ac.uk/museums-static/digitalegypt/chronology/index.html>; a series of essays, all in *Heilbrunn Timeline of Art History* (New York: The Metropolitan Museum of Art, 2000–): C. H. Roehrig, Egypt in the Old Kingdom (ca. 2649–2150 B.C.), <https://www.metmuseum.org/toah/hd/oking/hd_oking.htm> (dated October 2000); Roehrig, Egypt in the Middle Kingdom (2030–1640 B.C.), <https://www.metmuseum.org/toah/hd/mking/hd_mking.htm> (dated October 2000); J. Allen and M. Hill, Egypt in the Late Period (ca. 712–332 B.C.), <https://www.metmuseum.org/toah/hd/lapd/hd_lapd.htm> (dated October 2004); M. Hill, Egypt in the Ptolemaic Period, <https://www.metmuseum.org/toah/hd/ptol/hd_ptol.htm> (dated October 2016). All accessed June 2017.

Mesopotamia (Key Dates)[3]

Ur Royal Cemetery (Sumer): *c.* 2600-2100 BC (City-state occupied from *c.* 5500-400 BC[4])

Old Assyrian Period: *c.* 1813-1781 BC

Middle Assyrian Period: *c.* 1365-1056 BC

Neo-Assyrian Period: *c.* 883-609 BC

Achaemenid: *c.* 559/550-330 BC

Greece (art historical)[5]

Geometric Period: *c.* 900-700 BC

Archaic: *c.* 700-480 BC

Classical: *c.* 480-323 BC

Hellenistic: *c.* 323-31 BC

[3] A useful outline is provided by the Department of Ancient Near Eastern Art, List of Rulers of Mesopotamia, *Heilbrunn Timeline of Art History* (New York: The Metropolitan Museum of Art, 2000), <https://www.metmuseum.org/toah/hd/meru/hd_meru.htm> (dated October 2004), accessed June 2017. Again, reign dates are uncertain.

[4] University of Pennsylvania Museum of Archaeology and Anthropology, Iraq's Ancient Past: Rediscovering Ur's Royal Cemetery, <https://www.penn.museum/sites/iraq/?page_id=24>, accessed June 2017.

[5] Ancient Greece, 1000 B.C.–1 A.D., *Heilbrunn Timeline of Art History* (New York: The Metropolitan Museum of Art, 2000–), <https://www.metmuseum.org/toah/ht/?period=04&region=eusb> (dated October 2000), accessed June 2017.

Chinese Vessel Names[6]

Bianhu 扁壺 flat *hu*, similar in form to a circular flask

Ding 鼎 round-bodied tripod

Dui 敦 bowl-shaped vessel for serving grain

Dou 豆 a footed cup-like form with a wide mouth and shallow body, used for serving food

Fanghu 方壺 a *hu* with a body square in cross-section

Fou 缶 a pot to contain alcohol, similar to a *lei*

Guan 罐 (generic) pot (large body, little or no neck)

Gui 簋 pot-shaped vessel for serving grain

He 盒 box

He 盉 a teapot-like vessel for pouring alcohol

Hu 壺 vase-like form (relatively small body and long neck), commonly for storage of liquid

Jia 斝 elongated pouring vessel, usually without a spout (typically, with two knobbed stem-like attachments on the rim)

Lei 罍 typically, a broad-bodied vessel with a relatively narrow mouth, lidded, for the storage of alcohol

Pan 盤 platter/basin

Xuan 鋗 basin

Yan 甗 steamer

You 卣 a lidded container for alcohol

Yu 盂 a basin or broad pot

Zhong 鍾 vase (broader belly than the *hu*)

Zun 尊 of various forms, but often a broad, flaring-mouthed vessel for alcohol; sometimes identified as for heating alcohol

Zun-pan 尊盤 a *zun* set inside a basin

[6] Various guides are available in other works; see also Jean Lefeuvre, Récipients de bronze, d'après les inscriptions sur os et sur bronze, <chinesereferenceshelf.brillonline.com/grand-ricci/files/recipients-bronze.pdf>, accessed June 2017.

Introduction

The Han 漢 dynasty (206 BC-AD 220) stands at an historical juncture as the first unified dynasty to withstand succession between generations of rulers. Culturally poised between the Bronze Age (broadly, *c.* 1600-221 BC) and what I have termed the Age of Ceramics, it represents an era of transformation and innovation, building to varying extents on the developments of dynastic Qin 秦 (221-206 BC) and the Warring States (*c.* 475-221 BC). The relationship between Han social and political organization to Qin practices, retraceable through the comparison of received and excavated texts, has been recognized.[1] Much less has been done to examine Han art in an historical context. This may, in part, be due to the paucity of obvious links with earlier Chinese tradition. The few Eastern Zhou (*c.* 771-221 BC) motifs that may readily be identified (principally the meander/tendril or 'cloud' pattern), although widely used during the Han (cf., Figures 1, 13, 28), constitute only a relatively minor aspect of Han art as a whole. Dynastic Qin offers evidence important for an understanding of the transition away from Bronze Age norms, a process continued during the Han, but this evidence is highly fragmentary. In this context, Han art gives the impression of emerging largely ex nihilo. This is true in terms of the dominant media (clay and stone, rather than bronze), the dominant type of objects chosen for the most innovative and complex decoration (walls, rather than vessels), and especially the dominant subject matter: human activity and representations of deities, rather than largely abstract design (with some animal motifs).

Han use of bronze for utilitarian vessels[2] or luxury items,[3] rather than the bronze ritual vessels central in pre-imperial Chinese society to political legitimation and social status, is the expected result of social changes largely completed before the Han. Accordingly, the end of the social dominance of the bronze ritual vessel led to other expressions of affluence, as well as freeing décor from the limits of vessel tradition.[4] The strength of later Bronze Age vessel norms nonetheless persists throughout the Han in terms of the basic categories of vessel forms (*hu* 壺 vases and *ding* 鼎 tripods) and the basic compositional tenets of décor (horizontal banding around the body of the vessel – visible on Figure 10 – or the application of *pushou* 鋪首 animal masks on the side of vessels). At the same time, Han artisans, unlike their predecessors, clearly focused on the development of ceramic vessel production, with innovation in form, thickness

[1] E.g., Loewe 2010.

[2] Absent an inscription, it is difficult to ascertain the purpose for which the vessels found in Han graves were made. I assume that undecorated pots whose shapes are unrelated to earlier ritual ware are simply utilitarian. In some cases, the bottom of excavated pots (both bronze and earthenware) is marked with soot, indicating that they were used, presumably more than once. This suggests to me that such pieces were intended for practical purposes, rather than for ritual connected with the burial in which they were found. See Psarras 2015: 34, 76-77; see also Lin (ed.) 2012: 316-317, No. 190.

[3] As in examples from Mancheng 滿城 (Hebei): Zhongguo shehui kexueyuan 1980, Vol. 1: 40-41, Figs 23-24; Vol. 2: Col. Pl. 5, M1:5014, gold- and silver-inlaid bronze *hu*; Vol. 1: 44, Fig. 26, M1:5015, gold- and silver-inlaid bronze *hu*; Vol. 1: 47, Fig. 29, M1:5018, matching M1:5015.

[4] For the dominance of ritual bronzes on vessel forms and décors, see Falkenhausen 2006. Little early data in perishable media has survived, but examples of the application of bronze décor to other types of objects in other media include: Houjiazhuang 侯家莊 (Anyang 安陽 Municipality, Henan) HPKM1001 (*c.* 13th-12th centuries BC) and Lijiazui 李家嘴 (Panlongcheng 盤龍城, [Huangpi 黄陂, Wuhan 武漢 Municipality, Hubei]) M2 (*c.* 16th-14th centuries BC), both wood coffins (Beijing 1979: Pl. 27, Lijiazui M2 coffin imprint shown, top; comparative bronze décor from M1, bottom]; Pl. 28, Houjiazhuang); Shangcunling 上村嶺 (Sanmenxia 三門峽 Municipality, Henan) M2118 and 2119 coffin banners, *c.* 9th-early 8th centuries BC (Henan 1999b, Vol. 2: Col. Pl. 43, M2118; Col. Pl. 44, M2119); Xiadu 下都 (Yi 易 xian 縣, Hebei: *inter alia*, Hebei 1996, Vol. 2: Pl. 12-14, Laoyemiaotai 老爺廟臺 habitation site V, *c.* 4th century BC; Pl. 16:4-6, Laoyemiaotai habitation site V, *c.* 3rd century BC; Pl. 17:3-4, Laoyemiaotai habitation site 25, *c.* 4th century BC).

of the walls, and surface treatment (such as glazes).[5] More importantly, vessel décor no longer dominated the décor of objects in other media.

The most obvious Han innovation – often taken as defining Han art – is the development of figural or narrative art, most frequently known to us from tomb murals executed as stone bas reliefs and stamped bricks (paintings are more rare). Attempts to understand the development of this aspect of Han art are complicated not only by the paucity of earlier figural elements, but by the overwhelming association of composition and context: so strong is the association of Han narrative art and the tomb that the subject matter, as well as the use of murals, is often assumed to be ritual in character.[6] Subject matter and the context in which it is displayed thus become largely inseparable. In this way, despite obvious differences in context and media, a certain equivalence between the Bronze Age ritual vessel and the Han tomb mural tends to emerge. Han figural or narrative art thus tends to be viewed as a sociological concern, emphasizing the meaning of the images (or the reason they were used[7]), rather than their derivation.[8] This pursuit in turn largely depends on connecting images to passages in transmitted texts, which, in fact, offer remarkably little relevant information. Even the mythological geography of the *Shanhaijing* 山海經 is difficult to place in context;[9] certainly, it does not furnish a description of religious beliefs. This dearth of objective points of reference for Han dynasty interpretations of images applies all the more so to the Eastern Zhou era – and to the cultures beyond China through whom the images were transmitted. Furthermore, although connected at various stages in their history and combined into a harmonious whole by the Han, we have no reason a priori to view the images as a single, set unit throughout their history, in all of the cultures where variants appear. Their likely transmission to China through multiple cultures suggests the reverse. It would therefore be a mistake to interpret their diffusion as paralleling that of Buddhism, whose adoption in China exceeds the scope of the present work. Here, I propose to examine only questions surrounding the emergence of these images in China, a problem that can only be addressed archaeologically, leaving analysis of image meaning to other scholars. Indeed, archaeologically-based conclusions may ultimately modify the way the transmission and further development of image meaning will be seen.

In these terms, the Han tomb mural can be broken down into three components: context (the tomb), form (the mural), and subject matter. Each of these three components has a separate

[5] In ceramics, this is particularly visible in broad experimentation with surface treatment, as well as with the production of highly-finished variants of standard forms and experimentation with elaborate new structures, such as the multi-*guan* 罐 pot (miniature pots attached to the main vessel). Examples of highly-finished forms, fine clay bodies, or fine glazes include: Zhongguo taoci 2000: Pl. 123, Shaoxing 紹興 (Jiangxi), stoneware/porcelain (*ci* 瓷) *hu* or *zhong* 鍾; Pl. 141, Shanghai Museum; 142, Zaijiadun 宰家墩 (Hanjiang 邗江, Yangzhou 揚州 Municipality, Jiangsu); Pl. 144, Shangyu 上虞 (Zhejiang) Cultural Relics Management Committee, stoneware/porcelain, light-colored glaze. Examples of multi-*guan* pots include Zhongguo taoci 2000: Pl. 133, Shengzhou 嵊州 Municipality (Zhejiang) Cultural Relics Management Station; Pl. 134, Wangjiatang 王家塘 (Changzhou 常州 Municipality, Jiangsu); Pl. 135, Shahe 沙河 (Yin 鄞 xian, Zhejiang); Pl. 136, Fenghuang 鳳凰 (Xiaoshan 蕭山 Municipality, Zhejiang), heavy, deep chocolate glaze; Pl. 137, Ma'anshan 馬鞍山 (Huangyan 黃巖 Municipality, Zhejiang), with double-layered glaze: dripped dark color over a light base; Pl. 138, Shangyu (Zhejiang) Cultural Relics Management Station.

[6] An assumption visible, for instance, in Wang 2011, 2012. A substantial body of material is readily available on the meaning of Han art, including recent volumes which further provide extensive references (Wu Hung 1989, C. Y. Liu, M. Nylan, A. Barbieri-Low, *et al.* 2005., C. Y. Liu, M. Loewe, Zheng Yan, L. Thompson, *et al.* 2008).

[7] Powers 1991 suggests an association between political views and use of specific images; however, the images he cites may be found elsewhere in China, executed in different styles. For discussion, see Psarras 2015: 34-59.

[8] Hsing I-tien 2005 is a fine exception; Nickel 2012, 2013, in general terms.

[9] For annotations and discussion, see Mathieu 1983.

derivation. Although in this research I shall focus on elements of subject matter – specifically, on individual images that recur frequently in different compositions, a brief introduction to the problems of context and form helps to clarify the narrower analysis.

While the use of murals in tombs became popular during the Han, fragmentary evidence from the excavations of Qin palaces at Xianyang 咸陽 (Shaanxi)[10] indicates that murals (paintings and stamped bricks) were used at least during the dynastic Qin in living architecture. Although they provide only limited information about composition, the Qin fragments provide a prototype for the mural as a form, as well as for the use of narrative imagery, to which we will return. We have no evidence as to the possible use of murals in the pre-imperial period; in contrast, narrative scenes applied to other substrates do occasionally occur. Further, although again we lack evidence, the Qin fragments, which include figural décor, suggest that murals were also featured in Han dynasty palaces and (by extension) aristocratic residences. Indeed, some use of ornamented brick or stone in Han living architecture is confirmed by the stamped brick flooring in the Han city at Chongan 崇安 (Fujian),[11] with a geometric décor closely related to Bronze Age ornamental patterns.

The earliest Han murals now known are the figural paintings on silk which lined the wood box burial chamber of Mawangdui 馬王堆 (Changsha 長沙, Hunan) M3 (168 BC).[12] Given the fragility of the fabric and the pigments used in painting, such work may not have survived in other tombs. In addition, the high social rank of the deceased in Mawangdui M3, believed to be a son of the Marquis of Dai 軑(Mawangdui M1), raises the question of how widely such paintings may have been distributed in Han society. The widespread adoption of tomb murals attested later in the archaeological record appears to result from a decision to use more durable materials for such décor. This seems to have resulted in a broader range of quality, with documented examples of stones and bricks with a décor ranging from simply-drawn, single motifs (geometric or figural) to complex scenes sustained over several panels (read as representations of paradise or the residence of the deceased – or the two combined). Such variation suggests the availability of artisans of differing technical abilities, presumably at differing levels of cost. Although it is difficult to assess the social status of most decorated tombs (many, if not most, have been thoroughly robbed), the sheer number of murals known today leads me to conclude that such work must have become accessible to a broader cross-section of society than paintings on silk like those in Mawangdui M3.

The production of stone and brick murals seems to have emerged in connection with the development during the Han of what I have called architectonic tombs in stone and brick, a distinctive form approximating in many respects a miniaturized house. Although so strongly identified with the Han, architectonic tombs coexisted with the flat-topped, compartmented wood box tombs characteristic of Bronze Age aristocratic burials not only in the early Western, but through the early Eastern Han (*c.* late 3rd century BC-2nd century AD).[13] They vary in size and in complexity of layout (the number of rooms, the use of connecting hallways), as well as in the treatment of the roof. If the body of these tombs may be related to Han living architecture, this architecture, as we understand it primarily from the models and drawings of buildings

[10] Ma Jianxi 1990; Shaanxi 2004.
[11] Fujian 1990: 355, Fig. 13, building 1 (T7[3]:31).
[12] Zhang Zhenglang, Fu Juyou, and Chen Songchang 1992: 26-34.
[13] For a discussion of Han tomb structures, see Psarras 2015. For steppe influence on the Han aristocratic use of the burial mound, see Rawson 1999.

included in many tombs, offers no parallel for the use of the curved archways, vaulting, and domes characteristic of the architectonic tomb. Even more than Han art, the architectonic tomb seems a new invention, without Chinese precedent. This lack of precedent suggests to me the self-conscious development of new structures; the apparent lack of Chinese prototype for the roofing, in particular, convinces me that these tombs reflect the selective assimilation of foreign influence. The development of Han art may have been less self-conscious, but the role of foreign influence is at least equally significant and more readily traceable.

Eastern Zhou yields scattered examples of narrative or figural décor: hunting and other animal scenes featuring humanoid – rather than human – creatures (as in Figures 4, 5, 7, 10), people engaged in presumably ritual activities against an architectural background, animals interacting with other animals, and, even more rarely, a host of floral motifs (primarily represented on embroidered silks from Mashan 馬山 [Jiangling 江陵, Jingzhou 荆州 Municipality, Hubei][14]; see Figures 63, 64, 65). All of these constitute a sharp, intrusive departure from the norms of Chinese Bronze Age ornamentation. Direct carryover into the Han appears largely limited to more narrative depiction of animals (especially animal predation – as in Figures 6, 32, 38, in which a feline or other animal predator attacks a hooved animal such as a goat or horse) and, rarely, of humanoid figures assumed from their attributes (thunderbolts, for example) to represent deities (cf., Figure 1). The latter appear in an Eastern Zhou style in a mural fragment from the Qin dynasty palace site (Xianyang Municipality, Shaanxi) and again on a silk manuscript Mawangdui (Changsha Municipality, Hunan) M3.[15]

The animal-based images have been widely recognized as steppe-derived;[16] the floral motifs have, as far as I know, not attracted scholarly attention. No convincing origin has been proposed for the other elements. Close examination of Eastern Zhou figural work does, in fact, yield connections with Han narrative art. How this is so becomes evident only when both Eastern Zhou and Han art are broken down into discrete compositional elements that may be seen to have been used repeatedly in different contexts. As in the problem of identifying Eastern Zhou narrative elements in Han art, the question of the origin of these elements may be further obscured by the clearly Chinese context in which they are sometimes placed: in the depictions of people, for instance, the garments worn and the buildings shown are all identifiable as Chinese by comparison to depictions and three-dimensional models found in Eastern Zhou and Han tombs.[17] It is important, however, not to confuse the Chinese context applied to the scenes with the origin of specific components or, indeed, the composition as a whole.

---

[14] Hubei 1985.

[15] Shaanxi 2004: 220, Fig. 201, Qin palace find; Zhang Zhenglang, Fu Juyou, and Chen Songchang 1992: 35, Mawangdui (Changsha Municipality, Hunan).

[16] As recognized by Institute of Archaeology of Shanxi Province 1996: 16-17, 83-84, which also acknowledges in passing the possibility of iconographic influence from Egypt, the Near East, and Central Asia. Weber 1968 reviews then-available Eastern Zhou material, minimizing the potential for foreign influence. Bunker 1983-1985 and Jacobson 1988, for example, reprise aspects of the question of sino-steppe exchange. For steppe influence on the Han, including art, see Pirazzoli-t'Serstevens 1994, 2008; Rawson 2012.

[17] For three-dimensional models, for the Warring States, see Hebei 1996, Vol. 2: Col. Pl. 51, find from the Xiadu site, state of Yan 燕 (Yixian, Hebei), 64G:043, bronze figure; Col. Pl. 52-53, Xiadu find 67DG:0160, bronze fittings in the form of buildings; for the Han, see Hong Kong 2015: 82, Mawangdui (Changsha Municipality, Hunan) M1, painted wood figures; 83-85, Yangling 陽陵 site (Xianyang Municipality, Shaanxi), unnumbered tomb, earthenware figures with engobe décor; 102-103, Daiwangxiang 待王鄉 (Jiaozuo 焦作 Municipality, Henan), earthenware architectural model with engobe décor; 104, Hongqiling 紅旗嶺 (Hepu 合浦, Guangxi) M2, earthenware model house; 105, Tielu New Village 鐵路新村 (Guigang 貴港 Municipality, Guangxi) M3, earthenware model residence; 125, Mawangdui (Changsha Municipality, Hunan) M1, painted wood figures.

The most important of these elements are animal predation, typically a feline attacking a hooved animal (Figure 32); the animal master, a humanoid creature flanked or surrounded by animals (Figure 3); and the tree of life, a tree or tree-like shape, likewise flanked or surrounded by animals (Figure 25). In addition, a substantial number of floral or vegetal motifs also recur. Together, these form the core of one of the most fundamental of Han iconographies: the depiction of paradise. Although Chinese prototypes are lacking, these image components are readily recognizable in the context of the ancient Near East, Egypt, and the Mediterranean, as early as the 3rd millennium BC, followed later by the steppe. In these regions, the animal master, tree of life, and animal predation serve as central iconographies, remaining in use over millennia, recast in different ways, with different meanings attached at various times. In Han hands, these motifs again assume central iconographic importance, with a single image often being adapted in numerous ways: the animal master becomes not only the Queen Mother of the West (*xi wang mu* 西王母), sovereign deity of the western paradise, but simultaneously her consort, the King Father of the East (*dong wang gong* 東王公)[18] (Figure 14), as well as the various genii (to use the Western term) that inhabit the meanders of the Mawangdui (Changsha Municipality, Hunan) M1 black lacquered (outer) coffin[19] (Figure 1) and the Mancheng (Hebei) M1:5182 gilded bronze *boshanlu* 博山爐 mountain-shaped incense burner.[20] Thus, even though these creatures are not identical in Chinese terms, all represent adaptations of the image of the animal master. The tree of life, in turn, becomes, in sculptural form, the branching 'money trees';[21] while animal predation (together with related animal images) becomes the subordinate of both the animal master and the tree of life.

To these central elements, Han artisans add a variety of motifs – primarily animal and plant forms – which, outside of China, occupy a more purely ornamental status. Some are as old and as widely-adopted in the ancient world outside of China as the animal master; others emerged in the Hellenistic world (*c.* 323-31 BC). (Steppe art rarely makes use of floral forms.) Some, again like the animal master, first appear in Chinese work during the Eastern Zhou, but only rarely, becoming widespread during the Han. Indeed, Han development of these décors suggests that foreign motifs first adopted by Eastern Zhou artisans may well have been subsequently reintroduced, perhaps repeatedly. In this context, it is therefore likely that Chinese contact with foreign cultures, over an extended period and extended distances, was the norm, not the exception.

International contact remains little studied in the context of Bronze Age and early imperial China, apart from the advent of Buddhism and obviously-foreign imports, neither of which will be examined here.[22] In contrast, international exchange of various kinds has been intensely explored in recent decades for the Near East, Mediterranean, and adjacent territories. In these areas, long-distance trade in raw materials has been well documented, as has cultural

[18] As on the Wu 武 family shrines (Jiaxiang 嘉祥, Shandong): Liu Xingzhen and Yue Fengxia 1991: 16, Queen Mother of the West; 32, King Father of the East, both Wu Liang 武梁 shrine; 67, Queen Mother of the West (? image unclear); 55, King Father, both Front shrine; 92-93, King Father, Left shrine.

[19] Zhang Zhenglang, Fu Juyou, and Chen Songchang 1992: 6-11.

[20] Zhongguo shehui kexueyuan 1980, Vol. 1: 64-65, Fig. 44-45. For discussion of the *boshanlu* form, see Rawson 2006, 2012:27-28, as of Achaemenid censer shape.

[21] For multiple images (and a different approach), see Erickson 1995.

[22] Recent studies of note include Zhao Deyun 2016, Hong Quan 2012, Li Ling 2014, Li Jaang 2011, Liu Yang 2013. Such research is more common in the study of early Xinjiang (Li Shuicheng 1999; Wu 2009; Lin Meicun 2015), but of course Xinjiang was not Chinese.

influence transmitted by the flow of objects and artisans. To cite only one example of trade, lapis lazuli, mined in Afghanistan as early as the early 3rd millennium BC, was exported as a raw material to Egypt, Mesopotamia (Iraq-Syria),[23] as well as to Sistan (eastern Iran), where it was processed and subsequently exported in the form of finished goods.[24] The development of the animal master, tree of life, and animal predation, more complex than trade in raw materials or finished goods, covered similar distances. In the more familiar period of the Achaemenid (550-330 BC) and Alexander the Great (reigned 336-323 BC), if not before, Greek and Persian influence permeated northern India and parts of Central Asia, including Bactria (northern Afghanistan, Tajikistan, Uzbekistan),[25] and extended into the Altaian culture of Pazyryk (*c.* 5th-3rd centuries BC)[26] and the Xiongnu 匈奴 culture (*c.* 4th century BC-3rd century AD) of the Far Eastern steppe (primarily Inner Mongolia, Mongolia, south Siberia).[27] I shall not attempt to summarize here the complexities of these exchanges, but refer interested readers to readily-available scholarship.

The extent of these interregional exchanges, both geographically and chronologically, should raise parallel questions for China, all the more so given that territories contiguous to China (as in those of the Xiongnu and, indeed, Xinjiang) were part of the western equation. How can we assume that China did not have significant contact with, for instance, Central Asia long before Zhang Qian's 張騫 assignment (*c.* 138 BC) to the Western Regions (*xiyu* 西域, essentially modern Xinjiang)[28] or with India long before the introduction of Buddhism into China (traditionally, *c.* 1st century AD)? Certainly, Zhang's reports changed Han diplomacy, bringing a more detailed awareness of foreign cultures to the attention of the court (and, thus, the historian), but this change may well have affected primarily the central government and its immediate circles, not what might be termed private experience and private enterprise. Unfortunately, the current archaeological record in[29] and immediately around China rarely allows narrow identification of the paths of intercultural contact. As more field work and more analysis are completed, we may hope that greater precision becomes possible. Nonetheless, the effects of such contact are already clearly visible and awaiting examination.

---

[23] Moorey 1999: 86; see also Francfort 1993.

[24] E.g., at Shahr-i-Sokhta: Weiss (ed.) 1985: 153-154, No. 54 (entry by K. Kohlmeyer). Kohlmeyer also notes Afghanistan as a source of the carnelian exported as a raw material to Mesopotamia, where it was subsequently worked; and on p. 165, No. 71 and 166, No. 72, trade in steatite vessels from southern Iran, where evidence has been found of mines and workshops, with the vessels subsequently traded throughout Iran, Mesopotamia, and the Persian Gulf. All of these examples date to *c.* 2900-2500 BC. Other sources on the subject include (*inter alia*) Aruz, Benzel, and Evans (eds) 2008, Aruz, Graff, and Rakic (eds) 2013, Aruz, Graff, and Takic (eds) 2014, Collon 1987, 1995, Moorey 1999, Muscarella 1988.

[25] Substantial literature is readily available on these questions, including Sideris 2008; Bernard 1987.

[26] Rudenko 1970 emphasizes Achaemenid cultural influence on Pazyryk, primarily as a means of dating the site; cf., Curtis and Tallis 2005: 47-48; Boardman 2000: 200-202. It must be noted that the dating of Pazyryk remains highly controversial, with multiple new runs of radiocarbon analyses: consensus now seems to be *c.* 300-250 BC for the Pazyryk kurgans, with related Altaian sites presumably earlier (Parzinger *et al.* 2008: 15).

[27] For the Xiongnu, see Psarras forthcoming.

[28] Cf., Nickel 2013, especially 28.

[29] Since most extant figural data from the Eastern Zhou often occurs as vessel décor on pieces found in excavated tombs, dating is often possible by inscriptions on the vessel (subject to problems of interpretation) or, more frequently, through cross-dating established by other objects in the same tomb. In contrast, most Han murals occur in tombs which cannot be dated unless the structure has been inscribed with the date of the death or burial of the occupant, or the date of construction of the tomb. Most figured tombs are not date-inscribed and, thoroughly robbed over time, no longer yield objects which may provide a date. Thus, questions such as whether certain regions of China were more open to certain influences cannot now be answered.

The terminology I have adopted is commonly used in Western languages, particularly with reference to early versions of these images, before they became recognizably associated with specific gods, kings, heroes, or landscapes.[30] Such terminology thus allows for identification of the images with minimal cultural association. My use of the term "paradise" is similarly neutral, without reference to any school of thought, simply indicating the place where supernatural or fantastic beings and creatures may be found, whatever their relationship to the human world.

In this work, I offer analysis of the development of key images in Han figural art. Most of these reflect foreign influence, whether received in China during the Eastern Zhou, the Qin, or during the Han. Ideally, this discussion would be fully illustrated to allow easy comparison of relevant objects. Alas, this is impossible, not only because of the volume of illustrations required, but because of the high cost of reproducing images from some museums (the British Museum, for instance, considers scholarly publications to be commercial and therefore not exempt from fees[31]) and publishers (particularly Wenwu). I am grateful to the J. Paul Getty Museum (Malibu, CA) and The Metropolitan Museum of Art (New York), whose open access programs allow reproduction of photographs published online of specified objects in their collections. Research for this article was begun with a Summer Stipend grant from the National Endowment for the Humanities under grant no. FT-40420 (1994), gratefully acknowledged, and continued with the incalculable, unwavering support of my mother, the late Mrs. Mary E. Psarras. My thanks are also due to the editors and reviewers whose generous comments were most helpful as I prepared this manuscript for publication. As always, any errors are naturally my own.

[30] For questions of the meaning of these iconographies in the Near East, cf., Collon 1987; and, in the steppe, cf., Dumézil 1978.

[31] British Museum, terms of use of site images <https://www.britishmuseum.org/about_this_site/terms_of_use/copyright_and_permissions.aspx>, viewed June 2016; no waiver is allowed (personal communication, 14 June 2016).

I: Major Iconographies[32]

[32] See also Psarras 1998-1999 and, for questions surrounding tomb décor, Psarras 2015: 34-59.

Chapter 1

Eastern Zhou Context

It is well understood that, by the time of the Han, the bronze ritual vessel no longer defined Chinese art and society. This social development had repercussions beyond political and ritual reorganization: in the domain of art and material culture, the vessel as an object type was no longer the primary focus of artistic production and bronze was no longer the most important medium,[33] freeing both vessel production and décor in general. In Han décor, the use of geometric pattern preferred throughout much of the Bronze Age was replaced by the figural, developed into an extensive and consistent iconography consisting of human, animal, and hybrid figures, depicted individually and in narrative scenes. Although portions of this imagery, most commonly understood as depicting paradise, appear on a wide range of three-dimensional, as well as flat, objects,[34] the most complete development occurs in the stone and brick mural blocks known from Han architectonic tombs. These murals thus provide the greatest body of evidence for the study of Han narrative art.

In the face of such radical change, it can be difficult to connect Han art to that of the Bronze Age; connection to Qin remains largely impossible, given that dynasty's brief timespan. Nonetheless, we shall see that the changes visible in Han art did not come about as abruptly as it might appear; indeed, even Han narrative art does not represent a complete break with the past. The pre-imperial era remained physically visible to some extent, as some pre-imperial artifacts remained in circulation during the Han, as indicated by their burial in Han tombs; at times, Han artisans imitated Bronze Age vessels (although imitations are difficult to identify solely through published reports).[35] More importantly, significant areas of Han continuity with pre-imperial decorative motifs may be identified. These range from minor geometric motifs to Eastern Zhou examples of figural and narrative décor. As expected, with the exception of floral forms, most of these décors were originally used on bronze vessels. Curiously, the motifs which become most important in Han art are largely peripheral to the Eastern Zhou, where

[33] As an exception, a complex abstract décor characteristic of the Han Far South (that is, primarily Guangdong and Guangxi) appears in its most complicated versions on bronze ware. Variants of the décor applied to ceramic ware are generally less clearly executed and represent only a portion of the compositions known in bronze, indicating that in this case, bronze was the dominant medium. See Psarras 1997.

[34] Zhongguo shehui kexueyuan 1980, Vol. 1: 64-65, Figs 44-45; Vol. 2: Col. Pl. 9, Pl. 30 (Mancheng M1:5182); Erickson 1995, multiple examples (money trees); Zhang Zhenglang, Fu Juyou, and Chen Songchang 1992: 6-11 (Mawangdui M1 coffin).

[35] See Psarras 2015: 87-103; Rawson 1989. Pre-imperial pieces buried in Han tombs include the Late Western Zhou *gui* 簋 in Sandian (Xi'an 西安 Eastern Suburbs, Shaanxi: Zhu Jieyuan and Li Yuzheng 1983:34, Fig. 2) and the Middle Warring States *hu* Mancheng (Hebei) M2:4028 (Zhongguo shehui kexueyuan 1980, Vol. 1:247, Fig. 161). See also Jiangxi 2016: 62-63, Early Western Zhou *you* 卣; 64-65, Early Warring States (published broadly as Eastern Zhou) *fou* 缶, both from the tomb of Liu He 劉賀, Marquis of Haihun 海昏 (Xinjian 新建 [Nanchang Municipality, Jiangxi]), *c.* 1st century BC (Jiangxi 2015: 76); and Eastern Zhou bronzes from 大雲山 (Xuyi 盱眙, Jiangsu) M1 (Xu [ed.] 2017: 169, No. 78, *xuan* 鋗 basin, Springs-Autumns; 170-171, No. 79, *chunyu* 錞于bell, Warring States). See also Lin (ed.) 2012: 172-3, No. 61, referring to p. 293, No. 168, jade, possibly dating to the Warring States, in the tomb of the King of Nanyue 南越 (Xianggangshan 香港山 [Guangzhou 廣州 Municipality, Guangdong]), died 122 BC. In my view, examples of Han imitation of pre-imperial work include: Zhongguo shehui kexueyuan 1980, Vol. 1: 39, Fig. 22, M1:5019 *hu*, bronze, silvered and gilded, glass inlay; Vol. 1:61, Fig. 42:2-3, M1:4286, gilded bronze cup; Vol. 2: Col. Pl. 8, right, M1:4286; Pl. 28:1, far right (M1:4286), 2 (M1:4286); Vol. 2: Col. Pl. 5, M1:5014 *hu*, bronze, silvered and gilded, inner surface lacquered in red, all Mancheng; Guangzhou 1991, Vol. 1:283, Fig. 196; Vol. 2: Col. Pl. 27:2, King of Nanyue G41, bronze brazier.

they represent a startling – and limited – departure from Bronze Age norms. Given the further departure of Han art from that of the Bronze Age, the adoption of these specific motifs appears to reflect deliberate choice.

An understanding of the development of Han narrative art thus depends on understanding the origins of narrative motifs in the pre-Han period and the cultural forces they represent. The example of two minor geometric patterns carried over from the Bronze Age to the Han illustrates the complexity of the double problem of image origin and transmission.

A pattern of jagged lozenges occurs throughout the Bronze Age, from Shang bronze vessels to Late Warring States bronze mirrors.[36] When it appears on stamped hollow bricks from the Qin palace 1 (Xianyang Municipality, Shaanxi),[37] followed by use on a variety of Han objects, in a variety of media,[38] the motif represents the extension of a long tradition. Variations of the pattern, such as rhomboids enclosing dots, circles, or leaf-like shapes, also occur in Han work, often as a border on decorated brick (cf., Figure 40) or stone.[39] These variants undoubtedly derive from Warring States bronze décors of concentric rhomboids filled with dots,[40] followed by the dynastic Qin, as in the colored patterning (engobe?) of earthenware figures from the K9901 pit associated with the burial of Qin Shihuang 始皇 (Lintong 臨潼 [Xi'an 西安 Municipality, Shaanxi]).[41] The transmission of the pattern seems obvious and we have no reason to doubt a Chinese origin.

This situation contrasts with the example of a set of braid or rope patterns sometimes used to divide registers of décor on Eastern Zhou bronzes (Figures 4, 5, 7) and again during the Han to divide the registers of mural décor.[42] The braid and its variants first appear on Chinese work around the Middle Springs and Autumns (*c.* late 7th-early 6th centuries BC), without earlier precedent.[43] All variations are, however, common in Near Eastern work from as early

[36] Chronologically successive examples include: Rawson 1995, Vol. IIA:55, Fig. 62, *pan* 盤 platter (*c.* 13th-11th centuries BC); Bagley 1995: 504-505, No. 98, Arthur M. Sackler Gallery [Smithsonian Institution, Washington, DC] V-137 (*c.* 12th-11th centuries BC); 506, Fig. 98.1-3; 507, Fig. 98.4-5; 512-513, Fig. 101.1; 514, Fig. 101.2, all *yu* 盂 (*c.* 11th century BC); Hubei 1984:65, Fig. 51:7, Yutaishan 雨臺山 (Jiangling, Jingzhou Municipality, Hubei) M183:2 *hu* (*c.* 5th century BC); Pl. 24:4, Yutaishan M434:3 *dui* 敦 (*c.* 4th century BC), both engobe-decorated earthenware; Hubei 1976:120, Fig. 7, Qianping 前坪 Municipality (Yichang 宜昌, Hubei) M23:13, bronze mirror (*c.* 3rd century BC).

[37] Liu Yang (ed.) 2012: 287, No. 115.

[38] Han examples include the borders of the red lacquer inner coffin of Mawangdui (Changsha Municipality, Hunan) M1 (Hunan 1973, Vol. 2: Pl. 32), the brocade cloth covering the interior of that coffin (Hunan 1973, Vol. 2: Pl. 61), and a stamped brick from the Han habitation site of Chongan (Fujian) T7(3):31 (Fujian 1990: 355, Fig. 13, building 1).

[39] E.g., Zhou Dao, Lü Pin, and Tang Wenxing 1985: Pl. 1-3, Luoyang 洛陽, Henan; Pl. 64, Zhengzhou 鄭州, Henan; Kaifeng 2015: 21, Fig. 4, left and center columns; right column, second from bottom, Daxinzhuang 大新莊 (Kaifeng 開封 Municipality, Henan), all in brick; Yin Zenghuai and Jiang Feng 2010: 69, Fig. 9, Caomiao 曹廟 (Sihong 泗洪, Jiangsu), in stone; Guangzhou 1981, Vol. 1: 435, Fig. 270:5, Guangzhou (Guangdong) M5054:22 (as a border on a bronze *zun* 尊).

[40] Zhongguo qingtongqi 1995: 176, Pl. 197, *dou* 豆 (Early Warring States).

[41] Zhang Weixing 2002: 69, Fig. 16.2-3; 70, Fig. 17.2-3.

[42] As in Mengzhuang 孟莊 (Pingyin 平陰, Shandong) M1: Ji'nan 2002: 51, Fig. 23, carved stone. See also Yin Zenghuai and Jiang Feng 2010: 67, Fig. 2; 70, Fig. 12; 74, Fig. 21, Caomiao (Sihong, Jiangsu), carved stone; and Zhongguo meishu 1988: 4, Pl. 4, Wu Liang shrine (Jiaxiang, Shandong), carved stone (d. AD 151); Zhou Dao, Lü Pin, and Tang Wenxing1985: 69-70, Zhengzhou (Henan), stamped bricks.

[43] Examples include: Zhongguo qingtongqi 1995, wide braid: 66, Pl. 74, Jinsheng 金勝 (Taiyuan 太原 Municipality, Shanxi) *hu*, Late Springs-Autumns; 88, Pl. 98, Jinsheng (Taiyuan Municipality, Shanxi) *jian* 鑑, Late Springs-Autumns; 117, Pl. 133, Dongshe 東社 (Yuanping 原平 Municipality, Shanxi) canopy fixture, Late Springs-Autumns; twisted rope: 10, Pl. 11, Shangma 上馬 (Houma 侯馬 Municipality, Shanxi) *ding*, Middle Springs-Autumns; 162, Pl. 184, Liulige 琉璃閣 (Hui 輝 xian, Henan) *hu*, Early Warring States (following Zhongguo qingtongqi 1995; *c.* second half 6th century BC, per So 1995: 33, Fig. 38); herringbone: 122-123, Pl. 138-139, Fenshuiling 分水嶺 (Changzhi 長治 Municipality, Shanxi) *lei*, Early Warring States. Note that the dating of some sites remains debated: for example, see Falkenhausen 1999:

as the first half of the 3rd millennium BC and continuing through the Achaemenid (as Figure 2, shoulder), as well as being transmitted early to Greek cultures (as on Figure 69), where the motif remained common through the Hellenistic era.[44] Undoubtedly by extension with both Persian and Greek contact, the twisted rope likewise appears in steppe art particularly from the 4th century BC onward, in the context both of the Scythians (*c.* 7th-3rd centuries BC)[45] and of the Far Eastern steppe[46] (Figures 10, 25, 30, 48, 54). Again as the result of Persian and Greek contact, the motif spread to the general area of Pakistan and northern India, identified as the provenance of a carved steatite 'ringstone' in the Los Angeles County Museum of Art (*c.* 3rd century BC).[47] Thus, although the braid and related décors may have been transmitted directly to the Han from the Eastern Zhou, the origin of the motif is undoubtedly Near Eastern.[48]

506, footnote 89. The herringbone pattern on the Fenshuiling *lei* takes the appearance of a web of rope, with open, circular knots dividing segments of décor. While this gives the impression of a rope-suspended vessel (which it may, indeed, represent, cf., Wu Xiaolong 2017: 31, 95-96), such use of the pattern may represent less a depiction of actual non-Chinese vessel suspension than the adaptation of a decorative motif. Similar division of décor is also achieved by flat, plain bands, as Zhongguo qingtongqi 1995: 72, Pl. 80, Jinsheng (Taiyuan Municipality, Shanxi) *bianhu* 扁壺, Late Springs-Autumns; 127, Pl. 143, Shangguo 上郭 (Wenxi 聞喜, Shanxi) *bianhu*, Middle-Late Warring States; as well as through the use of thin, paired triangles, as Zhongguo qingtongqi 1995: 61, Pl. 69, collection of the Asian Art Museum (San Francisco) *hu*, Late Springs-Autumns. In this context, the choice of a cable pattern seems likely to reflect the demands of composition (see below).

[44] Multiple examples allow retracing of a Near Eastern chronological sequence, as in: Collon 1987: 12, No. 9, Uruk, before *c.* 3000 BC; 48, No. 177 (Chagar-Bazar [Syria]), 178 (Tell Leilan and Mari [Syria]), and 181 (Tell al Rimah [Iraq]), all *c.* 19th-18th centuries BC (all cylinder seals); Weiss (ed.) 1985: 166, No. 72a, Temple of Shamash, Mari (Syria), carved steatite vessel, *c.* 2900-2500 B.C; Crowley 1989: 449, Fig. 259 (seal impression, Brak, Mesopotamia [Syria]), Fig. 261 (steatite vase fragment, Mari, Mesopotamia [Syria]), Fig. 263 (lamp cover, Telloh, Mesopotamia [Iraq]), all *c.* 2800-2300 BC; Collon 1995: 158, Fig. 126, Southeastern (Burnt) Palace, Nimrud (Iraq), cylindrical ivory box, *c.* early 9th century BC; Godard 1950: 14, Fig. 5; 20, Fig. 10; 26, Fig. 16; 116, Fig. 101, Ziwiye (Kurdistan [Iran]) hoard, *c.* late 8th century BC *terminus ad quem*, using Muscarella's date for the cauldron in which the objects are said to have been found (Muscarella 1988: 347). In the Greek context: Aruz, Benzel, and Evans (eds) 2008: 411, Fig. 129, *c.* 14th century BC, ivory pyxis with herringbone pattern, Agora Museum (Athens). The twisted rope and related motifs are common in Achaemenid and Hellenistic toreutics: Smithsonian 1964-1965: 146, No. 434, Ziwiye gold bracelet (here dated *c.* 7th century BC), Archaeological Museum, Tehran, 7818; 148, No. 456, Achaemenid gold appliqué, Archaeological Museum, Tehran, 7953-7954, both with rope-like edging; Curtis and Tallis (eds) 2005: 140, No. 158, 159; 141, No. 163, all Oxus Treasure (Takht-i Sangin, Tajikistan), gold bracelets, British Museum (London) ANE 124041, 124042, 124034; Terenožkin and Mozolevskij 1988: 126, Fig. 140, gold tear-shaped plaques; 127, Fig. 141, gold gorytus cover, both, Melitopol'skij (Zaporož'e [Ukraine]) burial 2; both, Greek-produced; Schiltz 1994: 196-202, Figs 145-148, Tolstaja Mogila (Pokrov, Dnepropetrovsk [Ukraine]), Greek-produced torque, *c.* 4th century BC, all with twisting.

[45] As on the *c.* 4th century BC Scythian site of Melitopol'skij (Zaporož'e [Ukraine]): Terenožkin and Mozolevskij 1988: 89, Fig. 95:5, burial 1, gold plaques with herringbone border; and the *c.* 330-300 BC gold necklace from the Pavlovsky (Pavlovskij) kurgan (Bol'šaja Bliz'nica [Belarus]), the chain of which is woven in a herringbone pattern (Williams and Ogden 1994: 169-169, No. 106). For discussion of Greek and Achaemenid influence on the Far Eastern steppe, see Psarras forthcoming.

[46] E.g., Tian Guangjin and Guo Suxin 1986: 80, Fig. 47:3 (unprovenanced, in my estimation of Xianbei 鮮卑 attribution); 81, Fig. 48:1, Aluchaideng 阿魯柴登 (Hanggin [Hangjin] 杭錦 Banner, Inner Mongolia), Fig. 48:2, Xigoupan (Xigouban) 西溝畔 (Jungar [Zhunge'er] 准格爾 Banner, Inner Mongolia) M2:27; Pl. 63:1-2, Xigoupan M2:26, 27. Stylistically, Xigoupan M2:26-27 also seem likely to be of Chinese origin; certainly they once had a Chinese owner, as attested by the inscription on the back. The use of the rope border, however, is clearly steppe in origin.

[47] Pal 1986: 127, No. S3. Here again, the rope pattern is used to separate registers of décor.

[48] A conclusion also reached by Weber 1968:202-203, following Bernhard Karlgren, for the braid pattern. Weber remains unconvinced about the herringbone variant and use of the rope in a composition approximating netting. The netting in question refers to the use of (for instance) herringbone pattern on an Early Warring States *lei* from Fenshuiling (Changzhi Municipality, Shanxi: Zhongguo qingtongqi 1995:122-123, Pl. 138-139), where it is used to divide segments of vessel décor, as if framing it in a rope net (cf., Figure 7 of the present article). Similar division of décor is also achieved on other bronze vessels by flat, plain bands: Zhongguo qingtongqi 1995: 72, Pl. 80, Jinsheng (Taiyuan Municipality, Shanxi) *bianhu*, Late Springs-Autumns; 127, Pl. 143, Shangguo (Wenxi, Shanxi) *bianhu*, Middle-Late Warring States; or by thin, paired triangles: Zhongguo qingtongqi 1995: 61, Pl. 69, collection of the Asian Art Museum, San Francisco; *hu*, Late Springs-Autumns. In this context, the choice of a cable pattern seems likely to reflect the demands of composition. Accordingly, I conclude that the cable pattern is Near Eastern, but the way it is used on the Fenshuiling vessel is an extension of Chinese norms. See above, footnotes 43-44 for additional references.

Given continuous use in regions open to Near Eastern and Greek influence, we may assume transmission of the rope motif to Springs and Autumns China as a result of contact with the steppe, Central Asia, or India. However, gaps in the archaeological records of the non-Chinese north and northern India for much of the period corresponding to the Eastern Zhou (specifically, until the Middle or Late Warring States, *c.* 4th-3rd centuries BC) prevent identification of a specific path of transmission. Again given continuous use in Western-influenced regions, it is reasonable to expect that Han use of the rope patterns resulted not only from Eastern Zhou usage, but from repeated exposure to the motif on steppe – and perhaps northern Indian – art. Such reintroduction from the steppe to Han China appears likely in the case of a stamped brick from Nanguan 南關 (Zhengzhou 鄭州 Municipality, Henan),[49] on which a stylized twisted rope pattern (created by close-set diagonal lines of small squares) frames a rectangular area of geometric décor, immediately recalling the twisted rope border on rectangular northern non-Chinese plaques (as on Figure 54). A related convention characteristic of the eastern steppe is imitated on the Dayunshan大雲山 (Xuyi 盱眙, Jiangsu) M1 bronze chime stand in the form of a winged dragon,[50] where the twisted rope marks the dragon's spine in the manner of the spinal markings of predator and prey on gold live-prey predation plaques in the Siberian Collection of Peter the Great.[51]

The situation presented by the rope motifs, far from being isolated, is repeated in many of the figural décors that appear intrusive in the Eastern Zhou, only to become central in the Han. Two of the most common of Han décors illustrate the depth of the problem: the meander and a variety of motifs incorporating animals and divinities – in the terms of the original Near Eastern and steppe iconographies, the animal master (Figure 3), the tree of life (Figure 9), and animal predation (Figures 21, 32, 33). In Han art, these are combined to form the basis for a wide range of figural scenes, the most important of which is paradise.

[49] Henan 1960: 23, Fig. 20 (right); *c.* 65 AD, per Psarras 2015.

[50] Xu (ed.) 2017: cover, 64-65, No. 4, silver-inlaid bronze.

[51] The piece is frequently reproduced, as in Pfrommer 1993: 59, Fig. 44, State Hermitage Museum 1727-1/6, gold. The convention must derive from the line of beading (and related marks) on the throat of Scythian stags: e.g., Reeder (ed.) 1999: 160-161, No. 50, Illičeve (Leninski, Krim [Ukraine]) kurgan 1, burial 6, gold plaque, *c.* 5th century BC.

Chapter 2

The Animal Master

The loose meander ('vine') motif, characteristic of lacquer décor during the Han (Figures 1, 13, 28), has a long and varied history throughout the Bronze Age, beginning with the Shang.[52] During the Han, it occurs particularly on lacquerware,[53] on ceramics in cases where the décor is particularly close to pre-imperial bronze norms,[54] and on mural décor.[55] Unlike many Bronze Age prototypes, these Han variants tend to have a vegetal appearance (as 'vines'), or to be reworked in a more figural manner as 'clouds' or mountains, as on the black outer coffin from Mawangdui (Changsha Municipality, Hunan) M1 (Figure 1) and a series of small boxes from Dayunshan (Xuyi, Jiangsu) M2.[56] The meander may be drawn with a thin line in an open, wandering composition (as on the Dayunshan M2 boxes[57] and a stone bas relief from Yanjiacha 延家岔 [Suide 綏德, Shaanxi])[58] (Figure 13), or with a broad line in a relatively compact arrangement (as on stone bas reliefs from tombs at Yi'nan 沂南 [Shandong][59] and Lugou 路溝 [Suide, Shaanxi]).[60]

In addition, the Han continue the Western (*c.* 1050-771 BC)[61] and, especially, Eastern Zhou convention of meanders consisting of elongated animal bodies (frequently fantastic animals or snakes) or terminating in animal, including bird, heads (as on Figure 10, register 8).[62] A

[52] For Shang examples, see (*inter alia*): Bagley 1995: 78, Figs 45, Minggong 銘功 (Zhengzhou Municipality, Henan) M2 *gui* (Early Shang, *c.* 1600-1400 BC); 47, Panlongcheng (Huangpi, [Wuhan Municipality, Hubei]) *li*; 82, Fig. 57, Baijiazhuang 白家莊 (Zhengzhou Municipality, Henan) M2 *pan* (Middle Shang, *c.* 1400-1200 BC). A thinner interlace occurs on the handle of the Da Ke 大克 *ding*, Late Western Zhou (Rawson 1995, vol IIA: 113, Fig. 160).

[53] To cite only a couple examples: Nanjing 2013:50, Fig. 36, Dayunshan (Xuyi, Jiangsu) M2:95; Anhui 2007: 115, Fig. 83:1, Beishantou 北山頭 (Chaohu 巢湖 Municipality, Anhui) M1:20 *pan*.

[54] As in (randomly) several examples applied to different vessel forms: Dongdianzi 東甸子 (Xuzhou 徐州 Municipality, Jiangsu) M1E (Xuzhou 1999: 7, Figs 6:2 [M1E:15, *he* 盒 box], 6:3 [M1E:3, *hu*], 6:5 [M1E:35, *ding*], 6:8 [M1E:57, *fanghu* 方壺], 6:9 [M1E:41, *hu*]), and Tonghuagou 桐花溝 (Jiyuan 濟源 Municipality, Henan) M63 (Henan 1999a:22, Fig. 5:2 [M63:3, *ding*]; front cover [M63:1, 'egg-shaped' *hu*]; inner front cover:1 [M63:6, *fanghu*], 2 [M63:2, *hu*]; Col. Pl. 1:1 [M63:7, *hu*], 2 [M63:4, *yan* 甗 steamer]).

[55] To give only a few examples, see Zhongguo meishu 1988: 6-7, Pl. 6 (Wu Family front shrine [Jiaxiang, Shandong]), Pl. 7 (Qishan 齋山 [Jiaxiang, Shandong]); 52-53, Pl. 62-63 (Beisai 北寨 [Yi'nan 沂南, Shandong]); 69, Pl. 81 (Lugou 路溝 [Suide 綏德, Shaanxi]). These meanders continue into the Northern Wei 北魏 (AD 386-535) and Northern Qi 北齊 (AD 526-559), as do concentric rhomboids: Zhong Xiaoqing 1999: 54, Fig. 3:1; 55, Fig. 4; 56, Fig. 6:2; 58, Fig. 9:4-5; 59, Fig. 11; 60, Fig. 12, upper left, lower center, lower right.

[56] Hunan 1973, Vol. 2: Pl. 27-31, 38-57, Mawangdui (Changsha Municipality, Hunan) M1; Nanjing 2013: 45-49, Figs 30-35, Dayunshan (Xuyi, Jiangsu) M2:95.

[57] Nanjing 2013: 50, Fig. 36 (M2:95).

[58] Zhongguo meishu 1988: 67, Pl. 79.

[59] Zhongguo meishu 1988: 52-53, Pl. 62-63.

[60] Zhongguo meishu 1988: 69, Pl. 81.

[61] Gugong 1999: 170, Pl. 157, Zhui 追 *gui* (Middle Western Zhou).

[62] Use of the snake is often associated with southern bronzes because of its frequent occurrence in the *c.* 433 BC tomb of the Marquis Yi of Zeng 曾侯乙 (Leigudun 擂鼓墩 [Suizhou 隨州 Municipality, Hubei]), as throughout Hubei 1989, but it also occurs on northern work, as (*inter alia*): Zhongguo qingtongqi 1995: 6-7, Pl. 6-8, Liuquan 柳泉 (Xinzhong 新絳, Shanxi) cemetery find, *ding*, Middle Springs-Autumns; 51, Pl. 58, Liyu (Hunyuan, Shanxi), animal-shaped *zun*, Late Springs-Autumns, detail showing meander terminating in snake head; 62, Pl. 62, Shangma (Houma Municipality, Shanxi), Middle Springs-Autumns, *fanghu*, fantastic animals; 64, Pl. 72, Jinsheng (Taiyuan Municipality, Shanxi), *fanghu*, detail, fantastic animals; 66, Pl. 74, Jinsheng (Taiyuan Municipality, Shanxi), Late Springs-Autumns, *hu*, fantastic animals; 71, Pl. 79, Arthur M. Sackler Gallery, Early Warring States, *hu*, gold- and silver-inlaid bronze, with bird heads.

number of Han bronze mirrors,[63] as well as the Mancheng M1:5014 gilded and silvered *hu*,[64] closely follow Warring States mirror décor.[65] By extension, traceries made of elongated animal bodies occur frequently on jade work of various forms, as illustrated by a headrest and sword fittings from Mancheng (Hebei) M1.[66] Although it seems reasonable that Warring States mirror décor represents the immediate source for the Han parallels, some cases may be less straightforward. For instance, the articulated vine patterns painted on the walls and ceiling of the front chamber in the tomb of the King of Nanyue (Xianggangshan [Guangzhou Municipality, Guangdong]; 122 BC)[67] follow from Warring States norms. However, they also bear a striking stylistic resemblance to the pattern of antlers terminating in bird heads on the tattoos on the man interred in Pazyryk (Altai) kurgan 2 (*c.* 300-282 BC),[68] an image also incorporated into Xiongnu art (Figure 41).[69] The similarity of these steppe examples to the mural in the tomb of the King of Nanyue raises the possibility of steppe influence, absorbed by China either during the later Eastern Zhou or during the Han (and probably during both) as part of the further development of the Zhou animal meander.

Frequently, however, Han integration of the animal into the meander takes the form of simple juxtaposition, as when the meander, reworked as 'clouds,' is reinforced with bird heads, as on the Wu Family shrines (Jiaxiang, Shandong) and a number of tomb murals in Jiaxiang and Yanggu, Shandong – all undoubtedly from the same workshop.[70] In other cases, only a single line connects the tail of the animal to a cloud-like meander, as on the Dayunshan (Xuyi, Jiangsu) M2 lacquer box.[71]

Most strikingly, the Han combined the meander with images of animals paired with humanoid figures (Figure 1). The latter seem to have first appeared in China in the Middle or Late Springs and Autumns (*c.* later 7th-early 5th centuries BC; cf., Figures 4, 5, 7, 10). These figural décors represent a departure from earlier Chinese art,[72] which rarely utilized either humanoid form

63 E.g., Kong Xiangxing 1992: 164-165.
64 Zhongguo shehui kexueyuan 1980, Vol. 1: 40-41, Figs 23-24.
65 As in Kong Xiangxing 1992: 90, 92, 94, 96, 98, 103-129, etc.
66 Zhongguo shehui kexueyuan 1980, Vol. 1: 80, Fig. 53 (M1:5188, headrest); 104, Fig. 70, M1:5042 (sword fittings).
67 Guangzhou 1991, Vol. 2: Col. Pl. 1.
68 Rudenko 1970: 111, Fig. 53-54. I have followed Parzinger *et al.* 2008: 17 for the dating of Pazyryk.
69 Tian Guangjin and Guo Suxin 1986: 345, Fig. 2:1, Aluchaideng (Hanggin Banner, Inner Mongolia) gold plaques.
70 Liu Xingzhen and Yue Fengxia 1991: 75, 81 (Front shrine); 92-93, 100 (Left shrine); 124-126, 133-135 (Rear shrine), Wu Family shrines (Jiaxiang, Shandong; *c.* mid-first century AD); Liaocheng 1989:54, Fig. 11, Balimiao 八里廟 (Yanggu 陽谷, Shandong) M1 (*c.* 175 AD, per Psarras 2015); Zhu Xilu 1992:77, Fig. 104, Hualin 花林 (Jiaxiang, Shandong); 38, Fig. 45, Songshan 宋山 (Jiaxiang, Shandong) M1.
71 Nanjing 2013: 52, Fig. 41 (M2:158); 53, Fig. 45 (M2:161).
72 I will exclude discussion of neolithic Chinese manifestations of the animal master, known in the cultures of Longshan 龍山 and the more localized Liangzhu 良渚 (Jiangsu, Zhejiang, Shanghai regions), both of which yield jade carvings in the form of a human-animal hybrid grasping before him a large animal head. For Longshan: Du Jinpeng 1994: 55, Figs 1-3, Zhufeng 朱封 (Linqu 臨朐 , Shandong) M202:1, compared to Liangzhu on Du Jinpeng 1994: 63, Fig. 12, misread in the excavation report as depicting a single creature; for Liangzhu: Jiang Song 1994: 344, Fig. 3. On other Liangzhu representations, a central humanoid is shown grasping a stylized animal in each hand, as on Fanshan 反山 (Zhejiang) M15:7 (Jiang Song 1994: 344, Fig. 2:1). For excellent photographs of Liangzhu material where these variants are clearly visible, see: Zhejiang 1989: Pl. 13-14, Yaoshan 瑤山 (Yuhang 余杭, Zhejiang) M9:4, M10:15, respectively; Pl. 56, Fanshan (Zhejiang) M12:97; Pl. 115, Fanshan M17:8, all showing an animal head alone; Pl. 6-9, Fanshan M12:98; Pl. 120-121, Yaoshan (Yuhuang, Zhejiang) M2:1, showing the humanoid grasping an animal head. The peculiarities of the animal head alone are, as has often been noted, so close to the Bronze Age *taotie* 饕餮 that some relationship seems inevitable, even though too many lacunae remain in current data to allow any direct reconstruction through cultures and/or time (cf., Sun Zhixin 1993; Thote 1996). Childs-Johnson 1995: 80, Fig. 1, includes the drawing of a Shang bronze décor of an animal master holding two animals who share the same head. Regardless of the origins of the neolithic examples, there seems to be no continuity – and no direct relationship – between these early examples and Eastern

or narrative décor. In contrast, the new combination dominates Han art as the iconography of paradise and, by extension, influences much of Han figural work not belonging to depictions of paradise. Throughout this development, the essential elements of the Eastern Zhou versions of the animal-and-humanoid décor are closely maintained, although the style of execution is rarely retained. The origins of the Eastern Zhou versions may be identified because they in turn retain the essential elements of the animal master iconography widely and continuously used in the Near East from perhaps as early as the 4th millennium BC onward.[73] Directly or not, this long tradition must therefore provide the prototype for the Eastern Zhou manifestations. Indeed, application of the Near Eastern iconography to highly portable objects – seals, psalia,[74] vessels – would have facilitated diffusion; its use in both northwestern Iran and China on vessels with register-divided hunting and ritual scenes, framed by the braided-rope and egg-and-dart motifs,[75] suggests to me that the iconography may have traveled as a whole in vessel form from Iran to China (cf., Figure 2). Other types of objects would have provided additional examples of the iconography.

The title given to the image comes from the depiction of a humanoid figure (male or female[76]) in association with animals; the specifics of the association vary. The divinity of the humanoid is underscored by this association with animals (later recast as symbolic of royalty[77]), as well as by his frequent portrayal as half-animal, half-human. The dominant position routinely assigned to the figure in Near Eastern compositions conveys his authority and, by extension, implies the ritualization of the images with which he is associated. This divinity was retained in Han versions, as is made evident by the Mawangdui (Changsha Municipality, Hunan) M3 manuscript,[78] which names and describes various deities whose representations are recognizable as deriving from the animal master. It therefore appears clear that the Chinese recognized the sacred dimension of the animal master image from the time of its first, Eastern Zhou adoption: at least some aspect of that significance seems to have been absorbed with the iconography and maintained thereafter. Subsequent Han versions of this iconography may therefore reflect a new direction in Chinese religious thought, even though an iconographic

---

Zhou, Qin or Han art.

[73] Smith 1981: 36-37, attributing Egyptian use of the animal-master to contact with Mesopotamia in the 'Protoliterate' period, *c.* 4000-3200 BC; Collon 1995: 73, Fig. 56, cylinder seals; 67, Fig. 50, mosaic fragments from grave 779, Royal Cemetery of Ur (Tell el-Muqayyar, Dhi Qar [Iraq]), *c.* 2700-2600 BC; Collon 1995: 69, Fig. 51, chlorite vessel, found at Khafajeh, near Baghdad (Iraq), but described as of Iranian ('or further east') manufacture, British Museum 368359, *c.* 2600 BC (see also <https://www.britishmuseum.org/research/collection_online/collection_object_details.aspx?objectId=368359&partId=1&searchText=khafajeh&page=1>, viewed 30 June 2017); Collon 1987: 179, Fig. 842, Nippur (Iraq), seal impression (drawing), *c.* 1307-1282 BC, the body of the animal master (flanked by animals) becomes a mountain; Moorey 1974: 152-154, No. 134-135; 154, No. 136, from Ziwiye, and Muscarella 1988: 82-85, No. 145, Luristan, *c.* 10th-8th centuries BC (following the dating on <https://www.metmuseum.org/art/collection/search/325693>, viewed 30 June 2017, The Metropolitan Museum of Art [New York] 64.257.1a, reproduced in the present article as Figure 2); Galanina and Gratch 1987: Pl. 47-48, Kelermes ([Kuban,] Krasnodar [Russia]) kurgan 4, Ionian-Scythian mirror, silver, electrum-plated on the reverse, *c.* late 7th-early 6th centuries BC.

[74] Muscarella 1988: 86-88, No. 147, Metropolitan Museum of Art 1980.324.3; Moorey 1974: 124, Fig. 98; 137, Fig. 119, northwestern Iran, *c.* 10th-9th centuries BC.

[75] Moorey 1974: 152-154, Nos 134-135; 154, No. 136, from Ziwiye, and Muscarella 1988: 82-85, No. 145, Metropolitan Museum of Art 64.257.1a.

[76] For discussion of the feminine version, see Crowley 1989: 34-39; 416-418, Nos 77-92. Examples include the lid of an ivory pyxis from Ugarit (Minet el-Beida, Syria) tomb 3, *c.* 1250 BC; Louvre (Paris) AO 11601 <https://www.louvre.fr/oeuvre-notices/couvercle-de-pyxide-avec-maitresse-des-animaux>, viewed 7 March 2016; and Tillia-tepe M2 (*c.* 1st century AD), on which an animal-mistress grasps the hind legs of wolf-like animals, which in turn prey on a fish- or dolphin-like head (Sarianidi 1985: Pl. 44-47, M2:7).

[77] As in the lion (or animal) throne, below.

[78] Zhang Zhenglang, Fu Juyou, and Chen Songchang 1992: 35.

equivalence in the principles of composition was maintained between the Eastern Zhou and Han eras.

In the most basic iconography, the animal master holds a bull or lion in each hand, with the pair of animals flanking him in profile[79] (Figure 3). This composition is the most readily-identifiable guise of the animal master, continuing in essentially the same form through the first centuries AD, as in Tillia-tepe (Afghanistan) M6 (*c.* 1st century AD)[80] and a Xianbei 鮮卑 plaque from Bharatudu ([Beihalatuda] 北哈拉吐達, Inner Mongolia), *c.* 386-535 AD.[81] He is also portrayed as presiding over the killing of animals, whether by other animals (animal predation) or by humans (hunting).[82] By extension, the sacred nature imputed to the animal master implies that this killing may be considered animal sacrifice, tied to the regeneration of life; this may explain the particularly close association of the animal master with animal predation, as well as suggesting sacred significance for animal predation alone. Both principle variants – the animal master flanked by animals and the hybrid animal master – have a history essentially as old as the animal master with flanking beasts and follow much the same cultural distribution.[83] Tracing their transmission to China, together with their development during the Han, is complex, and made more so due to multiple waves of transmission at different times, involving multiple, related images.

Both the animal master with flanking beasts and the animal master hunting recur in Eastern Zhou bronzes. Examples of the former include the *c.* 4th century BC incised bronze fragment, Gaozhuang 高莊 (Huaiyin 淮陰 Municipality, Jiangsu) M1:114-2 (readily visible around the rope motif, shown as circular in this view)[84] (Figure 4). Association with the killing of animals likewise occurs on Gaozhuang M1:114-1,[85] where the animal master aims an arrow at a nearby feline or, elsewhere on the same fragment, at a bird. By extension, the scattered animals in some Eastern Zhou décors represent the hunt, originally supervised by the animal master, but shown in some cases without him, as on Jiagezhuang 賈各莊 (Tangshan 唐山 Municipality, Hebei)[86] (Figure 5) and Liyu 李峪 (Hunyuan 渾源, Shanxi) vessels.[87] In this context, we may assume that, in these early depictions, the hunt and the assembly of animals as independent narratives retain a sacred character. Eastern Zhou adaptations of the animal master similarly depict him in combination with animal predation on pieces such as a *pan* (platter) in the Palace Museum (Beijing; unprovenanced, *c.* the Early Warring States).[88] Further, all of these compositional associations are retained throughout the Han, as in the humanoid figures

[79] E.g., Collon 1995: 73, Fig. 56a, identified as resembling finds from Tell Fara (southern Iraq), *c.* 2700 BC; 69, Fig. 51, chlorite vessel found at Khafajeh (Iraq), 'made in Iran or further east,' *c.* 2600 BC.

[80] Sarianidi 1985: Pl. 48, M6:4.

[81] Personal observation, Inner Mongolia Archaeological Institute, Hohhot, August 1992.

[82] Collon 1987: 25, No. 61, Tell Agrab (Shara Temple [Iraq]); cylinder seal, *c.* 3000-2334 BC.

[83] The animal master combined with animal predation: Collon 1987: 25, No. 61, Tell Agrab (Shara Temple [Iraq]) cylinder seal, *c.* 3000-2334 BC; Godard 1950: 21, Fig. 11, Northwest Palace (Nimrud [Nineveh, Iraq]), stone relief image of patterns on the clothing of Ashurnasirpal II (r. 884/883-860/859 BC); and combined with both hunting and animal predation: Collon 1987: 25, Fig. 61, Shara Temple (Tell Agrab [Iraq]) cylinder seal, *c.* 3000-2334 BC, with a décor of two 'bull-men' spearing a lion who is attacking a bull; 29, Fig. 79, Fara (Iraq) seal impression (drawing), *c.* 3000-2334 BC, with similar décor.

[84] Huaiyin 1988: 209, Fig. 22.

[85] Huaiyin 1988: 207, Fig. 20.

[86] An Zhimin 1953: 84-86, Fig. 10.

[87] Zhongguo meishu 1992: 45, Pl. 54.

[88] Zhongguo meishu 1992: 48, Pl. 57-58 (on the vessel legs). Gugong 1999: 289, Pl. 287, dates the piece to the Early Warring States.

hunting on the Mawangdui (Changsha Municipality, Hunan) M1 black coffin (Figure 1),[89] the humanoid figure with animals and animal predation on the Mancheng (Hebei) M2:3004 partially-silvered bronze *boshanlu* incense burner (Figure 6),[90] and the scattered animals of the Mancheng M2:4024 lacquered *lian* 奩 toiletries box.[91]

A number of variant physiognomies are assigned to the animal master, both in the western world and in China, primarily identifiable as human or human-like and hybrid, human-animal. Multiple versions of each occur. Two distinct types used during the Eastern Zhou were retained by the Han: the cartoonish figures common on *c.* 5th century BC bronzes such as the Gaozhuang (Huaiyin Municipality, Jiangsu) fragments (Figures 4, 7), and the more human features of the crouching figure on the Palace Museum *pan*.[92]

The cartoonish animal master is pervasive in the Late Springs-Autumns and Warring States: examples on Chu 楚 lacquerware, such as on the inner coffin and the duck-shaped lacquer box of the Marquis Yi of Zeng 曾侯乙 (Leigudun 擂鼓墩 [Suizhou 隨州 Municipality, Hubei]),[93] correspond exactly to those on the Gaozhuang (Huaiyin Municipality, Jiangsu) M1:114-2 (Figure 4) and M1:0153 fragments.[94] The same type of figure is sometimes also shown carrying rods or plant-like stems, as on Gaozhuang M1:1114-2 (Figure 4, lower left). He recurs on a brick fragment from the site of a Qin palace in Xianyang (Shaanxi)[95] and, with multiple attributes, on a painted silk manuscript from Mawangdui (Changsha Municipality, Hunan) M3 (168 BC).[96] Although the composition of the animal master carrying a plant continues throughout the Han (as on Figure 8, executed in a different style),[97] the cartoonish manner of drawing the master seems to have been relatively rare during the Han. This is also the case for another Warring States variant, equally abstract, if less cartoonish, as on the Changtaiguan 長臺關 (Xinyang 信陽 Municipality, Henan) M1:158[98] lacquered zither (*c.* early 4th century BC), which reappears on the Bicun 畢村 (Hunyuan, Shanxi) M1, earthenware *hu* with engobe décor (*c.* 168 BC).[99] At present, I have found no prototype for the specific features of these cartoonish styles.

In contrast, the style of figure seen on the Palace Museum *pan*, which seems to be rare during the Eastern Zhou, becomes standard during the Han as the 'immortal,' *xian* 仙 (cf., Figure 8), with the same wide eyes and flowing hair featured on the *pan*. Like the Palace Museum prototype, Han versions are generally winged; in other variants, they lack wings, but appear to fly.[100] The connection with flight is further emphasized in some compositions by the use

[89] Hunan 1973, Vol. 1: Fig. 17 (insert after p. 16).

[90] Zhongguo shehui kexueyuan 1980, Vol. 1: 257, Fig. 171.

[91] Zhongguo shehui kexueyuan 1980, Vol. 1: 304, Fig. 205.

[92] Zhongguo meishu 1992: 48, Pl. 57-58; Gugong 1999: 289, Pl. 287.

[93] Hubei 1989, Vol. 1: 34, Fig. 20; Vol. 2: Col. Pl. 2:3, 4; Pl. 11:4 (the inner coffin); Vol. 2: Pl. 130 (the duck-shaped box, WC2:1). See also Teng Rensheng 1991: 63, Fig. 66, for the inner coffin.

[94] M1:114-2 and M1:0153 fragments: Huaiyin 1988: 209, Fig. 22 (M1:114-2, reproduced in the present article as Figure 4); 211, Fig. 25:1 (M1:0153).

[95] Ma Jianxi 1990: 101, Fig. 2.

[96] Zhang Zhenglang, Fu Juyou, and Chen Songchang 1992: 35.

[97] E.g., Zhongguo meishu 1988: 45, Pl. 54, Hanjiaqu 韓家曲 (Yishui 沂水, Shandong), stone bas relief; 46, Pl. 55, Qianyao 前姚 (Cangshan 蒼山, Shandong), carved stone; 91, Pl. 106, Shilipu 十里鋪 (Nanyang 南陽 Municipality, Henan), carved stone; Chongqing 1998: 82, Fig. 5, Dianfen 淀粉 Plant; 83, Fig. 7, Linfei 磷肥 Plant; 83, Fig. 8, Dianfen Plant, both Wushan 巫山 (Chongqing 重慶 Municipality, Sichuan), gilded bronze plaques, dated *c.* Eastern Han.

[98] Henan 1986: Col. Pl. 2:3.

[99] Shanxi 1980: 48, Fig. 13; 51, Fig. 25. Dating per Psarras 2015.

[100] As Zhongguo meishu 1988: 125, Pl. 148, Knitting Mill ([Zhenzhichang 針織廠,] Tanghe, Henan); 195, Pl. 259, Yu 禹 xian (Henan), stamped brick.

of the cloud meander, as background (as on the Mawangdui [Changsha Municipality, Hunan] M1 black coffin, *c.* 168 BC; Figure 1) or the markings on the garments of the *xian* on a three-dimensional bronze fitting from the Han city of Chang'an 長安 (Xi'an Municipality, Shaanxi).[101] This compositional association continues throughout the Han, as on stone bas reliefs from Dahuting 打虎亭 (Mi 密 xian, Henan) M1, considered to date to the Late Eastern Han.[102]

At least in the early years of the Western Han, the *xian* coexists with the cartoonish styles of animal master. For instance, the winged *xian* on the black (outer) coffin of Mawangdui M1 recurs on a Mawangdui M3 lacquered *lian* toiletries box, contemporaneous with the cartoonish animal master on the Mawangdui M3 manuscript.[103] Indeed, a motionless, half-nude figure on the Mawangdui M1 coffin may be identifiable as a cartoonish animal master (Figure 1, lower right, labelled 57). It thus appears that the Han preference for the *xian* resulted from deliberate choice, not through a more spontaneous, gradual disappearance of the cartoonish versions.

The origins of the *xian* type may be seen in Neo-Assyrian (western Iran, Iraq, Syria; *c.* 9th-7th centuries BC) 'genii,'[104] a winged and bearded male figure whose equivalence with the animal master is confirmed by its depiction with flanking animals[105] or together with flanking animals on either side of a tree of life[106] (Figure 9). The cat held by the genii on the Palace Museum *pan* recalls, in more domestic form, the association with animals, while the figure's round eyes may also underscore derivation from a non-Chinese prototype. The sinicized genii was in turn transmitted to the steppe, as visible on a gold diadem from the Kargaly Valley (Kazakhstan), dated to *c.* 2nd-1st centuries BC.[107]

The wings of the *xian* ultimately derive from hybrid (animal-human) animal masters in Near Eastern depictions, repeated in China. Chinese examples include Eastern Zhou work, as on the Liulige 琉璃閣 (Hui 輝 xian, Henan) bronze *hu* M59:23,[108] on which the humanoid has a bird head and/or wings (Figure 10, registers 2 and 6), a convention also visible on Gaozhuang M1:0138.[109] Separately, on the Gaozhuang M1:0137 fragment, the master is depicted with a humanoid head, while the pair of animals flanking him take the place of his body (as on Figure 7, on which some of the relevant images have been rotated 90°). On yet other Gaozhuang fragments, he is shown with snakes in his hands or through his ears,[110] a characteristic that reappears on the Qin palace example.[111] On Liulige (Huixian, Henan) M59:23, he has horns (Figure 10, second register).[112]

[101] Hong Kong 2015: 168-169. The wings on this *xian* appear to be an extension of its garment.

[102] An Jinhuai and Wang Yugang 1972: 58-59, Fig. 8-9; Pl. 7:4.

[103] Zhang Zhenglang, Fu Juyou, and Chen Songchang 1992: 6-11 (coffin), 62 (*lian*); Hunan 1973, Vol. 2: Pl. 27-31, 38-57 (coffin).

[104] The term 'genii' is commonly applied to Neo-Assyrian décors, as Frankfort 1996: 197, Fig. 224, Northwestern Palace of Ashurnasirpal II, stone relief mural, detail of the tunic of Ashurnasirpal II (reigned 884-859 BC); and Parrot 1961: 266, Fig. 341, Khorsabad (Dur Sharrukin [Iraq]) wall paintings (721-705 BC), of a male figure with wings and a beard. For an important note on the dangers of following the suggested restoration of the Khorsabad paintings, see Green 2012.

[105] Collon 1987: 185, Fig. 894, cylinder seals (*c.* 9th-7th centuries BC).

[106] Collon 1987: 184, Fig. 879, cylinder seals (*c.* 9th-7th centuries BC).

[107] Akišev 1983: Pl. 158-169; the date is open to debate. Cf., Pirazzoli-t'Serstevens 1994. In addition to the form of the *xian*, several elements of the piece are Chinese: the vegetal meander background, the bear, the winged dragon (visible on Linduff 2014: 161, Fig. 2). To me, the workmanship does not appear Chinese, but the composition must reflect Han influence.

[108] Guo Baojun 1959: Pl. 93.

[109] Huaiyin 1988: 205, Fig. 18:1 (lower register, far right), 3 (upper register, far right), both with a bird's head.

[110] Huaiyin 1988: 202, Fig. 15 (M1:0147); 211, Fig. 25:2 (M1:0154). For comments on meaning, see Lin 2012: 78.

[111] Ma Jianxi 1990: 101, Fig. 2.

[112] Guo Baojun 1959: Pl. 93.

Similarly, the hybrid (animal-headed) humanoid from Late Springs-Autumns Lijialou 李家樓 (Xinzheng 新鄭 Municipality, Henan), executed in the round, is horned and holds a snake (?) between his teeth; the flanking animals are replaced by the pair of snakes beneath his feet.[113] The horned animal master reappears not only on the coffin of the Marquis Yi of Zeng (Leigudun [Suizhou Municipality, Hubei]),[114] but among the peripheral figures of the somewhat later (*c.* 400 BC) Chu silk manuscript (from near Changsha Municipality, Hunan).[115] He likewise figures on the Mancheng (Hebei) M1:5196 iron shortsword,[116] with flame-like antlers (depicted on the blade) emerging from a hybrid human-animal head (the guard). These hybrids are retained in various styles throughout the Han, as in the example of the master with bird attributes on a stone bas relief from Balimiao (Yanggu, Shandong) M1 (*c.* 175 AD).[117] As an extension of these, the Han further developed a range of animal-headed or snake-bodied humanoid deities. While partially deriving from the animal master, these seem to fulfil a different role (see Chapter 3 Developments Related to the Animal Master, *Lesser Deities*).

In terms of composition, the Han-era *xian*-type animal master retains his association with animals: in some cases, they flank him (as on a carved stone from Hanjiaqu [Yishui, Shandong];[118] Figure 11). By extension, on a carved stone from a shrine in Liangcheng 兩城 (Weishan 微山, Shandong), the *xian* is shown in mirror image, facing a bird and a human-headed canine beast.[119] In this case, the mirror-image animal master functions as a single entity. He also retains the role of hunter, on work ranging from the Mawangdui M1 black coffin (Figure 1) to a stone carving from Shilipu 十里鋪 (Nanyang 南陽 Municipality, Henan).[120] More frequently, however, the master appears in conjunction with animals placed in less formal relationship to him (as on Figure 8). Rather than indicating dominance by the central position of the master, whether or not he grips the animals flanking him (as maintained on Figure 11, upper register, or 12, upper right), his authority is instead often expressed by his role as animal tamer, rider, or driver[121] (cf., Figure 16; 44, center right). In some cases, he appears to have a more ecstatic role, dancing with a sacred plant in association with magical animals, as with the rabbit compounding the elixir of immortality on a carved stone from the tomb of Wang Deyuan 王得元 (Suide, Shaanxi; AD 100) or the loose parade of fantastic animals on a stone from a Han tomb in Kuaihualing 快華嶺 (Housijiagou 後思家溝, Suide, Shaanxi)[122] (see also Figure 8; 68, center right). Many of these, like the Mawangdui M1 coffin, differ little from Eastern Zhou examples such as the Gaozhuang fragments in fundamental composition, with the exception of the Han development of various forms of landscape (including the stylized meanders of the Mawangdui M1 coffin).

113 Henan 2001: 142-145, bronze. Cf., Falkenhausen 1999: 479, footnote 38, *c.* early 6th century BC (*c.* 575 BC, suggested by Falkenhausen).
114 Hubei 1989, Vol. 1: 34, Fig. 20; Vol. 2: Col. Pl. 2:3, 4; Pl. 11:4 (the inner coffin).
115 Barnard 1973.
116 Zhongguo shehui kexueyuan 1980, Vol. 1: 107, Fig. 72:5; Vol. 2: Col. Pl. 13:1; Pl. 66 (reconstructed); Zhixin J. Sun (ed.) 2017: 124, No. 46.
117 Liaocheng 1989: 53, Fig. 9, center. Dated per Psarras 2015.
118 Zhongguo meishu 1988: 45, Pl. 54.
119 Zhongguo meishu 1988: 41, Pl. 48 (dated by inscription to AD 139). See also Zhongguo meishu 1988: 37, Pl. 43, Panjiatong 潘家疃 (Fei 費 xian, Shandong), carved stone.
120 Zhongguo meishu 1988: 91, Pl. 106.
121 Nanyang 1990: Pl. 181, Nanyang (Henan) stamped brick. See also Zhongguo meishu 1988: 32, Pl. 36, Liangchen (Weishan, Shandong), carved stone; 70-71, Pl. 82, Sishipu 四十鋪 (Suide, Shaanxi), carved stone; 70-71, Pl. 84, Liujiawan 劉家灣 (Suide, Shaanxi), carved stone; 123, Pl. 146, Yingzhuang 英莊 (Nanyang Municipality, Henan), carved stone; 196, Pl. 260, Yanling 鄢陵 (Henan), stamped brick.
122 Shaanxi 1959: 23, Pl. 12, tomb of Wang Deyuan, AD 100; 45, Pl. 36, Housijiagou (both, Suide, Shaanxi).

The *xian* is also incorporated into formalized scenes of worship. In these, which undoubtedly reflect numerous later influences, the animal master takes on two roles, simultaneously: as a subordinate to the Queen Mother of the West (or King Father of the East) or subsumed into these more dominant deities. In terms of the former, *xian* appear in the court of the Queen Mother of the West, whether in the background, as on a stone from Xinsheng 新勝 (Pidu 郫都 [formerly Pi 郫 xian], Chengdu 成都 Municipality, Sichuan), on which two *xian* play a *liubo* 六博 board game,[123] or as an acolyte to the Queen Mother, as on carvings from Hejiagou 賀家溝 (Suide, Shaanxi) and Songshan 宋山 (Jiaxiang, Shandong)[124] (Figure 12, upper right, far right).

In contrast, the equivalence of the Queen Mother and the *xian* as two renditions of the animal master is superficially less clear: certainly, the Queen Mother is regularly portrayed as a massive, immobile figure, sometimes winged,[125] but never flying. Nonetheless, the equivalence becomes visible in terms of composition. Regardless of whether *xian* appear with her, the Queen Mother of the West (or King Father of the East) takes the place in the composition of earlier animal masters: she is flanked by animals (often magical; Figure 14), as well as presiding over scattered animals[126] (Figure 12, upper right in conjunction with the scene on the left), hunting, and animal predation.[127] On an openwork jade screen from Dingzhou 定州 ([formerly Ding 定 xian,] Hebei) M43, the enthroned Queen Mother is shown surrounded by *xian* and animals: in the upper plaque, the animals are placed immediately beside her; in the lower register, the *xian*.[128] Unlike the *xian*, however, the Queen Mother of the West does not herself hunt; she is also less likely than the *xian* to be associated with animal predation.

Again, as in Eastern Zhou parallels, scenes of the hunt or of scattered animals maintain the sacred nature of the association with the animal master as scenes of paradise, even when the animal master is not shown. This is clear from numerous carved stones from Suide (Shaanxi), on which the hunt or scattered animals are shown in the same way whether or not a deity (Queen Mother of the West or *xian*) is included[129] (Figures 12, 13). Thus, the scattered animals

[123] Zhongguo meishu 1988: 77, Pl. 91.

[124] Shaanxi 1959: 37, Pl. 26-27, Zhaojiapu 趙家鋪; 39, Pl. 28, Hejiagou (all, Suide, Shaanxi); Zhongguo meishu 1988: 2, Pl. 2; 3, Pl. 3, both Songshan (Jiaxiang, Shandong).

[125] As in Zhongguo meishu 1988: 2, Pl. 2; 3: Pl. 3, both Songshan (Jiaxiang, Shandong). I am assuming that the symmetrical, single curves emanating from her shoulders in these cases are wings, rather than flames (represented by symmetrical, multiple curves). The Songshan examples are marked with fine striations, like the wings of the adjacent *xian*. However, the distinction between wings and flames may be blurred. See below, *Kavaem Khvareno*.

[126] Zhongguo meishu 1988: 40, Pl. 47, Hongdaoyuan 宏道院 (Chengli 城里, Tengzhou 滕州 [formerly Teng 滕 xian], Shandong), carved stone; 70-71, Pl. 83, Sishipu (Suide, Shaanxi); 77, Pl. 91, Xinsheng (Pidu, Chengdu Municipality, Sichuan), stone coffin; 191, Pl. 248, Qingbai 清白 (Xinfan 新繁, Chengdu Municipality, Sichuan). On stones from Suide (Shaanxi), the associated animals may also be scattered throughout the bordering meanders: Shaanxi 1959: 38, Pl. 28, Zhuanyaoliang 磚窑梁 (Hejiagou, Suide, Shaanxi); 56, Pl. 45-46, Yihepu 義河鋪 (Suide, Shaanxi) M1; 98, Pl. 93, Suide (Shaanxi).

[127] For example, hunting: Zhongguo meishu 1988: 18, Pl. 21, Jiaxiang Village (Jiaxiang, Shandong), carved stone; animal predation: Zhongguo 2000: 170, Pl. 221, Yi'nan (Shandong), octagonal carved stone pillar. We shall return to the question of animal predation below (*Animal Predation*).

[128] Dingxian 1973: Pl. 1.

[129] Examples with a deity: Shaanxi 1959: 39, Pl. 28, Zhuanyaoliang (Hejiagou, Suide, Shaanxi); 45, Pl. 36, Kuaihualing (Housijiagou, Suide, Shaanxi); 65, Pl. 56, Ban Buddhist Temple 板佛寺 (Kuaihualing, Suide, Shaanxi), scattered animals; 21, Pl. 10, tomb of Wang Deyuan (Suide, Shaanxi). Without a deity: Shaanxi 1959:22, Pl. 11, tomb of Wang Deyuan (Suide, Shaanxi); 84-86, Pl. 76-78; 88-94, Pl. 80-86, 88, Suide (Shaanxi), all hunting; 36, Pl. 25, Zhaojiapu (Suide, Shaanxi); Zhongguo meishu 1988: 67, Pl. 79, Yanjiacha 延家岔 (Suide, Shaanxi), all scattered animals. Equally, the scattered animals without a deity applied as a band of low-relief décor on glazed *hu* in the Early Eastern Han (*c.* 1st century AD), as in: Xianyang 1982: 234, Fig. 13:2, Xianyang (Shaanxi) M36:19; Cheng *et al.*1992: 27, Fig. 5:1, Fangxin 房新 (Xi'an Municipality, Shaanxi) M6:4; both dated via Psarras 2015, *hu* 91, *c.* 67 AD.

tangled in vegetal meanders on carved stones from Suide (Shaanxi), for example (as Figures 12, 13), form the same composition as that most commonly applied to Han lacquerware and jade.[130] Compositionally, apart from the addition of the meander landscape, Han versions of the sacred hunt or scattered animals are not far removed from their Eastern Zhou antecedants.

Frequently, the flanking animals become part of the Queen Mother's throne, in an adaptation of the Near Eastern 'lion throne,' denoting kingship. The animal throne is closely identified with Kushan Buddhist sculpture (*c.* 1st-3rd centuries AD),[131] deriving from much earlier Near Eastern usage ultimately connected to images of the animal master, such as Neo-Assyrian cylinder seals.[132] Since the motif seems to have been incorporated into Chinese art only during the Han, we may reasonably assume that it reflects influence transmitted via Bactria or northern India, whether during the Kushan Empire or before, possibly as part of Buddhist iconography. The Queen Mother of the West is typically enthroned between a dragon and a tiger, as on a stamped brick from Xindu 新都 (Sichuan)[133] (Figure 14). The role of the throne as a sign of domination is more starkly shown on stone carvings from Weishan 微山 (Shandong), where the entwined bodies of the primordial hybrid (snake- or lizard-bodied) beings, Fuxi 伏羲 and Nüwa 女媧, serve as throne.[134] In other examples, such as a stone from Qilingang 麒麟崗 (Nanyang Municipality, Henan), Fuxi and Nüwa again flank the seated, but not obviously enthroned, Queen Mother of the West.[135] In this case, however, the human upper bodies of the primordial deities are shown frontally, in much the same posture as the Queen Mother. This composition accords them considerable importance, but still subordinates them to the Queen Mother of the West, whose role as animal master is further reinforced by a flanking set of felines. A similar duplication of subordinate elements occurs in other compositions, where animals flanking the deity may be retained in addition to the animal throne – as, for instance, on the Weishan carving, where a pair of birds is shown below the throne.[136]

Similarly, repeated motifs of an enthroned figure flanked by snake-like open spirals on a stone bas relief from Baishan 白山 (Pei 沛 xian, Xuzhou Municipality, Jiangsu) reprise the deity (that is, the animal master) enthroned[137] – and recall the earlier animal master with snake-like

[130] E.g., Anhui 2007: 60, Fig. 40 (FM1:282); 62, Fig. 42:1 (FM1:311); 63, Fig. 43 (FM1:389); 65, Fig. 45, top (FM1:314, lid), all Fangwanggang 放王崗 (Chaohu Municipality, Anhui) lacquer; 127, Fig. 92:2 (BM1:113), Beishantou (Chaohu Municipality, Anhui) jade ring-disc.

[131] Rosenfield, 1993: 183-186, positing a Western Asian origin for the throne; Figs 9 and 10 (Mathura [Uttar, India], figure standing immediately in front of a lion *couchant* partially wrapped around the figure's feet), 96 (Khair Khaneh [Afghanistan], throne platform supported by leaping horses], 107 (Shotorak [Afghanistan], half of a lion throne). Pugachenkova *et al.* 1996: 375, views Mathura as a source for the Gandharan lion throne. For connections between the enthroned Queen Mother of the West and the enthroned Buddha, see Wu 1987. Wu further explores the influence of Buddhism on Han art in Wu 1986.

[132] Collon 1987: 166, No. 773, British Museum 89769, cylinder seal.

[133] Zhongguo meishu 1988: 173, Pl. 216. See also Zhongguo meishu 1988: 77, Pl. 91, Xinsheng (Pidu, Chengdu Municipality, Sichuan) stone coffin; 83, Pl. 98, Pengshan 彭山 (Sichuan) stone coffin. For the equivalence of the dragon and tiger, see below, *Animal Predation*.

[134] Zhongguo meishu 1988: 33, Pl. 37; see also 27, Pl. 31, Wangkai 王開 and 28, Pl. 32, Xihukou 西户口 (both Tengzhou, Shandong). The fans wielded by Fuxi and Nüwa in the Weishan scene may be identified as an attribute of the servant, here reinforcing the status of Fuxi and Nüwa as subordinate to the Queen Mother of the West. By 'lizard-bodied,' I mean those snake bodies that have feet, as on Zhongguo meishu 1988: 95, Pl. 112-113, both Nanyang (Henan) stone carvings; 96, Pl. 115, Huyang 湖陽 (Tanghe 唐河, Henan) carved stone.

[135] Wang Yu 2014: 69, Fig. 1. In this composition, the Queen Mother of the West is further flanked by constellations.

[136] Zhongguo meishu 1988: 27: Pl. 31, Wangkai; 28, Pl. 32, Xihukou (both Tengzhou, Shandong).

[137] Xuzhou 1985: Pl. 262.

dragon on the Changtaiguan (Xinyang Municipality, Henan) M1:158 lacquered zither.[138] The same iconography is unambiguously identifiable on a harness ornament (*danglu* 當盧) from the horse and carriage pit associated with the tomb of the Marquis of Haihun 海昏 (Xinjian 新建 [Nanchang Municipality, Jiangxi]), *c.* 1st century BC).[139] On this piece, the *xian* animal master, in his usual mobile stance, is shown flanked by entwined dragons. On another harness ornament from the same pit, the *xian* is not portrayed and the two dragons represent the hybrid Fuxi and Nüwa,[140] identified by the the sun (with the associated bird inside) and moon (inhabited by a rabbit and toad) above their heads.[141] This series of décors serves to illustrate the interchangeability of the various incarnations of animal master. It further suggests that the snake-like elements on the Baishan relief may also represent Fuxi and Nüwa. Indeed, this equivalence may carry over to the knotted dragons framing the abbreviated scene of human activity on a carved stone from Guoli 郭里 (Zou 鄒 xian, Shandong).[142] From these equivalencies, it appears that the heraldic flanking animals of the animal master, regardless of species, may have been understood in China as representing (like Fuxi and Nüwa) dualistic forces of nature.

The image of the animal throne may well have been further reinforced by contact with depictions of the goddess Nana (Nanaia), frequently shown riding a lion, particularly in cases where the throne of the Queen Mother of the West is placed on the back of a single animal, rather than two, as on a stamped brick from Chengdu 成都 (Sichuan).[143] Often merged with other goddesses, Nana has an ancient history, from approximately the late-third millennium BC Uruk (near As-Samawah [Al-Muthanna, Iraq]) through 6th century AD Sogdiana (Tajikistan).[144] Contemporaneously with the Han, she occurs in various media in Bactria,[145] where she is further echoed by a male figure on a lion from Tillia-tepe tomb 4.[146] Coincidentally, when not shown with a lion, Nana may be identified by the crescent moon attribute which she acquired through her association with the Greek Artemis,[147] recalling the connection between Nüwa and the (full) moon, later assumed by the Queen Mother of the West.[148] This similarity may have facilitated transmission to China.

138 Henan 1986: Col. Pl. 2:3.
139 Jiangxi 2015: 71, bottom.
140 Jiangxi 2016: 105, left, gold-inlaid bronze.
141 Examples of hybrid Fuxi and Nüwa with their respective sun and moon attributes include: Zhongguo meishu 1988: 172, Pl. 213-214, Taiping 太平 (Pengzhou 彭州 [formerly, Peng 彭 xian], Sichuan; as hybrid bird-humanoids); 173, Pl. 215, Chongqing 崇慶 (Sichuan; as snake-humanoid hybrids). All, stamped bricks.
142 Zhongguo meishu 1988: 48, Pl. 58.
143 Zhongguo meishu 1988: 191, Pl. 248, enthroned on a tiger.
144 Grenet and Marshak 1998.
145 Mukerjee 1969; Rosenfield 1993: 84, text Fig. 10, seals; Fig. III:44 (#134); Fig. IV (#78); Fig. VII (#135-142), all coins.
146 Sarianidi 1985: Pl. 88-97, M4:2, gold belt plaque.
147 Grenet and Marshak 1998: 8.
148 Cf., Wu Hung 1989: 127.

Chapter 3

Developments Related to the Animal Master

Less obviously, the animal master iconography further generated a number of minor figures and compositional elements common in Han art: animal-humanoid hybrid deities, man-animal combat, scenes of human activity, and specific conventions of depiction. As with the animal master, these images reflect complex patterns of foreign influence.

Lesser Deities

In addition to renditions of the hybrid animal master, the Han developed an extensive pantheon of animal-headed and snake-bodied deities. These entities frequently appear as supplicants in the courts of the Queen Mother of the West and King Father of the East, as in the Left Wu family shrine (Jiaxiang, Shandong; *c.* mid-second century AD), or as guardians of paradise, as on the stone relief post of doors in Mamaozhuang 馬茂莊 (Lishi 離石, Shanxi) M2 (*c.* 175 AD).[149] Although they are not the only anguiped deities,[150] Fuxi and Nüwa retain a special status. Embodying *yang* 陽 and *yin* 陰, respectively, as well as the regulation of human society,[151] they may be shown alone (without reference to the Queen Mother of the West), as in the ceiling paintings at Qianjingtou 淺井頭 (Luoyang Municipality, Henan) CM1231 (*c.* 24 AD) and in the tomb of Bu Qianqiu 卜千秋 (Luoyang Municipality, Henan; *c.* 9 AD),[152] or as subordinate to the Queen Mother of the West, as in bas reliefs from the Left Wu family shrine (Jiaxiang, Shandong),[153] where they serve to illustrate the Queen Mother's supremacy over all creation. Despite their derivation from hybrid animal masters, the Han development of these deities seems to incorporate additional influence apparently not absorbed by China before the Han,[154] from both Western and, undoubtedly, Indian sources.[155]

The representation of animal-humanoid hybrids, particularly those associating a human head on an animal body, occurs as early as the 3rd millennium BC in Egypt, with the development

[149] Liu Xingzhen and Yue Fengxia 1991: 92-93, upper left, Left Wu family shrine, second stone; Shanxi 1992: 25, Fig. 28; 26, Fig. 31, Mamaozhuang (Lishi, Shanxi) M2 (dated per Psarras 2015).

[150] Anguipeds also serve as subordinates to Nüwa and Fuxi, as on the fourth stone of the Left Wu family shrine (Liu Xingzhen and Yue Fengxia 1991: 100, top).

[151] Indicated by Fuxi's carpenter's square and Nüwa's compass (Wu Hung 1989: 245).

[152] Luoyang 1993: 12-13, Fig. 25, Qianjingtou (Luoyang Municipality, Henan); Luoyang 1977: 10-11, Figs 33-34, tomb of Bu Qianqiu (Luoyang). Dates per Psarras 2015.

[153] Liu Xingzhen and Yue Fengxia 1991: 92-93, Left Wu family shrine (Jiaxiang, Shandong), second stone. On the Wu Liang shrine, they are depicted as part of a series of early cultural heroes (Liu Xingzhen and Yue Fengxia 1991: 16-17).

[154] Michael Loewe provides a late imperial woodcut illustration of the *juedi* 角抵 games (Loewe 1994: 239, Fig. 16; 237), in which dancers assume animal masks for the reenactment of mythological battles between divinities with animal attributes. He cites references to such performances in extant histories for both the Western and Eastern Han. Similarly, Anette Bulling (1966-67, 1967-68) argues that Han depictions of many, if not all, figural scenes were based on dramatic performances. This theory has parallels in some Greek vase painting (cf., Neer 1995) and may be accurate for some Han images. We have no reason, however, to assume that Bulling's theory applies to all Han images or even to all representations of a single image. The context of banquets with acrobatic and dance performances, where we might expect to see animal-masked human figures, is distinct from the scenes of paradise with which the animal-headed figures discussed here are associated. In both contexts, however, depiction of the hybrids implies that they belonged to the mythological landscape.

[155] Cf., Animal-human hybrid deities in Mathura: Pugachenkova *et al.* 1996: 369.

of the sphinx,[156] as well as in Ur (Tell Muqqayan, Dhi Qar [Iraq]), with the image of human-headed bulls.[157] These figures are widely in use during the 2nd millennium in both the Near East and Greece,[158] and remain in use through the Achaemenid and Hellenistic periods.[159] The impact of Persian and and particularly Hellenistic art on Gandhara (northern Pakistan, eastern Afghanistan) and Bactria is well-known,[160] as demonstrated by excavations at the Bactrian city of Aï Khanoum (Takhar Province [Afghanistan]; *c.* early 3rd-mid 2nd centuries BC)[161] and, later, by the development of Gandharan Buddhist art (*c.* 1st century BC-7th century AD), incorporated into the Kushan Empire. In this context, the hybrid worshippers of the enthroned Buddha on a Kushan-era stone carving[162] are placed in a composition reflecting stylistic influence filtered through Persia and Greece, perhaps combined with the Hindu pantheon of hybrid beings. In turn, both in terms of hybrid deities and of formalized worship, this Kushan piece may also reflect the kind of influence visible in similar scenes centering on the Queen Mother of the West in the Left Wu shrine (*c.* mid-second century AD) and Mamaozhuang (Lishi Municipality, Shanxi) M2 (*c.* 175 AD)[163] (Figure 15). The direction of influence in this case must have been toward China, indicating that new developments must have both traveled quickly and been quickly absorbed.

However, Hellenized Central Asian art is not the only likely source of new influence reflected in Han hybrids. Despite the popularity of the snake or serpentine dragon in Eastern Zhou art, in association with the animal master or, far more frequently, in zoomorphized meanders or interlace (which continue to a lesser extent during the Han[164]), the anguiped image used during the Han most markedly for Fuxi and Nüwa seems to have no Eastern Zhou prototype. Anguipeds do, however, occur in Greek art, as in late-fifth century BC depictions of the Scylla (a

156 The Encyclopaedia Britannica's entry on the sphinx (<https://www.britannica.com/topic/sphinx>, viewed 31 December 2018) cites the Great Sphinx at Giza as the earliest extant example, *c.* 2575-2465 BC.

157 Collon 1995: 224, Fig. 192, upper panel, Royal Cemetery at Ur (Tell Muqqayan, Dhi Qar [Iraq]), sound-box of a lyre, shell-inlaid bitumen, *c.* 2600 BC (University Museum, Philadelphia).

158 Collon 1987: 127, No. 551, Syria, blue glass cylinder seal showing the Egyptian Seth (*c.* 1300 BC); Harper, Aruz, and Tallon (eds) 1992: 141-143, No. 88, multi-brick relief (baked clay) showing a deity with a human head and bull body, Apadana mound (Susa [Shush, Khuzestan, Iran]), Middle Elamite (*c.* 1200 BC), Louvre Sb 14390 (see also <https://www.louvre.fr/en/oeuvre-notices/panels-molded-bricks, viewed 31 December 2018); Godard 1950: 22, Fig. 12, detail of decoration on the clothing of Ashurnasirpal II (r. 884-859 BC), stone bas relief, British Museum; Collon 1987: 121, No. 519, lapis lazuli cylinder seal originally Near Eastern, recut in Thebes (Greece), *c.* 1000-500 BC. Harper, Aruz, and Tallon (eds) 1992: 143, discusses the development of the lamassu figure (human-headed bull deity) in first-millennium BC Iraq and Syria.

159 E.g., Harper, Aruz, and Tallon (eds) 1992: 228-230, No. 157, Apadana (Susa) central court, multi-brick glazed relief showing a sphinx, Achaemenid (*c.* late 6th- early 5th centuries BC), Louvre Sb 3324 (see also the photograph on the Louvre site, <http://cartelfr.louvre.fr/cartelfr/visite?srv=car_not&idNotice=12400>, viewed 31 December 2018, which provides a date of *c.* 510 BC); Williams and Ogden 1994: 248, No. 185, Marion (Polis Chrysochous [Cyprus]) tomb K28, gold pendant in the form of a sphinx, *c.* 400-350 BC; Pfrommer 1993: 17-18, for discussion of Scythian and Parthian depictions of the sphinx.

160 To cite only a few of a substantial body of references: Boardman 1994, 2000; Schlumberger 1960a, b; Pugachenkova *et al.* 1996.

161 These excavations have yielded a multitude of reports and analytical articles, as (to name only a few) Bernard 1987, 1996. See Claude Rapin's references for Aï Khanoum, <http://claude.rapin.free.fr/1BibliographiesPDF/1FAKhBiblio.pdf>, viewed 22 March 2017, and the Encyclopaedia Iranica, Ay Kanom, <http://www.iranicaonline.org/articles/ay-kanom-or-a-khanum-tepe-a-local-uzbek-name-lit>, viewed 22 March 2017, for extensive bibliography.

162 Rosenfield 1993: Fig. 81.

163 Liu Xingzhen and Yue Fengxia 1991: 92-93, upper left, Left Wu family shrine, second stone; Shanxi 1992: 25, Fig. 28; 26, Fig. 31, Mamaozhuang (Lishi, Shanxi) M2. Cf., Wu Hung 1989: 134-141.

164 Han examples include: Anhui 2007: 115, Fig. 83, Beishantou (Chaohu Municipality, Anhui) BM1:20 (lacquer *pan*); Xu (ed.) 2017: 136, No. 52, Xiaoguishan 小龜山 (Xuzhou Municipality, Jiangsu), gilded bronze globular incense burner; 154, No. 68, Dayunshan (Xuyi, Jiangsu) burial goods pit 1 (associated with M1), gilded bronze belt plaques inlaid with carved jade. Eastern Zhou examples are ubiquitous: e.g., throughout So 1995.

woman with the tail of a sea serpent).[165] Like some Han versions of anguipeds,[166] these images of Scylla depict small, lizard-like forelegs below her human torso and may also include the head of a dragon.[167] This dragon head has no counterpart in Han figures. A further comparison is provided by Greek tritons, male or female with serpentine body (*c.* 200 BC).[168] The Scythians depicted a similar deity, Api, also a woman with the lower body of one or more snakes. In *c.* fourth-century BC Greek-influenced Scythian work, the curve of Api's two snake legs mimicks her curling skirts, which in turn consist of serpentine animals terminating (per steppe convention) in tiger or eagle heads.[169] The intruding lizard legs and skirt-like wings appear on a Han stone bas relief from Shuanggou 雙溝 (Suining 睢寧, Xuzhou Municipality, Jiangsu), in addition to wings attached near the shoulders,[170] suggesting that some version of the Api image may have reached China.

Man-Animal Combat

Like hunting, man-animal combat is associated from an early date with the animal master.[171] Unlike hunting, in which the killing of the animals takes place from some distance, the human protagonist in man-animal combat is in direct physical contact with the animal: man and animal are of roughly the same size and both thus appear equal adversaries in the confrontation. This mutuality lends a mythic, if not religious, dimension to the iconography, underscored by the identification of the male figure as a manifestation of the animal master (half-man, half-animal)[172] or, by extension, a hero, whether king or perhaps priest.[173] The image appears on *c.* 6th century BC bronzes with animal master iconography, as on the third and fourth registers of the Liulige (Huixian, Henan) M59:23 *hu* (Figure 10),[174] and frequently during the Han – with a typically loosened spatial relationship – in the depiction of *xian* chasing or confronting various animals (often a dragon or tiger), as on a Yingzhuang 英莊 (Nanyang Municipality, Henan)[175]

165 Nikulina 1994: Pl. II:123, Bibliothèque Nationale (Paris), rock crystal stamp seal; Pl. II-124, Staatliche Museen (Berlin) T.II.94, glass seal. These depictions recall the *c.* sixth-century BC Attic Greek 'composite monster' with an animal head, wings, a human (masculine?) upper body, lion forelegs, and the same fish body utilized on the Scylla (Osborne 1996: 172, Fig. 43, Olympia [Greece], bronze shield blazon). As with Scylla, the human torso is simply attached to the side of the fish, rather than emerging where the fish's head would be. (Note that, confusingly, Nikulina at times reuses plate numbers.)

166 As in 'lizard-like' variants of Fuxi and Nüwa: Zhongguo meishu 1988: 95, Pl. 112-113, Nanyang (Henan); 96, Pl. 115, Huyang (Tanghe, Henan), all carved stone.

167 As noted, Nikulina 1994: Pl. II:123, 124. On these pieces, the woman's torso appears to have been attached to a full dragon (with a fish-like tail).

168 Williams and Ogden 1994: Pl. 37, noted as probably northern Greece.

169 Galanina and Gratch 1987: Pl. 144, gold plaque covering wood frontal piece, Greco-Scythian caparison, Bol'šaja Cumbalka (Zaporož'e [Ukraine]); Pl. 203, gold appliqué, Scythian manufacture, Kul'-Oba (Kerč', Crimea [Ukraine]).

170 Jiangsu 1959: Pl. 70, Fig. 90, right.

171 Collon 1987: 30, No. 84, southern Mesopotamia, lapis lazuli cylinder seal, *c.* 2600 BC.

172 As on the seal noted above, e.g., Collon 1987, described as a 'bull-man.'

173 E.g., Collon 1987: 91, No. 421 (Marathon [Greece]) and No. 428 (Borsippa [Iraq]), both chalcedony cylinder seals, post-500 BC; Boardman 2000: 154, Fig. 5.1, Phoenician green jasper scaraboid, Achaemenid period (Cambridge E.O.36); 183, Fig. 5.64, Kamini 'stele' (identified by Boardman as a table support), Athens, stone relief. The latter also includes the representation of live-prey predation. The specific identity assigned to animal-master figures certainly varies and is not always known.

174 Guo Baojun 1959: Pl. 93.

175 Wang Jianzhong and Shan Xiushan 1990: Pl. 248. See also Zhengzhou 1972:48, Fig. 14:3, Xintongqiao 新通橋 (Zhengzhou Municipality, Henan), stamped hollow brick; Wang Jianzhong and Shan Xiushan 1990: Pl. 252, Nanyang (Henan) find, stone bas relief; Pl. 253, Huyangxindian 湖陽辛店 (Tanghe, Nanyang Municipality, Henan), stone relief dated to AD 18; Pl. 254, Caodian 草店 (Nanyang Municipality, Henan), stone relief; Pl. 255, Wangzhai 王寨 (Nanyang Municipality, Henan), stone relief; Pl. 256, Dongguan 東關 (Shiqiao 石橋, Nanyang Municipality, Henan), stone relief; Pl. 259, Kuixinglou 奎星樓 (Dongguan, Nanyang Municipality, Henan), stone relief, etc.; Nanyang 1980: 244, Fig. 8:1.

stone relief (Figure 16) or the Baonüdun 寶女墩 (Hanjiang 邗江, Yangzhou 揚州 Municipality, Jiangsu) M104:16[176] bronze ornament. This use of the *xian* clearly places the image in relation to the paradise iconography, but a more human – perhaps more secular – version also occurs, as on a stamped brick from Luoyang (Henan),[177] featuring a man taming a tiger.

As with the animal master, man-animal combat appears in the Near East by the late 4th millennium BC[178] and remains in use, not only in Persia,[179] but in Greece through at least the late 4th century BC.[180] The image is rare in the steppe, even in Greek-produced Scythian work, although examples of animals hunting people occasionally occur.[181] In such cases, the distinction between hunting and man-animal combat can be difficult. Man-animal combat occurs, however, in Xiongnu art on essentially identical bronze plaques from the partially-Xiongnu non-Chinese site of Xichagou 西岔溝 (Xifeng 西豐, Liaoning) and the non-Xiongnu non-Chinese site of Daodunzi 倒墩子 (Tongxin 同心, Ningxia), both broadly dated to the Han[182] (Figure 17). On these pieces, a helmeted man on foot fights an animal standing on its hind legs (both shown in profile), while a mounted warrior appears beside them (in full frontal view), flanked by a cart beneath a tree. The mounted warrior and the helmeted man on foot clearly reprise the décor of a *c.* fourth-century BC Scythian gold plaque from Geremessovskij (Zaporož'e [Ukraine]).[183]

In this context, the source for the image is certainly Western, transmitted to China by the 5th century BC. We may view Han renditions as the result of some degree of Eastern Zhou influence, reinforced by Xiongnu influence, which itself maintained Greek influence. The role of the steppe in this transmission is more obvious in the case of exotic Han pieces, such as an unprovenanced Chinese-type garment hook of turquoise-inlaid gilded bronze in the form of an armed man being attacked by a feline (Kunstindustriemuseet, Copenhagen).[184] Beyond the composition, the use of inlay follows steppe ornamental practices closely associated with Sarmatian taste (*c.* 4th century BC-5th century AD), echoed in Tillia-tepe, but only rarely in Xiongnu work.[185] It is often difficult to assess where inlaid gold pieces found in Han tombs

[176] Yangzhou 1991:47, Fig. 20:5, Fig. 21 (*c.* 90 AD, per Psarras 2015). See also, for instance, Nanyang 1980: 251, Fig. 21:1, tomb of (the consort of) Lord Feng 馮君 (Tanghe [Nanyang Municipality, Henan]), d. AD 18, stone relief; Liu Songgen and Xue Wencan 1993: 53, Xinzheng (Henan), stamped brick with a décor of a man kneeling in front of a tiger.

[177] Huang Minglan 1986: 44-45.

[178] Collon 1987: 27; 29, No. 79, Fara (Iraq); *c.* late 4th millennium BC; 30, No. 85, southern Mesopotamia, *c.* 2600 BC; Collon 1995: 78, Fig. 59a-c, Akkadian, *c.* late 3rd millennium BC. All cylinder seals.

[179] Collon 1995: 158, Fig. 26, Southeast (Burnt) Palace at Nimrud (Iran), *c.* early 9th century BC, cylindrical ivory box with depictions of man-animal combat as well as hunting by chariot.

[180] Collon 1987: 91, No. 421, chalcedony cylinder seal, Marathon (Greece), *c.* 500 BC or later; Reeder (ed.) 1999: 287, Nos 141 (Herakles and Cerberas), 142 (Herakles and the Nemean lion), from the Scythian kurgan Babyna Moxila (Taraso-Xryxorivka, Dnepropetrovsk [Ukraine]), silver phalerae, *c.* 350-300 BC.

[181] Galanina and Gratch 1987: Pl. 226-228, Scythian tomb at Bol'šaja Bliznica (Krasnodar [formerly Kuban, Russia]), gold, Greek-produced *kalathos* (feminine headdress) depicting men being attacked by griffins, *c.* 4th century BC; *L'Or* 1995: 64, No. 91, Kobjakovo (Rostov [Russia]) kurgan 10, Sarmatian torque, gold with polychrome inlay, men battling a winged dragon with one of the dragons biting one of the men, *c.* late 1st-early 2nd centuries AD.

[182] Tian Guangjin and Guo Suxin 1986: 96, Fig. 64:6, Xichagou (Xifeng, Liaoning); Ningxia 1988b: 345, Fig. 10:6; Pl. 16:3, Daodunzi (Tongxin, Ningxia) M10:33.

[183] Galanina and Gratch 1987: Pl. 136, *c.* 4th century BC.

[184] Deydier 1980: 95, Pl. 70, Kunstindustriemuseet, Copenhagen. Chinese-type garment hooks generally have an attachment button on one end of the reverse side and a hook on the opposite end of the face: see Wang Renxiang 1985.

[185] *L'Or* 1995 (Sarmatians); Sarianidi 1985 (Tillia-tepe); Tian Guangjin and Guo Suxin 1986: Col. Pl. 16:1; Pl. 69:4, Aluchaideng (Hanggin Banner, Inner Mongolia; Xiongnu). Schiltz (1994: 314) dates the Sarmatians from *c.* 4th century BC. *L'Or* (1995: 118-121), identifying the Alans as a Sarmatian tribe, cites a *c.* 5th century AD end-date for both Alans and Sarmatians. *Minami Rosia* 1991: 168-169, provides a *c.* 3rd century AD date for the end of the Sarmatians as such and a

were produced.[186] The Kunstindustriemuseet garment-hook nonetheless appears to be of Han manufacture. The man, depicted with a broad face and large eyes, presumably represents a foreigner; his shortsword may mark him as Xiongnu, although he could belong to any of the northern non-Chinese peoples. As in the prototypes (including the Liulige *hu*), the feline is virtually as large as the man, conferring near-equal status to predator and prey.

Human Activity

The impetus for Han depictions of landscape has been long been debated.[187] The development of realistic landscape, as in the rice fields and tiered mountains shown on stamped bricks from Sichuan,[188] seems a natural result of Han interest in portraying human activity. However, although they may figure as independent compositions, social scenes are often incorporated into larger compositions culminating in the enthroned Queen Mother of the West or King Father of the East, whose position at the top of the composition readily translates their domination of all the spheres of activity shown, whether human or divine.[189] This association of secular and sacred is visible in Near Eastern animal master iconography[190] and is retained in Eastern Zhou versions. It is in this context, moreover, that it is apparently first documented in Chinese art.

On fragments from Gaozhuang (Huaiyin Municipality, Jiangsu), human reality intrudes in hunting scenes primarily through the use of real equipment, more specific in type than the generic bows and arrows with which animal masters are often equipped. Some fragments, for instance, depict wheeled vehicles, in most cases apparently manned by animal masters in various guises (visible on Figure 4, lower right).[191] On the M1:0155 fragment, hunters on foot carry a specifically Chinese weapon, the halberd (*ge* 戈).[192] On these examples, the hunters appear to be animal masters; certainly, they fulfil the role of animal masters. However, the Gaozhuang M1:27 *pan* fragment, executed in the same incised style as the other figured pieces, clearly depicts humans in a series of social scenes: hunting on foot, views of a temple or other building in which some activity is taking place, a procession outside this building, horses being led toward the structure, all set in a landscape of rows of trees.[193] In this case, I find no specific depiction of the animal master, but inclusion of the hunt, elsewhere closely identified with him, confers an element of the sacred to the collection of scenes. In addition, if the building shown is indeed a temple, it exemplifies the sacred context proper to animal master hunting scenes.

---

c. 4th century AD end-date for the Alans, here also identified as a branch of the Sarmatians.

186 Cf., Lin (ed.) 2012: 283, No. 158.

187 For instance, Jacobson 1985, 1988.

188 E.g., Zhongguo meishu 1988: 158, Pl. 191, Anren 安仁 (Dayi 大邑, Sichuan), Pl. 192, Sanjie 三界 (Pengzhou, Sichuan); 159, Pl. 193, Huapaifang 花牌坊 (Qionglai 邛郲, Sichuan), Pl. 194, Bailong 柏隆 (Deyang 德陽, Sichuan).

189 As in Zhongguo meishu 1988: 2, Pl. 2, Songshan (Jiaxiang, Shandong), with kitchen scenes (carved stone); 10, Pl. 11, Hongshan 洪山 (Jiaxiang, Shandong), with wheel wrights (stamped brick).

190 E.g., cylinder seals: Collon 1987: 29, No. 82, Abu Salabikh (Iraq) tomb 173; 29, No. 83, Ur (Tell Muqqayan, Dhi Qar [Iraq]), both *c.* 3000-2334 BC; 38, No. 130, Knossos (Crete) palace, *c.* 2300-1900 BC *ante quem*; 48, No. 178, Tell Leilan and Mari (Syria), Sippar (Iraq), *c.* 2000-1500 BC (drawing of seal impression); 64, No. 274, Perati (Greece) chamber-tomb 1, *c.* 1500-1000 BC; 164, No. 758, Susa (Iran), *c.* 3000-2334 BC (drawing of seal impression); 166, No. 773, *c.* 1000-500 BC (British Museum 89769), the latter dated to *c.* 720-700 BC on the British Museum website: <https://www.britishmuseum.org/research/collection_online/collection_object_details.aspx?objectId=369250&partId=1>, viewed 31 December 2018. The same principle of combining domestic and ritual also appears on Greek work in a Scythian context, as in the gold torque from Tolstaja Mogila (Pokrov, Dnepropetrovsk [Ukraine]), on which scenes of everyday life figure on one register, juxtaposed with animal predation, on the other (Schiltz 1994: 196-202, Figs 145-148).

191 Huaiyin 1988: 209, Fig. 22 (M1:114-2); 210, Fig. 24 (M1:114-4).

192 Huaiyin 1988: 211, Fig. 25:3.

193 Huaiyin 1988: 199, Fig. 12:1.

Similarly, although an Early Warring States (*c.* 5th century BC) copper-inlaid *hu* from Baihuatan 白花潭 (Chengdu Municipality, Sichuan)[194] depicts primarily human activities (war, hunting, music-making), the lowest register depicts the animal master flanked by animals and, in leaf-shaped cells below, paired animals in mirror-image heraldic pose. Notably, the composition of the war scenes parallels that of the animal master-related hunting scenes on pieces like the Gaozhuang fragments. In fact, the relationship of war to the animal master is illustrated by the sixth register of the essentially contemporaneous Liulige (Huixian, Henan) *hu* M59:23[195] (Figure 10), on which one animal master hunts another. This juxtaposition of secular and sacred activities becomes characteristic of Han narrative art, where scenes of paradise are frequently associated with processions, feasting, entertainment, and the like, with little apparent demarcation between divine and human spheres.

At least by the late 4th century BC, scenes of human activity appear without obvious reference to any deity, as on lacquered wood bows from Jiuliandun 九連墩 (Zaoyang 棗陽 Municipality, Hubei), depicting hunting on foot or from a carriage and with a variety of weapons, as well as people in procession and meeting each other.[196] A simpler composition of processions (on foot or in carriages) occurs on the Baoshan (Jingmen Municipality, Hubei) M2:432 lacquered *lian* toiletries box (*c.* 316 BC).[197] These pieces suggest that, by the later Warring States, considerable development of images ultimately deriving from the animal master iconography, but without necessarily any associated sacred character, may have taken place in media less laden with ritual significance (and more ephemeral) than bronze. Such developments would presumably have been known to the Han.

Specific Artistic Conventions

Corollary to Chinese versions of the animal master are a number of specific stylistic devices which undoubtedly reflect foreign influence. These often occur in hunting or scattered animal scenes or as part of the depiction of the Queen Mother of the West, all of which may be associated with images of paradise.

Kavaem Khvareno

John M. Rosenfield associates the *kavaem khvareno* ('flaming shoulders,' flaming halo), with Iranian royalty, particularly during the Islamic period.[198] Undoubtedly a mark of divinity, the motif appears at least as early as *c.* 2334-2000 BC on Near Eastern cylinder seals.[199] It likewise occurs in Greek-derived work of the Hellenistic period, as on depictions of Artemis and Zeus-Mithra with a radiant halo at Aï Khanoum (Kondoz [Afghanistan])[200]; in Kushan art, on deities such as the Indian goddess Sri and the Kushan god Pharro,[201] as well as on Buddha figures.[202]

194 Zhongguo 1976: Pl. 67; Zhongguo meishu 1992: 81, Pl. 94; cf., Thote 1999: 182, Fig. 2. Another example is provided by Hebei 1987: 178, Fig. 29, Sanji 三汲 (Pingshan 平山, Hebei) M8101:2.
195 Guo Baojun 1959: Pl. 93.
196 Hubei 2017.
197 Hubei 1991, Vol. 2: Col. Pl. 7:2; Col. Pl. 8.
198 Rosenfield 1993: 198.
199 Collon 1987: 34, Nos 102, 103, 104 (Tell al Rimah [Iraq]), 105 (Ur [Tell Muqqayan, Dhi Qar, Iraq]); 166, Nos 765 (Nippur [Iraq]), 766.
200 Bernard 1996: 114.
201 Rosenfield 1993: 200.
202 Rosenfield 1993: 198; cf., Rosenfield 1993: Fig. 106, Paitava (Parwan, Afghanistan).

It may therefore have reached China through Bactria, not necessarily in association with Buddhism.

In Han art, it is used not only as a halo for the Queen Mother of the West (and King Father of the East), as on stone bas reliefs at Mamaozhuang (Lishi, Shanxi)[203] (Figure 18, top), but on the shoulders of the *taotie* on the door of Mamaozhuang M4[204] and on the shoulders of a human-like figure standing on a fish at Wangcun王村 (Xia 夏 xian, Shanxi) XWM5.[205] On some circular plaques in gilded bronze from Wushan (Sichuan) depicting the seated Queen Mother of the West at the gates of heaven (identified by inscription), the flames are represented by highly vegetal meanders.[206] This evolution of the *kavaem khvareno* undoubtedly explains the tendrils surrounding the bodies of some immortals, as well as around a cluster of coins, on the bronze money tree from Guijiayuanzi 桂家院子 (Zhaotong 昭通 Municipality, Yunnan),[207] suggesting that the coins themselves have a divine aspect in such representations. Its use on Late Eastern Han ceramic model wells with no décor overtly associated with paradise from tombs such as Lixian 蠡縣 (Hebei)[208] and Xinggu 興固 (Shahe 沙河 Municipality, Hebei)[209] is less straightforward: does it indicate association with paradise or only an aesthetic choice?

Flying Gallop

Han hunting (and related) scenes frequently make use of motifs such as the flying gallop (the horse or other animal with hind legs extended backward, forelegs extended or bent toward the front), and the Parthian shot (the mounted bowman turning to aim behind his mount). Both motifs, obviously foreign to China,[210] are well-attested in the ancient western world over a long period of time. The flying gallop reached China by the 5th century BC, where it is occasionally applied to random animals in scattered animal compositions, as on the Jiagezhuang (Tangshan Municipality, Hebei) M5 *hu*[211] (Figure 5, lower register, panels 1-3, 6, lower left corner). In this composition, the effect is largely overwhelmed by the décor of scattered animals, most of which appear to be in motion, regardless of their stance. Following more recent excavations, however, the flying gallop appears markedly in hunting scenes on *c.* late-fourth century BC lacquered bows from Jiuliandun (Zaoyang Municipality, Hubei).[212] This application obviously parallels Han use and suggests Han continuity with Eastern Zhou, undoubtedly further reinforced by contemporaneous non-Chinese influences. In contrast, I have not found pre-Han examples of the Parthian shot; one may appear as more ephemeral art (lacquer, paintings) comes to light.

Janice L. Crowley, tracing the flying gallop to Minoan art of the late 19th century BC, emphasizes its divergence from contemporaneous Near Eastern and Egyptian conventions depicting

[203] Shanxi 1992: 17, Figs 8, 9; 22, Figs 20-21; 25, Fig. 28; 26, Fig. 31 (M2); 32, Fig. 49 (M3); Shanxi 1996: 16, Fig. 6:2; 17, Fig. 7:2 (M14, AD 175). See also Wang Yu 2014:72, Fig. 6:1, Qilingang (Nanyang Municipality, Henan), carved stone; Zhongguo meishu 1988: 77, Pl. 91, Xinsheng (Pidu, Chengdu Municipality, Sichuan).
[204] Shanxi 1992: 39, Fig. 70, *c.* 176 AD, per Psarras 2015.
[205] Shanxi 1994: 36, Fig. 5, painting, *c.* 90 AD, per Psarras 2015.
[206] Li Meitian 2014: 73, Fig. 2 (several sites), coffin ornaments; also 72, Fig. 1, on an openwork, gilded bronze plaque showing the Queen Mother of the West seated on the animal throne.
[207] Yunnan 1962: 398, Fig. 6:3, 6 (immortals), 2 (coins), *c.* 65 AD, per Psarras 2015.
[208] Hebei 1983: 49, Fig. 19 (drawing); 50, Fig. 20 (photograph), *c.* 174 AD, per Psarras 2015.
[209] Hebei 1992: 14, Fig. 4:8; Pl. 3:2, *c.* 176 AD, per Psarras 2015.
[210] E.g., Ghirshman 1962: 266; 267, Figs 345 (Siberian Treasure of Peter the Great, gold boar hunt plaque), 346 (Han stamped brick), also concludes that the Han depiction of the flying gallop is of Parthian derivation.
[211] An Zhimin 1953: 86, Fig. 11.
[212] Hubei 2017: 45, Fig. 19 (M1:815); 46, Fig. 20 (M1:817); 47, Fig. 21, bottom (M2:130).

speed.[213] According to Crowley, the motif spread to Syria as the result of Minoan influence and later appeared in Egypt (Dynasty XVIII, *c.* 1539-1295 BC). It remained in use in the Near East and Greece at least through the Classical period.[214] In some examples, it is used in hunting scenes where the horses pulling a carriage appear in flying gallop,[215] as is also the case on the essentially contemporaneous Jiuliandun bows. This near-contemporaneity suggests that little time was required for transmission of the motif and that such influence was readily absorbed by the Chinese.

The role potentially played by the steppe in either the initial transmission or in reinforcement during the Han is ambiguous. The flying gallop implicit in the stance of the small bronze horse statuette, described as depicting a Mede horseman,[216] is repeated on a nearly-identical gold statuette in the Siberian Collection of Peter the Great.[217] Further Far Eastern steppe examples are provided by wood harness ornaments from Pazyryk kurgan 1[218] and the boar, with legs fully outstretched, and horse, with forelegs bent, on the gold boar hunt plaques from the Siberian Collection of Peter the Great.[219] Although work such as this may well have reached the Han, the flying gallop is otherwise rare in steppe art. Han examples are plentiful, applying the motif to a variety of animals, including a hooved animal without horns, a rabbit, and a deer on the lacquered *lian* toiletries box from Maquan (Xianyang Municipality, Shaanxi)[220] (Figure 19); deer on a stone bas relief from Qinglongshan 青龍山 (Peixian, Xuzhou Municipality, Jiangsu)[221] (Figure 29); horses on a stone bas relief from Gaoli (Zoucheng Municipality, Shandong).[222]

Parthian Shot

The Parthian shot, despite its name, is common in Near Eastern work from the Achaemenid, well before the Parthian (247 BC-AD 224).[223] It remains in use thereafter, appearing, for instance, on a painted clay wall frieze in the Khaltchayan (Uzbekistan) palace, attributed to the Yuezhi 月氏 and dated *c.* 50 BC-50 AD.[224] A Bactrian transmission to China seems likely.

In Han work, the motif is not limited to the depiction of nomad warriors, as on a stamped brick from Fanye (Xinye, Henan),[225] but frequently occurs in hunting scenes, as on a stone relief from

[213] Crowley 1989: 113-119.

[214] Examples include, for the Near East: Collon 1995: 154, Fig. 122, Northern Palace of Assurbanipal, reigned 668-627 BC, Nineveh (Kuyunjik, Iraq); Nikulina 1994: Pl. II:20, *c.* late 5th-4th centuries BC seal; Pl. II:22, *c.* late 5th-4th centuries BC; Pl. III:496, right, *c.* 4th century BC; Pl. III:511, *c.* late 5th-early 4th centuries BC; Pl. III:512, *c.* late 5th-early 4th centuries BC, State Hermitage Museum Gl. 885, all seals. For Greek examples, see: Nikulina 1994: Pl. II:19, *c.* late 5th century BC; Pl. III:496, *c.* 4th century BC, Cambridge E.21864; Pl. III:499, *c.* 4th century BC, British Museum BM 89816.

[215] Nikulina 1994: Pl. III:511, seal, *c.* late 5th-early 4th centuries BC.

[216] Collon 1995: 221, Fig. 187, dating the piece to *c.* 5th-4th centuries BC; Colledge 1977: Pl. 11a, dating it to *c.* 300-150 BC.

[217] Schiltz 1994: 246-247, Figs 179-181, traditionally dated to *c.* 4th-3rd centuries BC. The Siberian Collection piece has separate bases for the horse's front and rear hooves; the 'Mede horseman' sets on a single base.

[218] Rudenko 1970: Pl. 88. Parzinger *et al.* 2008: 17 dates Pazyryk kurgan 1 to *c.* 295 BC.

[219] Schiltz 1994: 242-243, Fig. 178.

[220] Xianyang 1979: 133, Fig. 11:3, 4 (right side), 6, 7; *c.* 67 AD, per Psarras 2015.

[221] Nanjing 1984: 25, Fig. 8.

[222] Zoucheng 1994: 26-27, Fig. 7.

[223] As noted by Collon 1987: 155. Examples: Nikulina 1994: Pl. III:498, Achaemenid lentoid seals, *c.* 4th century BC; cylinder seals, Collon 1987: 154, No. 690, unprovenanced, British Museum BM 89816, *c.* 500 BC.

[224] Colledge 1977: 95, Fig. 40c, Toprak-Kala (Uzbekistan).

[225] Henan 1990B: 505, Fig. 5:3.

Qinglongshan (Peixian, Xuzhou Municipality, Jiangsu)[226] (Figure 29, lower register, far right). In some cases, as on a stamped brick from Yuxian (Henan),[227] the hunter draws on a tiger larger than his horse. This merging of the hunting scene with man-animal combat is further reinforced by the *xian* dancing on the tiger's back. Although the nomad figures are largely generic, they are often identified by scholars as Xiongnu. As in the West, the northern non-Chinese in battle scenes are most readily identified by the 'Scythian' or 'Phrygian' 'bonnet,'[228] a headgear echoed, incidentally, by the upswept hair of many *xian*.[229] Indeed, rather than being purely coincidental, this convergence of headgear and hair may speak to a shared foreign identity; curiously, it echoes an Etruscan statuette of a mounted 'Scythian.'[230] In any case, the two entities are at times interchangeable, as on a Yingzhuang (Nanyang, Henan) stamped brick, where a nomad with Phrygian bonnet takes the place of the *xian* as animal-tamer next to an elephant and tiger, the meander background suggesting paradise.[231] The hunter on the Yuxian brick, in contrast, appears to be Chinese: his short tunic and pants presumably follow nomad convention, but his flat hat seems Chinese.[232]

Three-Quarter View

The Han likewise made use of another western convention: the three-quarter view, developed in the Attic black-glazed ware during the 6th (particularly the mid-sixth) century BC,[233] but more readily used in the early 5th century BC (Late Archaic period, *c.* 500-480 BC), with the emergence of red figure ware[234] (Figures 20, 46 [on the carriage, not the harnessed griffins]). In Han terms, it is applied to the narrative scenes on mirrors from Bojishan 簸箕山 (Tianqi 天齋, Xuzhou Municipality, Jiangsu) XBM3:67[235] and the tomb of the King of Nanyue (Xianggangshan [Guangzhou Municipality, Guangdong])[236], as well as commonly in mural images of horse-drawn carriages[237] (Figures 22, 23).

[226] Nanjing 1984: 25, Fig. 8. See also Huang Minglan 1986: 102, 130-131; Zhongguo meishu 1988: Pl. 262, Dongzhao 東趙, all Luoyang (Henan) stamped bricks.

[227] Zhongguo meishu 1988: 195, Pl. 259.

[228] As on the three-dimensional, half-kneeling figure that functions as the base of the Mancheng (Hebei) M1:4112 bronze lamp: Zhongguo shehui kexueyuan 1980, Vol. 1: 72, Fig. 49:2. For a Late Middle-Late Warring States (*c.* late 4th-3rd centuries BC) example, see Hebei 1996, Vol. 2: Col. Pl. 23:2, Xinzhuangtou 辛莊頭 (Yixian, Hebei) XZHM30:229, earthenware basin with feet in the form of nomads.

[229] E.g., Zhongguo meishu 1988: 196, Pl. 260, Yanling (Henan) stamped brick. On Zhongguo meishu 1988: 132, Pl. 160, Yingzhuang (Nanyang, Henan) stamped brick, a nomad takes the place of the *xian* as animal-tamer next to an elephant and tiger, with a meander background.

[230] <https://www.metmuseum.org/art/collection/search/255955>, viewed 31 December 2018, *c.* early 5th century BC, Metropolitan Museum of Art 1989.281.78, Gift of Norbert Schimmel Trust, 1989.

[231] Zhongguo meishu 1988: 132, Pl. 160.

[232] Cf., the hat on the bowing figure in Chinese robes on a stamped brick from Luoyang (Henan): Huang Minglan 1986: 136.

[233] Boardman 1995: Pl. 75, *c.* mid-sixth century BC, Painter of the Louvre krater, Ashmolean (Oxford) 190; Pl. 120, Neandros (signed) cup, *c.* mid-sixth century BC, Museum of Fine Arts (Boston) 61.1073; Pl. 138, Princeton Painter amphora, *c.* 550-540 BC, Princeton 168 (date per Boardman 1995: 234).

[234] Cook 1997: 163.

[235] Xuzhou 1997: 12, Fig. 18; Li Yinde and Meng Qiang 1997: 23, Fig. 1; back cover (color photo). An essentially identical mirror in the collection of the Freer Gallery (Smithsonian Institution, Washington, DC) is published in Deydier 1980: 99, Pl. 75.

[236] Guangzhou 1991, Vol. 1: 86, Fig. 58, C145-73, polychrome-inlaid bronze.

[237] Zhongguo meishu 1988: 66, Pl. 77, Yanjiacha (Suide, Shaanxi), carved stone; 73, Pl. 87, unprovenanced rubbing, collection of Chang Renxia 常任俠; 86-87, Pl. 102, Yangzishan 羊子山 (Chengdu Municipality, Sichuan) M1, carved stone.

Although limited in scope (as, of course, were narrative compositions), the convention is documented in the Middle-Late Warring States on a mirror reportedly from Jincun 金村 (Luoyang Municipality, Henan), *c.* 4th century BC,[238] followed by another from Shuihudi (Yunmeng, Hubei) M9:60,[239] dating to dynastic Qin (or Qin *terminus post quem*). Both bear the image of a man hunting a tiger in three-quarter view. On Shuihudi M9:60, the man, on foot, carries a full-length sword; on the Jincun piece, he is mounted, in nomadic dress, carrying a shortsword. If the Shuihudi décor may derive in part from the Jincun, the latter recalls *c.* fourth-century BC Achaemenid seals with scenes of a man on horseback, equipped with a spear, and depicted in three-quarter view, in the Greek manner.[240] By the same token, contemporaneous Ionian seals[241] showing warriors on foot with spear and shield, again in three-quarter view, provide a compositional model for the hunter on foot on Shuihudi M9:60. Given the limited application of the three-quarter view during the Warring States, I suspect that its appearance on the Jincun mirror results from imitation of a similar composition, rather than assimilation of this use of perspective.

The manner in which perspective is addressed in other Warring States figural work shows growing sophistication in the handling of narrative spatial relationships, but not adoption of the three-quarter view. For instance, the figures on the Gaozhuang (Huaiyin Municipality, Jiangsu) fragment M1:114-2 are shown in a mixture of profile and full frontal; the juxtaposition of horses harnessed side-by-side is indicated by mirror image: the near horse is shown in profile; the far horse, also in profile, is shown upside-down (Figure 4, lower center-right).[242] However, on the Jiuliandun (Zaoyang Municipality, Hubei) lacquered bows, the horses harnessed side-by-side are shown in overlapping profile,[243] with the carriage also in profile. In the mural painting from the Qin Palace 3 (Xianyang Municipality, Shaanxi), although the horses are in profile, not enough remains of the carriage to determine the perspective used.[244] It therefore appears that three-quarter perspective was repeatedly introduced into China, perhaps more widely – or more relevantly – during the Han.

In the Han-era Far Eastern steppe, three-quarter frontal perspective is visible on some Xiongnu bronze plaques with a décor of human activity from the mixed Xiongnu-Xianbei-Wuhuan site of Xichagou (Xifeng, Liaoning)[245] (Figure 24), as well as on Xiongnu-associated bronze rectangular plaques depicting an ox in three-quarter profile,[246] an example of which occurs in the Han tomb of Shiyang 石羊 (Chengdu Municipality, Sichuan).[247] It is therefore possible that the convention was transmitted to China via the steppe. However, a simpler use of perspective,

[238] Kong Xiangxing 1992: 152, gilded and gold-inlaid bronze; detail, Tian Guangjin and Guo Suxin 1986: 136, Fig. 100.

[239] Hubei 1981: 46, Fig. 62 (rubbing); Pl. 4 (color photo); Pl. 30:1 (black and white photo), bronze. See also Kong Xiangxing 1992: 153.

[240] Nikulina 1994: Pl. III:499 (British Museum 89816), 500 (Staatliche Museen Berlin FIG. G. 182).

[241] Nikulina 1994: Pl. 358, State Hermitage Museum Ž-574, *c.* third quarter 4th century BC.

[242] Huaiyin 1988: 209, Fig. 22. The same convention occurs on a carved bone plaque from the Upper Xiajiadian 夏家店 site of Nanshan'gen 南山根 (Ningcheng 寧城, Inner Mongolia) M102:18 (Zhongguo shehui kexueyuan 1981: 307, Fig. 6). The dating of Upper Xiajiadian remains problematic, with some scholars maintaining a broad span from the Late Western Zhou through the Warring States, largely on the basis of the Chinese ritual bronzes found in some burials. I remain unconvinced that the bronzes were contemporaneous with burial (e.g., Psarras 1999). See Psarras in preparation.

[243] Hubei 2017: 39, Fig. 1 (M1:728); 45, Fig. 19: (M1:815); 46, Fig. 20 (M1:817); 47, Fig. 21 (M2:130).

[244] Shaanxi 2004: Col. Pl. 5; Liu Yang (ed.) 2012: 284.

[245] Tian Guangjin and Guo Suxin 1986: 73, Fig. 39:2. For Xichagou, see Psarras 1994.

[246] Tian Guangjin and Guo Suxin 1986: 84, Fig. 52:1, 2.

[247] Sichuan 1983: 27, Fig. 2:6 (drawing), Fig. 3:1 (rubbing), *c.* 190 AD, per Psarras 2015.

with the horses in profile and the carriage in three-quarter view, was also adopted in Han work.[248] This same variant may be seen on a bronze vase from Gondla (Punjab), dating to *c.* 2nd-1st centuries BC,[249] suggesting that additional Hellenized influence may have reached the Han through India.[250]

Transmission of the full rear (or full frontal[251]) view, applied occasionally to Han horses[252] (Figure 15, bottom left), is likely to have followed a similar path from the Greek world.[253] Such influence is visible in the full frontal horse on a lentoid Achaemenid seal, dating to the first half of the 4th century BC, with the image of a mounted boar hunter.[254] Similarly, depiction in full frontal view of a horse pulling a carriage on the late-fourth century BC Scythian gold headdress plaque from Karagodjuasx (Krasnodar [Russia])[255] undoubtedly stems from Greek contact. The convention subsequently spread across the steppe to the Xiongnu, as on bronze plaques from Xichagou (Xifeng, Liaoning)[256] (Figure 24) and Daodunzi (Tongxin, Ningxia) M10:33,[257] which include and expand upon the décor of a Scythian plaque from Geremessovskij (Zaporož'e [Ukraine]).[258] Xiongnu, as well as potentially Indian or Bactrian, influence is therefore likely in the transmission of this perspective to the Han.

[248] Zhongguo meishu 1988: 6-7, Pl. 8, Lianling 蘭陵 (Cangshan, Shandong), carved stone; 212, Pl. 211, Qingbai (Chengdu Municipality, Sichuan) M1, stamped brick.
[249] Rapin 1992: Pl. 94:2 (drawing): Pl. 124:1 (photo), dated to *c.* 2nd century BC (late Maurya/early Shunga); Errington, Cribb, and Claringbull (eds) 1992: 162-164, No. 163, dated to *c.* 1st century BC.
[250] Scythian-produced work of the *c.* 4th-3rd centuries BC also employs various forms of perspective (three-quarter frontal and full frontal) in the representation of horse-drawn carriages, as on the Karagodjuašx (Krasnodar) headdress plaque cited above (Galanina and Gratch 1987: Pl. 232), and on a related bronze plaque from Slonovskaja Bliznica (Ukraine; Meljukova 1989: 342, Fig. 37:20).
[251] Wu Hung 1989: 197, suggests that the full frontal view in Han homage scenes may also have been used in imperial portraits to indicate authority (no such portraits are currently known), deriving from Buddhist iconography (Wu Hung 1989: 134-141).
[252] Liu Xingzhen and Yue Fengxia 1991: 81, 83 (Front shrine), 92 (Left shrine, with detail on p. 95), 107 (Left shrine, with detail on p. 111), 119 (Left shrine), Wu family shrines (Jiaxiang, Shandong), carved stone; Liaoning 1985: 37, Fig. 42, Dongmenli 東門里 (Liaoyang 遼陽 Municipality, Liaoning), painted murals (*c.* 67 AD, per Psarras 2015); Nanyang 1990: Pl. 148, 150, 164-165, Nanyang (Henan) stamped bricks.
[253] E.g., Boardman 1995: Pl. 75, Painter of the Louvre krater, *c.* mid-sixth century BC, Ashmolean 190.
[254] Nikulina 1994: Pl. III:471, top center, Metropolitan Museum of Art L1812; Pl. III:472, upper left, lentoid seal, Metropolitan Museum of Art 49.43.7; Pl. III:489, lentoid seal, private collection (Moscow).
[255] Galanina and Gratch 1987: Pl. 232, State Hermitage Museum 249217.
[256] Tian Guangjin and Guo Suxin 1986: 96, Fig. 64:6.
[257] Ningxia 1988b: 345, Fig. 10:6; Pl. 16:3.
[258] Galanina and Gratch 1987: Pl. 136, gold, *c.* 4th century BC; State Hermitage Museum Dn 1859 ½.

Chapter 4

Tree of Life

The tree of life appears in Eastern Zhou Chinese art at the same time as the animal master and exercises a similarly long-reaching influence. As with the animal master, the immediate transmitter of the iconography to the Eastern Zhou is unclear. Again as with the animal master, it is likely that multiple versions reached China both before and during the Han. Sources are likely to include not only the Near East and the steppe, but northern India, given the importance of the tree in Buddhist compositions, as on the stone reliefs on the east gate of Stupa I at Sanci (Madhya [India]; second half of the 1st century BC).[259] If Eastern Zhou adoption of the animal master heralds the beginning of narrative art in China, the adoption of the tree of life heralds the beginning of the depiction of landscape.

The tree of life (Figure 2, registers 1, 3; Figure 9), understood as representing the axis mundi connecting the living and the dead, is attested in the Near East in at least the 3rd millennium BC and continues through the Parthian era (247 BC-AD 224).[260] The most readily-recognized version of the iconography remains in use throughout its history: a tree flanked by mirror-image animals, as on the *c.* 2600 BC shell plaque from Pu-abi's grave in the Royal Cemetery of Ur (Tell Muqqayan, Dhi Qar [Iraq]), with a décor of ibex in mirror-image on each side of a flowering tree set on the summit of scale-form mountains.[261] Arguably, this plaque proves the most enduring prototype both in the steppe and in China. In some Near Eastern versions, half-man, half-animal divinities flank the tree, thus effectively combining the animal master with the tree of life.[262] The longevity of this combination is attested by the Hellenized décor of the woven garment of the man buried in Yingpan 營盤 (Yuli 尉犁 [Lopnor], Xinjiang) M15 (*c.* 2nd-3rd centuries AD, according to the excavators).[263] On alternating registers of this cloth, the tree of life is flanked by pairs of bulls and deer (or goats) or by pairs of armed heroic figures in Hellenized style. I interpret the latter as deriving ultimately from Neo-Assyrian images of the hero (or king) fighting a bull or a lion, a composition which recasts the hunting animal master as a semi-divine human.[264] In iconographic terms, the tree and the body of the animal master are interchangeable.

---

259 Ray 1975: Pl. 53. Craven (1991:45-46) describes 'aboriginal' (pre-Harappa, *c.* 3rd millennium BC) fertility gods and goddesses (yaksa, yaksi) associated with the worship of trees (*inter alia*); 64, Hindu use of yaksa/yaksi.

260 Collon 1995: 192, Fig. 155, British Museum 118896, which Collon here dates to *c.* 3rd century AD. See also Bushnell 2008.

261 Collon 1995: 65, Fig. 47.

262 E.g., the fourth register of the sandstone stele commissioned by the Elamite king, Untash-Napirisha, *c.* 1340-1300 BC, originally in Chogha Zanbil, moved to Susa (both, Iran) in *c.* 12th century BC (Harper, Aruz, and Tallon [eds] 1992: 127-129, No. 80; especially 128, Fig. 42 [reconstruction]; Louvre Sb12; cf., <https://www.louvre.fr/en/oeuvre-notices/stele-untash-napirisha-king-anshan-and-susa>, view 4, viewed 1 January 2019). Similarly, winged men (i.e., animal masters) flank a tree of life on the garment worn by Ashurnasirpal II (r. 884-859 BC) on a relief in the Northwestern Palace at Nimrud (Frankfort 1996: 197, Fig. 224). Note that Frankfort describes the men as 'genii.'

263 Xinjiang 1999: 10, Fig. 10; Col. Pl. 2; inside front cover.

264 E.g., Collon 1987: 124, Fig. 522, Ur (Tell Muqqayan, Dhi Qar [Iraq]), seal impression, *c.* 2550 BC; 124, Fig. 526, Tello (Girsu [Iraq]), seal impression, *c.* 2350 BC; 123, 125, descriptions; 194, Fig. 943, seal, British Museum BM 89538, *c.* 3000-2334 BC (description, Collon 1987: 193).

A range of more abstract examples was also developed, as on a stone relief from Nineveh (*c.* the early centuries AD), depicting two dragons flanking a vegetal form interpreted as a vase or an altar.[265] In this instance, while little remains formally of the tree of life, the heraldic composition of the original is nonetheless maintained. Indeed, a Neo-Assyrian (*c.* 900-612 BC) faience vase from Ashur (Iraq), with a décor of goats in mirror image leaping down the side of a mountain,[266] provides an early example of such abstraction. On the Ashur vase, although no tree is depicted, the heraldic positioning of the goats together with the close relationship of this composition to that of the Pu-abi plaque (for instance) imply the tree of life.

In the steppe, the image is widespread in both literal and more abstract forms. Sarmatian examples include the Xoxlač kurgan (Novočerkassk) gold crown, with deer executed in the round flanking a tree (also in the round) on the upper rim of the crown,[267] and the gold foil diadem ornaments from an unidentified tomb in the Don Valley.[268] Although rare in Xiongnu art, the tree is central to Xianbei work attributed to the Eastern Han period (AD 25-220), where the tree may be depicted between mirror-image animals turned to face it or may merely be implied by the vertical line of symmetry dividing mirror-image animals (Figure 25).[269] In some versions, the tree instead frames the outer edges of the plaque.[270] By extension, any mirror-image depiction of an animal in steppe art (on crowns, bracelets, animal plaques worn in mirror-image pairs, etc.[271]) may be understood as implying the tree of life. Especially in the case of plaques and bracelets, the wearer's body may therefore be seen as implicitly replacing the tree of life or, indeed, the animal master.

As in foreign precedents, Chinese versions from the Middle-Late Springs and Autumns through the Han range from literal to implicit: explicit (and, here, in the manner of the Pu-abi composition), on the Gaozhuang (Huaiyin Municipality, Jiangsu) M1:114-2 bronze vessel fragment,[272] where the tree stands on a hill, flanked by animals (Figure 4), and implicit on the bronze *hu* Liulige (Huixian, Henan) M59:23[273] (Figure 10), on which the tree is replaced by paired triangles, a convention also adopted on a copper-inlaid square *dou* from Hougudui 侯古堆 (Gushi 固始, Henan),[274] with repeated pairs of facing tigers aligned in registers separated by darts. On these examples, it is above all the mirror-image pairing of animals or other scenes that reflects the tree of life, particularly in its steppe manifestations. That the triangles or darts on these vessels represent the tree of life, rather than serving only to divide registers, is

[265] Collon 1995: 192, Fig. 155, British Museum 118896, which Collon here dates to *c.* 3rd century AD.

[266] Frankfort 1996: 198, Fig. 225.

[267] Tian Guangjin and Guo Suxin 1986: 66, Fig. 35 (drawing); *L'Or* 1995: 59, Nos 85 (photo, reproduction), 86 (photo, original).

[268] *L'Or* 1995: 66, No. 97.

[269] E.g., Tian Guangjin and Guo Suxin 1986: 76, Fig. 44; 77, Fig. 45; 79, Fig. 46:3-4, all Xiongnu; and for Xianbei examples, 79, Fig. 46:1-2 (in my attribution).

[270] Tian Guangjin and Guo Suxin 1986: 79, Fig. 46:3-4.

[271] For Sarmatian examples: e.g., *L'Or* 1995: 81, No. 108, Dači (Azov District, Rostov [Russia]) kurgan I, cache gold bracelet with polychrome inlay, *c.* second half 1st century AD; 35, Nos 43-44, Treasure of Stavropol' (Kazinskoje, Stavropol' [Russia]) gold torques, *c.* 4th century BC. For Scythian examples: e.g., Galanina and Gratch 1987: Pl. 239, Čertomlyk kurgan (Dnepropetrovsk [Ukraine]), gold torque, *c.* last quarter 4th century BC. Bactrian examples include: Sarianidi 1985: Pl. 104, 106, Tillia-tepe M6:15; Pl. 105, 107, Tillia-tepe M2:4, both: gold bracelets inlaid with turquoise and carnelian. Two circular silver ornaments from Nalin'gaotu 納林高兔 (Shenmu 神木, Shaanxi) provide highly westernized examples of the form (Dai Yingxin and Sun Jiaxiang 1983: 25, Fig. 4:2).

[272] Huaiyin 1988: 209, Fig. 22. See also the tree of life flanked by tigers on a bronze tripod *hu* from Hougudui 侯古堆 (Gushi 固始, Henan: Zhongguo meishu 1992: 26, Pl. 31), which identifies the tigers as 'dragons.'

[273] Guo Baojun 1959: Pl. 93.

[274] Zhongguo meishu 1992: 25, Pl. 30.

made clear by the first register of Liulige M59:23, where the triangles are placed in the middle of the register, dividing, rather than framing, the pair of mirror-image birds. At the same time, all of the compositions on Liulige M59:23 and the Hougudui *dou*, including the consistent use of mirror-image, echo the compositional norms elsewhere associated with the tree of life. This is true as well of the triangles or darts, all of which, whether between single animals or between pairs (or mirror-image scenes), likewise correspond to the placement of the tree of life in these other compositions. Thus, the triangles and darts here form an integral – if optional – part of the iconography. In a more direct parallel to the Ashur vase noted above, although no tree is shown on a series of *bo* 鎛 bells from Lijialou (Xinzheng Municipality, Henan), the open interlace of the attachment loop takes the form of a stylized mountain, surmounted by a goat (represented by its head) and flanked at the base by two, heraldically-placed goats.[275] Similarly, on the Liulige (Huixian, Henan) M76:85 *hu*,[276] a double twist (of snakes?) separates mirror-image birds (Figure 26). Both explicit and implicit versions may be seen on roof tiles from the Qin palace site (Xianyang Municipality, Shaanxi).[277]

In Han versions, the Pu-abi-type animal-flanked tree on a mountain is retained and more fully developed, as on the lid of a bronze *zun* from Guangzhou (Guangdong) M5054:22.[278] In other cases, as in Eastern Zhou, Han depictions may be explicit, as in the tree flanked by animals on stone bas reliefs on the Qimu 啓母 memorial towers (*que* 闕) (Songshan 嵩山, Henan) and in the tomb of Jiunüdun 九女墩 (Suining, Xuzhou Municipality, Jiangsu)[279] (Figure 18; see also Figure 19:4, 9), or implicit, as in the pairs of mirror-image animals on stamped, hollow bricks from Xianyang (Shaanxi)[280] (Figure 19:6). Highly abstract forms of the tree may also be identified, as in the strongly vertical vegetal meander, flanked by pairs of animals, on a series of harness ornaments from Mancheng (Hebei), some of which include the animal master[281] (Figure 27). In a frequent variation, the tree of life is also rendered in Han representations as a single animal beneath a tree (Figures 39, 67), the connection with paradise sometimes emphasized by the presence of an immortal[282] or a plant with weeping leaves, associated with immortality[283]

[275] Henan 2001: 156-160. The bottom of the loop consists of a row of bird heads, echoing steppe tradition (see below, *The Bird Head*).

[276] Guo Baojun 1959: Pl. 103:1.

[277] Shaanxi 2004: 225, Figs 205:2 (83XYCL:5), 205:4 (74XZB:2), explicit; 225, Fig. 205:5 (81XYN:4), implicit in the paired heraldic animals.

[278] Guangzhou 1981, Vol. 1: 435, Fig. 270:5.

[279] Henan 1990a: 123, Pl. 95; cf., 31, Fig. 24; 132, Pl. 120; cf., 25, Fig. 17, Qimu (Songshan, Henan), carved stone; Jiangsu 1959: Pl. 23, Fig. 27, Jiunüdun (Suining, Xuzhou Municipality, Jiangsu), carved stone; Huang Minglan 1986: 32-33, 46-47, 70-71, 76-77, 96-97, Luoyang (Henan), stamped bricks.

[280] Xianyang 1982: 232, Fig. 11:1-4, 6-9, M36, *c.* 67 AD, per Psarras 2015.

[281] Zhongguo shehui kexueyuan 1980, Vol. 1: 201, Fig. 136:1-3, Mancheng (Hebei) M1:2250, 1003, 2027, respectively; 328, Fig. 222:1-2, Mancheng M2:1041, 1021 (respectively); 329, Fig. 223:1-2, Mancheng M2:1039, 1171 (respectively); all silvered bronze with partial gilding, except M1:2250 (gilded bronze). M1:2250, M2:1021, and M2:1039 include animal masters.

[282] As in riding a ram *couchant* beneath a tree on examples from Taishang 臺上 (Tongshan 銅山, Xuzhou Municipality, Jiangsu; Xuzhou 1985: Pl. 177), and common in Chulan 褚蘭 (Suxian 宿縣, Anhui) M2 (AD 171; Wang Buyi 1993: 542, Figs 38-39, bottom; 541, Figs 35, 36, 37 bottom, stone bas reliefs).

[283] Examples include a stone bas relief in the Wang Deyuan tomb (Suide, Shaanxi), depicting a deer beneath a plant with weeping leaves (Shaanxi 1959: 28, Fig. 19, bottom), or more clearly associated with immortality and scenes of paradise, as on Zhongguo meishu 1988: 60, Pl. 70, Zhuji 朱集 (Suining, Jiangsu), carved stone; 190, Pl. 247, Xindu 新都 (Sichuan), stamped brick. This plant appears to have a northern Indian origin, where examples include reliefs from Sanci (*c.* 1st century BC: Meister, Dhaky, and Deva [eds] 1988: Pl. 2). It is also known in bronze from the non-Chinese, non-Xiongnu cemetery of Maoqinggou 毛慶溝 (Liangcheng 涼城, Inner Mongolia; Tian Guangjin and Guo Suxin 1986: Pl. 113:6, M58:3, in the round). The date of Maoqinggou M58 may ultimately not be early enough to allow interpretation of this piece as a prototype for Han examples. A related, irregularly-shaped plant (e.g., Wang Deyuan

(Figure 23). This includes the unhitched horse tethered to a tree, best-known from the Wu family shrines (Jiaxiang, Shandong)[284] (Figure 67; see also Figure 39), its rein tangling with the branches in the same way that the antlers of the deer on some Xiongnu or Xianbei plaques tangle with the branches of surrounding trees.[285]

In a further development, the image of the jade *bi* 璧 disc is used as a substitute for the tree, again as on hollow bricks from Xianyang (Figure 19:2, 3, 7, 8) or in the mirror-image dragons holding a central *bi* surmounting a *bi* from Dingzhou (Hebei) M43.[286] Ultimately, the *bi* merges with the Indian image of the wheel, representing the Buddha. Although the wheel as an independent motif rarely occurs in Han depictions,[287] iconographic equivalence with both the tree of life and the animal master is demonstrated both by stonework from Mathura (*c.* 2nd century AD)[288] and by some Xianbei[289] bronze belt plaques, on which the wheel is flanked by animals. In some cases, the disc must be a substitute for the Queen Mother of the West (animal master), as on a carved stone coffin from Xinsheng (Pidu, Chengdu Municipality, Sichuan),[290] where a dragon and tiger (in profile) support a *bi* disc undoubtedly representing the animal throne. This reading is reinforced by the submissive stance of the kneeling humanoid figure on whose shoulders (like the Greek Atlas[291]) the disc is braced.[292] Often, however, it is not clear how much distinction may – or should – be made in derivation from the tree of life or the animal master. The two are essentially the same.

This merging of entities is visible from the earliest Chinese versions of both iconographies, but again falls within Near Eastern conventions, as illustrated by a seal from Nippur ([Iraq]; *c.* 1307-

tomb [Suide, Shaanxi]: Shaanxi 1959: 19, Fig. 8; 20, Fig. 9; 21, Fig. 10; 22, Fig. 11; 24, Fig. 13; 26, Fig. 16; 28, Figs 18-19), repeats a form often used in Pazyryk felt appliqué work and carved wood pieces (Rudenko 1970: Pl. 101:A-C; Pl. 102:A-C, kurgan 3, wood; Pl. 154, kurgan 5 felt appliqué hanging [detail]; Pl. 161, kurgan 5 felt appliqué saddle blanket).

284 Liu Xingzhen and Yue Fengxia 1991: 41, Wu Liang shrine; 79, Front shrine; 112-113, top, Left shrine. See also Balimiao (Yanggu, Shandong) M1 (Liaocheng 1989: 54, Fig. 11, bottom), stone bas reliefs from Baishan (Peixian, Xuzhou Municipality, Jiangsu: Xuzhou 1985: Pl. 262), Zhangxu (Suining, Xuzhou Municipality, Jiangsu; Xuzhou 1985: Pl. 254), and Suide (Shaanxi; Shaanxi 1959: 82-83, Pl. 74-75).

285 Ningxia 1988a: 19, Fig. 6:2 (two deer, bodies in profile, heads *en face*, in mirror-image beneath trees; the deer's antlers merge with the tree branches). See also northern non-Chinese plaques on which the reins of mirror-image camels are entangled with the surrounding trees (Tian Guangjin and Guo Suxin 1986: 77, Fig. 45:3-4, no provenance)

286 Dingxian 1973: Pl. 2:1.

287 But see Henan 1960: 23, Fig. 20, right, Nanguan 南關 (Zhengzhou Municipality, Henan) M159, stamped hollow bricks (*c.* 65 AD, per Psarras 2015); Jiaxing 1983: 9, Fig. 14, Haining 海寧 (Zhejiang), stone bas relief (*c.* 175 AD, per Psarras 2015), which shows a circle supported by a stand.

288 Rosenfield 1993: Fig. 32, 33, 82; following Rosenfield's dating, per Rosenfield 1993: 229-230.

289 Tian Guangjin and Guo Suxin 1986: 80, Fig. 47:1; Wu En 1981: Pl. 5:2 (collection of C.T. Loo, Paris).

290 Zhongguo meishu 1988: 76, Pl. 90. Note the image of man-animal combat, carved upside-down above the throne. The humanoid figure in Chinese garments is nonetheless identifiable as a *xian* because of his three-pointed diadem, a more formalized version of the four-pointed horns on the hybrid animal master on a carved stone from Nanyang (Zhongguo meishu 1988: 130, Pl. 157). These in turn follow examples with three or four points on Gaozhuang (Huaiyin Municipality, Jiangsu) M1:114-2 (Huaiyin 1988: 209, Fig. 22; here, Figure 4), followed by the hybrid animal master on a carved stone from Nanyang (Zhongguo meishu 1988: 130, Pl. 157).

291 Cf., *Greek Art* 1979: 228-229, No. 184, a globular bronze incense burner held on the shoulders of a woman, substituted for Atlas, *c.* mid-fifth century BC, Sacred Way, Delphi (Greece), Delphi Museum 7723.

292 This figure recalls the northern Indian crouching 'demon dwarf' (Poster 1986: 106, No. 38, earthenware sculpture, *c.* 2nd century BC-2nd century AD, Cleveland Museum of Art); its position below the throne further recalls Indian use of the human form as an architectural support: in the round, as with the yakshis (female earth spirits) of the Great Stupa at Sanci, *c.* late 1st century BC-early 1st century AD (Craven 1991: 70, Fig. 38), or in high relief, as in Stupa I at Sanci, *c.* 10-25 AD (Craven 1991: 71, Fig. 40; Ray 1975: Pl. 55). This practice is adopted on the Shen 沈 family *que* (Qu 渠 xian, Sichuan), whose pediment is supported by kneeling or seated human figures in high relief (Chongqing 1992: Pl. 165, 168), and on the Gao Yi 高頤 (Ya'an 雅安, Sichuan) *que* (Chongqing 1992: Pl. 111-112). It may not be coincidental that the Gao Yi dwarf appears to represent a nomad, with a moustache and facial features recalling Kushan princes.

1282 BC), on which the body of the animal master (flanked by animals) becomes a mountain.[293] This rendition is essentially followed in highly stylized form on an Early Warring States bronze *hu* from Fenshuiling 分水岭 (Changzhi 長治 Municipality, Shanxi),[294] with its repeated pattern of a snake-like form with a head at each end forming a mountain with a central tree (arrow). In this case, the two heads of the serpent replace the animals flanking the tree.

In both Eastern Zhou[295] and Han[296] versions, the tree of life also occurs in combination with the animal master, when the animal master becomes part of a plant or is shown holding a plant. On the Gaozhuang (Huaiyin Municipality, Jiangsu) M1:0147 fragment, a tree of life emerges from the animal master's head,[297] so that, in essence, the divinity literally becomes the tree of life. This convention is also followed on the Mancheng (Hebei) M1:2250 harness ornament, with its hybrid animal master (reinforced by the humanoid eyes at the top of the plaque)[298] (Figure 27). A similar composition occurs on a stone from Guojiagou (Suide, Shaanxi).[299] The plant with weeping leaves, associated with immortality, in the hands of *xian*-type animal masters like that on a stamped brick from Nanyang (Henan)[300] (Figure 3) expresses the same concept in attenuated form, as does the plant throne of the Queen Mother of the West/King Father of the East (Figures 12, 18). The latter occurs in different forms: as the mushroom thrones from Mamaozhuang (Lishi, Shanxi) M2 or as the tree-like thrones from northern Shaanxi, on which the tree and the divinity are largely obscured by *kavaem khvareno* flames[301] (Figure 18). While the mushroom is associated with immortality in Han China (as on a Huchang 胡場 [Hanjiang, Yangzhou Municipality, Jiangsu] lacquered tray),[302] the use of a plant as a throne recalls the Indian lotus throne, a convention not limited to Buddhist work.[303] Indian influence may also have reached China through a more obviously Hellenized, probably Bactrian, interpretation

[293] Collon 1987: 179, Fig. 842, seal impression (drawing).

[294] Shanxi 2010: 309, Fig. 104H:17 (M126:128).

[295] As on Huaiyin 1988: 202, Fig. 15 (M1:0147).

[296] As on Jiangsu 1959: Pl. 24, Fig. 29, Jiunüdun (Suining, Xuzhou Municipality, Jiangsu), carved stone; Shaanxi 1959: 14, Pl. 1, tomb of Wang Deyuan (Suide, Shaanxi), carved stone; Huang Minglan 1986: 40-41, on which the animal master is cast as a horse-herder; 96-97, on which the animal master takes the form of a horse tamer, all Luoyang (Henan), stamped bricks.

[297] Huaiyin 1988: 202, Fig. 15.

[298] Zhongguo shehui kexueyuan 1980, Vol. 1: 201, Fig. 136:1. Eyes like these figure near the bottom of a bronze beaker shown in Amiet 1976: Pl. 83 (northwestern Iran, *c.* 10th-9th centuries BC, dating by comparison to Muscarella 1988: 247); they appear to represent the face of a lion, whose highly-schematic body curves around the vessel. They also compare to images of the Egyptian god Bes; for Achaemenid-related examples: Curtis and Tallis 2005: 147, No. 184, Oxus Treasure [Takht-i Sangin, Tajikistan], gold appliqué (British Museum ANE 123933); 172, No. 263, Persepolis (near Shiraz [Iran]), faience pendant; Rudenko 1970: Pl. 91-92, Pazyryk kurgan 1, carved wood bridle ornaments. The quite human faces on these ornaments from Pazyryk are not unrelated to carved wood feline heads from the same site: Rudenko 1970: Pl. 104D, F, G (kurgan 3); Pl. 115C-F; Pl. 116C, E, F (all kurgan 5). Parenthetically, the horns and ears of the Pazyryk feline heads are closely echoed in the horned feline heads on the legs of Shangwang 商王 (Linzi 臨淄 Municipality, Shandong) M1:105 bronze *ding* (Linzi 1997: 18, Fig. 8; tomb dated by its excavators to *c.* 266-221 BC).

[299] Shaanxi 1959: 79, Fig. 72.

[300] Nanyang 1990: Pl. 181. See also Shaanxi 1959: 14, Fig. 1; 17, Fig. 6; 23, Fig. 12, all, tomb of Wang Deyuan (Suide, Shaanxi); 49, Fig. 39, Nanliang 南梁 (Guchengtan 古城灘, Yulin 榆林, Shaanxi).

[301] Shanxi 1992: 17, Figs 8-9; 22, Figs 20-21; 25, Figs 27-28; 26, Fig. 31, Mamaozhuang (Lishi, Shanxi); Shaanxi 1959: 64-65, Pl. 54-56, Kuaihualing Ban Buddhist Temple site (Suide, Shaanxi); 109, Pl. 111-112, Suide (Shaanxi); all, stone bas reliefs.

[302] Powers 1991: 55, Fig. 33.

[303] I am grateful to Mrs. Mary E. Psarras† for suggesting this connection (February 1997). Rosenfield 1993: Figs 90-92, Kushan Buddhist high relief stone carving, where the lotus sometimes has a stem; Pal 1986: 39-41, re: northern India; 138, No. S17, Kaushambi (?), molded terra cotta votive plaque, of Sri-Lakshmi, the earth mother, *c.* 1st century BC.

of the Indian convention, as in the putti seated on rosettes on embroidery from Noyon uul ([Noin-Ula,] Batsumber, Tuv [Mongolia]) kurgan 6.[304]

Mountainous Landscapes

Much Han landscape is suggestive, rather than realistic, often relying on a few trees and ground lines to set the scene. The mountain, like the meander, emerges as a shorthand reference to paradise. The reasons for this lie in its close association with both the tree of life (in the manner of the Pu-abi plaque[305]) and the animal master iconographies, combined on pieces such as Gaozhuang (Huaiyin Municipality, Jiangsu) M1:114-2[306] (Figure 4). While seemingly incidental during the Eastern Zhou, this symbolic identification emerges in a wide range of Han compositions, whether as *boshanlu*, scenes of scattered or paired animals (themselves indicating the animal master or related iconographies), images of the animal master in the guise of immortals or the Queen Mother of the West, or depictions of hunting. The close association of the mountain with the hunting animal master established in the Eastern Zhou is carried over in Han scenes of hunting in mountainous territory, whether or not[307] these include immortals[308] or the Queen Mother of the West (Figure 13).[309]

The mountain itself thus evokes paradise, with or without supporting images, as on *boshanlu* unadorned by supporting images.[310] The same association with paradise is undoubtedly true for the meander, used by the Han interchangeably with the mountain form. This equivalence is demonstrated by a stone relief from Qinglongshan (Peixian, Xuzhou Municipality, Jiangsu), featuring an essentially continuous hunting scene set in a landscape of meanders in one section and inverted-U-shaped mountains in another[311] (Figure 12, upper and lower registers, respectively), as well as by the gilded bronze incense burner Mancheng (Hebei) M1:5182, where the mountains (with their animals and humanoid figures) are accentuated with an inlaid pattern of the vine (meander).[312] On a gilded bronze *boshanlu* from the tomb of the Marquis of Haihun (Xinjian [Nanchang Municipality, Jiangxi]), a wave-like meander is used to create

---

304 Rudenko 1969: Pl. LXV:1, LXVI, LXVII:3.

305 Collon 1995: 65, Fig. 47, Tell Muqqayan (Iraq), *c.* 2600 BC.

306 Huaiyin 1988: 209, Fig. 22.

307 Without immortals, e.g., Shaanxi 2004: 680, Fig. 550:1 (XYNIIM17:2); 681, Figs 551:1 (XYNIIIM8:1), 551:2 (XYNIIM5:3), Qin palace II and III (Xianyang Municipality, Shaanxi) Han tombs, glazed earthenware vessels with low relief décor.

308 As on stamped brick at Xinye (Henan: Wang Baoxiang 1964: 91, Fig. 3) and Mamaozhuang (Lishi, Shanxi) M2 (Shanxi 1992: 22, Fig. 21, second register). In stone bas reliefs at Yingzhuang 英莊 (Nanyang Municipality, Henan; Nanyang 1984: 34, Fig. 22:1; *c.* 109 AD, per Psarras 2015), the mountain frames a deer and what may be an animal master (a standing figure with outstretched hand). The same type of craggy, cleft mountains appear in the round with parallel imagery on *boshanlu* censers such as Mancheng (Hebei) M1:5182 and M2:3004 (Zhongguo shehui kexueyuan, Vol. 1: 64-65, Figs 44-45; Vol. 2: Col. Pl. 9; Pl. 30, gilded bronze [M1:5182]; Vol. 1: 256-257, Figs 170-171; Vol. 2: Col. Pl. 22; Pl. 175, silver-plated bronze [M2:3004] ; here, reproduced as Figure 6).

309 As on Yangzhou 1988: 38, Fig. 30, Yaozhuang 姚莊 (Hanjiang, Yangzhou Municipality, Jiangsu) M101:190, lacquer *lian* with silver fittings and carnelian inlay; *c.* 70 BC, per Psarras 2015. Here, reproduced as Figure 28.

310 E.g., Zhongguo qingtongqi 1998: 128, Pl. 126, Hanjiang (Yangzhou Municipality, Jiangsu), gilded bronze.

311 Nanjing 1984: 25, Fig. 8, AD 150. Zhongguo meishu 1988: 126, Pl. 150, Nanyang (Henan), carved stone depicting a *xian* animal master flanked by live-prey animal predation with an additional prey (see below, *Animal Predation*), a mountain under half the composition, a meander-mountain on the other half. For the use of the meander to describe a mountain, see also Zhongguo meishu 1988: 128, Pl. 152, Nanyang (Henan), carved stone; Xianyang 1979: 133, Fig. 11, especially Fig. 11:1, 4, 7, 8, Maquan 馬泉 (Xianyang Municipality, Shaanxi), lacquered *lian* toiletries box from *c.* 67 AD, per Psarras 2015 [here, Figure 19]; Jiangxi 2016: 173, tomb of the Marquis of Haihun (Xinjian [Nanchang Municipality, Jiangxi]), lacquered box with gold foil décor, silver fittings.

312 Zhongguo shehui kexueyuan 1980, Vol. 1: 64-65, Figs 44-45; Vol. 2: Col. Pl. 9; Pl. 30.

the lower segment of the mountain.[313] Similarly, the waves of meanders populated by various animals (some mythicized) on a lacquer *zun* from Fangwanggang (Chaohu Municipality, Anhui) M1[314] at times assume distinctly mountain-like form. This convention is already visible, as we have seen, on the attachment loops of Lijialou (Xinzheng Municipality, Henan) *bo* bells.[315] The Han meander, more flexible than the mountain, also designates clouds or other heavenly bodies, as on the Mawangdui (Changsha Municipality, Hunan) M1 coffin (Figure 1) and related compositions[316] (such as Figure 13); it figures as well as in explicit depictions of constellations, as on a number of stone reliefs from Nanyang (Henan).[317] In this context, it is often difficult to assign a specific value to the meander, other than as referring to paradise or space beyond the human world. Similarly, when the mountain is used to frame a seemingly secular landscape,[318] as in the hunting scene on the Qinglongshan relief, it may not be possible or necessary to distinguish between the depiction of mortal life and that of activities in paradise.

The prominence of the mountain in Han art suggests that the image may have been reintroduced from the Eastern Zhou onward, undoubtedly multiple times and from varying sources. The influence of renditions like that of the Pu-abi plaque persists through the Han era, as witnessed by silver harness plaques from Noyon uul (Batsumber, Tuv [Mongolia]) M6 (Figure 30),[319] with a décor of a yak standing on wooded, scale-form mountains. If the date and producer of the Noyon uul pieces remain uncertain, these plaques belong to a compositional tradition maintained in the Near East from the Pu-abi piece through the *c.* 15th-14th centuries BC 'Atchana' or 'Nuzi' painted pottery (Mitanni, southern Turkey-northern Syria)[320] and early 1st millennium BC Iran, as witnessed by a beaker attributed to northwestern Iran, depicting a man hunting a bull on scale-form mountains (Figure 31).[321] Indeed, this composition is central to a décor associated with the Han Far South (i.e., Guangdong, Guangxi, Guizhou), with an all-over pattern of upright scales containing an abstract tree. In cases such as the circular earthenware box from the Main Depot site ([Zongcangku 總倉庫,] Guigang Municipality, Guangxi) M10, the incised tree-and-mountain pattern appears on the lid of the box, while the associated animals are depicted in the round (and *couchant* [recumbent]) on top of the lid.[322] In broader applications, the combined influence of steppe[323] and more immediately Near Eastern versions of the Pu-abi plaque is further evident in Han use of the scale-form mountain alone, as an element in a variety of compositions, including hunting scenes from Qinglongshan (Peixian,

313 Jiangxi 2016: 83.

314 Anhui 2007: 60, Fig. 40 (FM1:282).

315 Henan 2001: 156-160.

316 Zhang Zhenglang, Fu Juyou, and Chen Songchang 1992: 6-11; cf., Zhongguo meishu 1988: 67, Pl. 79, Yanjiacha (Suide, Shaanxi); Shaanxi 1959: 84-85, Figs 76-77, Suide (Shaanxi); all, carved stone.

317 Wang Yu 2014: 69, Fig. 1, Qilingang (Nanyang Municipality, Henan), carved stone; Zhongguo meishu 1988: 144, Pl. 175, Yingzhuang; 146, Pl. 178, Xiguan 西關; 147, Pl. 179, Wangzhuang 王莊; all Nanyang Municipality (Henan), carved stone.

318 See also Zhongguo meishu 1988: 130, Pl. 156, Wangzhuang (Nanyang Municipality, Henan), carved stone.

319 Trever 1932: Pl. 25:1 (M6:254, irregularly shaped plaque), 2 (M6:253, round plaque); Rudenko 1969: Pl. XXXVI:3 (M6:253): Pl. XXXVII:3 (M6:254). (All Noyon uul inventory numbers are taken from Trever 1932.) Noyon uul is generally attributed to the Xiongnu (but see Psarras forthcoming), however these pieces are not in Xiongnu – or any currently-recognizable – style. An abstract geometric pattern resembling the scale-form mountain likewise occurs on a Pazyryk kurgan 5 felt appliqué saddle blanket (Rudenko 1970: Pl. 161). However, although it is combined with a vegetal motif on this piece, we have no reason to interpret the pattern as representational.

320 Collon 1995: 112. Aruz, Benzel, and Evans (eds) 2008: 198, No. 119, prefer the term 'Nuzi ware.'

321 Muscarella 1988: 244-248, No. 342, Metropolitan Museum of Art 48.178.1.

322 Hong Kong 2015: 94. Cf., Psarras 1997.

323 As suggested through a different line of reasoning by Jacobson 1985, who argues against a Near Eastern source for Han representations of hunting in mountains.

Xuzhou Municipality, Jiangsu; Figure 29) and Gaolicun 高李村 (Zoucheng 鄒城 Municipality, Shandong),[324] or battle scenes on a stamped brick in Fanji 樊集 (Xinye 新野, Henan) M37.[325]

Nonetheless, because of the close association of the mountain with animals – and hence with the tree of life – in the art of the eastern steppe,[326] Han China must also have received influence from sources other than the steppe for compositions incorporating human activity. These are again provided by the Near East and, later, Greece,[327] in examples extending from approximately the late 3rd millennium BC through the Sasanian era (*c.* 224-651 AD),[328] for both hunting and other animal scenes[329] in a mountainous setting. In this context, influence from Hellenistic Central Asia is likely to have reached the Han. As an example, the Qinglongshan hunting scene (Figure 29) is closely related to that on a bone belt plaque from the Temple of the Oxus (Takht-i Sangin, Tajikistan), whose date remains debated as falling potentially between *c.* 1st century BC-1st century AD and the 3rd century AD.[330] Even if the Oxus plaque proves to be later than Qinglongshan, its décor fits well with Near Eastern traditions; the piece therefore represents the kind of influence undoubtedly known to the Han.

[324] Nanjing 1984: 25, Fig. 8, Qinglongshan (Peixian, Xuzhou Municipality, Jiangsu); Zoucheng 1994: 26-27, Fig. 7 Gaolicun (Zoucheng Municipality, Shandong), both carved stone.

[325] Henan 1990b: 505, supplemental Fig. 5:3; *c.* 109 AD, per Psarras 2015.

[326] Jacobson 1985: 175, Fig. 21, Tuekta (Altai), wood headdress (current consensus dates Tuekta to *c.* 440-400 BC: Parzinger *et al.* 2008: 17); Akišev 1978: 219 (drawing), Issyk (Semireč'e [Kazakhstan]), gold headdress (Akišev proposes a date of *c.* 5th century BC for Issyk, extended to *c.* 5th-4th centuries BC in Akišev 1983: Pl. 66-87; Schiltz 1994: 299, adopts a date of *c.* late 4th-early 3th centuries BC); Ko Pej (Tuva) kurgan 1, gold foil ornament, *c.* 4th century BC (following the excavators' dating: Semionov 1994: 42, Fig. 3); Martynov 1991: 221, Fig. 93, Tisul' (Kemerovo [Russia]) and the Minusinsk Basin (Xakasija, Krasnojarsk [Russia]), bronze finials, Tagar culture. The form of the Ko Pej ornament is echoed, in the round, on the Tagar finials. Note that Tagar is commonly dated *c.* 7th-3rd centuries BC, but the occurrence of Xiongnu or Xiongnu-derived plaques on Tagar sites indicates at least partial contemporaneity with the Xiongnu and hence with the Han.

[327] Crowley 1989: 146-147, identifies the mountainous landscape as a feature of Greek and Cretan art from *c.* 1550 BC onward.

[328] Collon 1987: 154, No. 685, serpentine cylinder seal, *c.* 2334-2000 BC; 155; Collon 1995: 206, Fig. 172, Sasanian silver bowl.

[329] Collon 1987: 189, No. 913, Khafajeh (Iraq), fired steatite cylinder seal, *c.* 3000-2334 BC; Collon 1995: 78, Fig. 59e, Akkadian cylinder seal, *c.* 2300-2200 BC; Collon 1987: 189, No. 915, chalcedony cylinder seal, *c.* 1500-1000 BC; Parrot 1961: 258, Fig. 331, ivory carvings mounted on a silver plaque, Mesopotamian manufacture (? not specified), *c.* early 1st millennium BC; Nikulina 1994: Pl. III:144, palace of Sennacherib (Nineveh), stone bas relief, *c.* 705-680 BC; Pfrommer 1993: 218-219, No. 127; Pl. 7, Hellenized Near East, gilded silver bowl, *c.* 2nd-1st centuries BC.

[330] Gruber, Il'yasov, and Kaniuth 2012: 363, Fig. 19.

Chapter 5

Animal Predation

Distinct from animal combat (involving animals of the same species), animal predation refers to a predator animal, usually feline, attacking its natural prey, usually hooved (horse, deer, goat, sheep). In the western world, the predator is generally represented by the lion, maintaining Near Eastern norms; in the Far East, by the tiger. Secondary predators, typically an eagle or additional felines, may be added to the composition (Figure 32, cf., Figure 42).[331] In some cases, bird and feline are combined into a griffin as predator.[332] Collectively, the feline, the prey, and the bird are sometimes referred to as the iconographic 'Scythian/steppe triad.'[333] The image of predation appears in the Near East at least by the first half of the 3rd millennium BC,[334] remaining in continuous use thereafter. Like the tree of life, it is associated from an early date with the animal master, as demonstrated by a cylinder seal from Tell Agrab (Shara Temple [Iraq]), *c.* 3000-2334 BC, depicting two animal masters (half-human, half-bull) attacking a feline attacking a bull.[335] As an independent motif, animal predation subsequently becomes emblematic of cultures across the steppe through the Han period. The dominance of the image in steppe cultures suggests that some religious significance was assigned to it, prefigured in the ancient Near East by its pairing with the animal master.

I distinguish between two dominant versions of predation: live prey, showing the prey at the moment of attack (as in Figure 32),[336] and dead prey, depicting moments after the attack, when the predator carries away the dead prey (as in Figure 33).[337] Live-prey predation is by far the most common variant across the steppe. In some versions, the prey retaliates against the

[331] *Inter alia*: Tian Guangjin and Guo Suxin 1986: 80, Fig. 47:4, cf., Ivolga (Burjatija) M100 (Artamonov 1973: 161, Pl. 213; Davydova and Minyaev 2008: 101, Fig. 105); Siberian Collection of Peter the Great (Schiltz 1994: 236, Fig. 172); and unprovenanced Ordos examples (Tian Guangjin and Guo Suxin 1986: 95, Fig. 63:2, 3), all of which I consider likely Xiongnu products. For what I suggest may be a Wuhuan version, see Tian Guangjin and Guo Suxin 1986: 95, Fig. 63:1. Such variants have an ancient history beyond the scope of the present study, but see as an example Aruz, Benzel, and Evans (eds) 2008: 411-412, No. 264, tomb of Ahiram, Byblos (Lebanon), ivory plaque, *c.* 13th century BC.

[332] E.g., Reeder (ed.) 1999: 197, No. 84 detail, Piščane (Čerkasi [Ukraine]) find, bronze Greek louterion, *c.* 5th century BC; Tian Guangjin and Guo Suxin 1986: 96, Fig. 64:2, 'Ordos bronze' plaque.

[333] This is distinct from the cultural 'Scythian/steppe triad,' referring to the presence of animal sacrifice, shortswords, and 'animal style' art in burials associated with nomads.

[334] Parrot 1961: 257, Fig. 328A, Lagash (Iraq), ivory plaque, *c.* first half 3rd millennium BC.

[335] Collon 1987: 25, No. 61, followed chronologically by Amiet 1976, plate inserted between pp. 72-73, Luristan bronze pin (predation implicit in the juxtaposition of felines and goat heads to each side of the animal master), *c.* 8th-7th centuries BC (per Muscarella 1988: 177); Godard 1950 :21, Fig. 11, Northwestern Palace (Nimrud [Nineveh, Iraq]), stone relief image of patterns on the clothing of Ashurnasirpal II (r. 884/883-860/859 BC).

[336] E.g., Rudenko 1969: Pl. XXXVIII:1, Dyrestuj (Burjatija [Russia]), bronze plaque. Dyrestuj is attributed to the Xiongnu by its excavators (e.g., Minjaev 1998); for discussion, see Psarras in preparation.

[337] E.g., Tian Guangjin and Guo Suxin 1986: 94, Fig. 62:2, unprovenanced ('Ordos') bronze plaque, which I attribute to the Xiongnu.

predator, [338] perhaps reflecting the influence of the animal combat iconography.[339] In other versions, predation may be inferred, rather than explicitly depicted, as in the juxtaposition of the tiger (upper band) and the horse and ram (lower band) on a gold headdress from the Xiongnu site of Aluchaideng (Hanggin Banner, Inner Mongolia)[340] (Figure 48). There may be little difference in size between predator and prey, although, more rarely, there are also cases where the prey is larger than the predator.[341] Relative size appears to reflect stylistic choice, rather than degree of realism.

Live-prey predation iconography initially appears in Chinese art in the Late Western Zhou (*c.* early 8th century BC), in the loose grouping characteristic of subsequent Chinese renditions. On a *he* 盉 pitcher in the Yangjia 楊家 (Mei 眉 xian, Baoji Municipality, Shaanxi) cache,[342] a feline, attached between the vessel's body and lid, attacks a bird on the lid. This arrangement is repeated on a Han-era bronze pitcher from Xuzhou (Jiangsu).[343] Although the predatory relationship depicted on the Yangjia example represents a new development, both the bird and the feline figure frequently in Western Zhou art,[344] a coincidence which may have facilitated adoption of the new iconography. The predation image becomes more common in the Middle-Late Springs and Autumns, at approximately the same time as the animal master and the tree of life, with which it may be combined. Because the animal master is rarely shown in steppe art, it is likely that this dual usage indicates introduction of the iconography to China via two different sources: from the steppe, beginning by the Late Western Zhou, reflected in predation used as an independent image, and through Central Asian adaptations of the Near Eastern convention by the Middle-Late Springs-Autumns, as reflected in the association of predation with the animal master.

Again as with the animal master, Eastern Zhou interpretations may be more or less explicit: on the third register of Liulige (Huixian, Henan) M59:23,[345] for instance, the central composition depicts an animal master hunting a feline; predation is implied by the juxtaposition of a recumbent deer behind and below the hunted feline (Figure 10). In contrast, on the suspension hook of a *bo* bell from Ronghe 荣河 (Shanxi; *c.* Late Springs-Autumns), predation is explicit, while the animal master is implicit: a twisted helix (snakes) replaces the animal master between mirror-image predator and prey.[346] On the Palace Museum *pan*, however, both the

[338] Galanina and Gratch 1987: Pl. 118-119, Tol'staja Mogila (Dnepropetrovsk [Ukraine]), Greek-produced in a Scythian tomb, *c.* 4th century BC; *L'Or* 1995: 57, No. 78, Xoxlač (Novočerkassk, Rostov [Russia]), chance find; Sarmatian tubular box, glass-paste-inlaid gold; *c.* 1st century-first half 2nd century AD; Sarianidi 1985: Pl. 160-161, Tillia-tepe M4:8, turquoise-inlaid gold scabbard; Tian Guangjin and Guo Suxin 1986: 95, Fig. 63:3 (unprovenanced); Rudenko 1969: Pl. XXXVIII:1 (Dyrestuj), Xiongnu (?) bronze plaque (reproduced here as Figure 33). Note that the same composition is used on the lid of a gold sphere from the Sarmatian Xoxlač kurgan (Novočerkassk, Rostov; *L'Or* 1995: 53, bottom; 57, No. 80), with the eagle clearly attacking the deer, rather than the tiger.

[339] For Sarmatian examples: *L'Or* 1995: 51, No. 58; for Xiongnu examples: Tian Guangjin and Guo Suxin 1986: 82, Figs 49-50, unprovenanced.

[340] Tian Guangjin and Guo Suxin 1986: 344, Fig. 1:4.

[341] E.g., Marazov 1998: 124-125, No. 44, Lukovit (Bulgaria), Thracian gilded silver appliqués, *c.* 4th century BC; Boardman 2000: 171, Fig. 5.37a-c, Taxila (Pakistan), Parthian-era seals; Pfrommer 1993: 158-160, Nos 32-33, Parthian gilded silver phalerae, *c.* 2nd century BC.

[342] Shaanxi 2003b: 16-19, 2003MYD:010. Both animals are executed in the round. On the closely related Gansu 2002: 14, Fig. 14 (photo); 17, Fig. 19:1 (drawing), Yuandingshan 圓頂山 (Li 禮 xian, Gansu) 98LDM1:21 *he* pitcher, the head of the feline predator is turned to look back.

[343] Zhongguo qingtongqi 1998: 74, Pl. 72.

[344] As in Rawson 1990, throughout.

[345] Guo Baojun 1959: Pl. 93.

[346] Zhongguo meishu 1992: 22, Pl. 27.

animal master (*xian*) and the predation scene are explicitly shown.[347] In cases where the animal master is omitted, the predation image may be explicit, as on a bronze *hu* from Liyu (Hunyuan, Shanxi)[348] with décor in low relief (*c.* Early Warring States) or the gold-inlaid bronze stands from the tomb of King Cuo of Zhongshan 中山 (Sanji 三汲 [Pingshan 平山, Hebei] M1, *c.* 309 BC).[349] In a number of cases, however, predation is instead implicit: on another Liulige *hu*,[350] for instance, a bird is shown above a tiger,[351] with a pair of deer behind them both. All four animals are *couchant*; their relationship is implied by the proximity of these specific species (feline, hooved prey, bird).

Late Springs-Autumns *fanghu* from Lijialou (Xinzheng Municipality, Henan) offer a different type of implicit predation, pairing dragons and tigers (both predators, cast in the round as flanges or vessel feet) with a crane-like bird (also in the round, on the lid).[352] While the Lijialou pieces effectively omit the prey, their composition echoes the more explicit *fanghu* from the Springs-Autumns-era Yuandingshan (Lixian, Gansu) 98LDM2, on which the feline flanges attached to the vessel lid face animals of a different species attached to the vessel body.[353] The latter, despite being somewhat feline, appear to represent prey. The predation iconography is further reinforced by the placement of tigers around the vessel foot and horned animal heads on the vessel body, the latter reflecting a merging of predator and prey also known in the steppe (below, *The Bird Head*). In the context of the Yuandingshan vessel, the horned tiger could equally well substitute for a horned, hybrid animal master. Significantly, the equivalence of dragon and tiger established on the Lijialou pieces is maintained throughout the Han, not only in predation (and animal combat), but also the animal master iconography, particularly with the enthroned Queen Mother of the West (as above, *The Animal Master*).

Despite frequently being associated with northern Chinese states, the depiction of live-prey predation is shared by both northern and southern China. Indeed, Zhongshan, traditionally considered a non-Chinese (Xianyu 鮮虞) state and thus the likely point of entry for steppe influence during the Warring States, may not dominate sino-steppe exchange: it has proved difficult to isolate a non-Chinese stratum in Zhongshan or to identify non-Chinese elements not shared with contemporaneous Chinese states. In this context, the role of Zhongshan in transmitting steppe influence remains questionable. In addition, while northern examples of predation such as the stands from the tomb of King Cuo are undoubtedly better known, southern variants may also be cited. These include a lacquered screen from Wangshan 望山

---

347 Zhongguo meishu 1992: 48, Pl. 57-58; Gugong 1999: 289, Pl. 287.

348 Zhongguo meishu 1992: 47, Pl. 56. The mold fragment from Houma (Shanxi; Shanxi 1987: 76, Fig. 13; 78, Fig. 19 [T2102H2222:4]) depicting a large boar and, beneath its muzzle, a small boar cannot be considered to represent animal predation, although the Houma composition undoubtedly derives from predation.

349 Zhongguo meishu 1992: 91, Pl. 105-106; Hebei 1979: Pl. 2. Note that on these pieces, the prey is far smaller than the predator.

350 Zhongguo meishu 1992: 23, Pl. 28.

351 Echoing the Chu bird: e.g., Hubei 1989, Vol. 2: Pl. 83, tomb of the Marquis Yi of Zeng (Leigudun [Suizhou Municipality, Hubei]) E37, bronze sculpture. Note that this bird occurs on northern work, as well, as on the stem of the small bronze *fanghu* from the tomb of Zhao Qing 趙卿 (Jinsheng [Taiyuan Municipality, Shanxi]; Late Springs-Autumns/Early Warring States: Zhongguo qingtongqi 1995: 12); cf., Mancheng (Hebei; Zhongguo shehui kexueyuan 1980, Vol. 1: 263, Fig. 176; Vol. 2: Col. Pl. 24, Pl. 178, M2:3102, bronze lamp; Vol. 1: 267, Fig. 179; Vol. 2: Col. Pl. 25, Pl. 182, M2:3032, cups on stand; gilded bronze, inlaid turquoise, jade rings).

352 Henan 2001: 108-109 (two types of dragons as flanges, one winged and more western in execution); 110-112, 114-117 (tigers as feet, dragons as flanges).

353 Li 2004: 82-83, Pl. 20; in modified form: 78-81, Pl. 18-19, 98DLM1; 84-85, Pl. 21, 98DLM2.

(Jiangling, Jingzhou Municipality, Hubei) M1[354] (Late Warring States), on which a bird of prey represents the predator; and snakes, the prey. Deer remain part of the composition as duplicate prey, in contrast with the steppe convention of duplicate predators.

All these Eastern Zhou Chinese variations persist during the Han: live-prey predation (Figure 6),[355] with or without the animal master or tree of life,[356] with or without retaliatory live-prey predation,[357] and, as an alternative, animal combat.[358] Han art likewise makes use of dead-prey predation. This last seems to have been adopted in China during the Han, suggesting a late (re)introduction from the steppe. In its most complex form, stylistically attributable to the Xiongnu, the hooved prey, significantly smaller than the feline predator,[359] is draped limply over the tiger's shoulders and the tiger's tail is drawn forward between its hind legs, as on a bronze plaque from Yanglang 楊郎 (Guyuan 固原, Ningxia)[360] (Figure 33). Both conventions ultimately derive from Greek work, where they appear separately in the predation scenes on a gold plaque from the sanctuary of Apollo at Delphi (*c.* first half of the 6th century BC).[361] I have not found any earlier history of the prey over the feline's shoulders, but the convention of the predator's tail between its hind legs has a long history, from Predynastic Egypt (*c.* 4000-3200 BC) through the Parthian era.[362] Although rare in the Far Eastern steppe, this complex handling of the predator's tail does occur in the western world in combination with live-prey predation, as on an ivory scabbard of heavily Achaemenid style from the Treasure of the Oxus (Takht-i Sangin, Tajikistan; *c.* 5th-4th centuries BC) and on Parthian-era seals from Taxila (Pakistan).[363]

354 Hubei 1996: cover; Col. Pl. 2. See also Zhonghua 1973: Pl. 60.

355 E.g., Zhongguo shehui kexueyuan 1980, Vol. 1: 257, Fig. 171, Mancheng (Hebei) M2:3004, partially-silvered bronze *boshanlu* (here, Figure 6), explicitly on the upper register, right side, combined with the animal master, and implicitly on the lower register, throughout, combined with the tree of life. The latter follows the same compositional arrangement as Sarianidi 1985: Pl. 160-161, Tillia-tepe M4:8, turquoise-inlaid gold scabbard.

356 E.g., Zhongguo meishu 1988: 125, Pl. 148, Knitting Mill ([Zhenzhichang,] Tanghe, Henan); 126, Pl. 150, Nanyang (Henan), both carved stone, both with the *xian* animal master.

357 Watson 1962: Pl. 84c, Mount Trust, gilded bronze semispherical ornament with a décor of a tiger and a donkey-head (?) biting each other.

358 Nanjing 2013: front cover; 39, Fig. 23:5, Dayunshan (Xuyi, Jiangsu) M2:31, weight, bronze inlaid with gold, silver, turquoise, carnelian.

359 Except on the Dian-culture Shizhaishan 石寨山 (Jinning 晉寧, Yunnan) M12:38 bronze plaque (Lutz 1986: 127, No. 77), where the prey (lying rigidly along the tiger's back) is of nearly the same size as the predator. The larger size of the prey in this case may reflect the importance of oxen in the culture of Dian, but may also reflect the original source from which the image was adapted: in fact, both the position and the relative size of the prey repeat one of the dead-prey predation scenes on a gold plaque from Delphi: Nikulina 1994: Pl. II:136, upper right; see also Aruz, Graff, and Takic (eds) 2014: 310, No. 182A, third row, right; and, on a companion plaque not shown in Nikulina 1994, Aruz, Graff, and Takic (eds) 2014: 310, No. 182B, third row, left, Delphi Archaeological Museum, inv. 9797.

360 Ningxia 1978: 87, Fig. 1; repeated in Tian Guangjin and Guo Suxin 1986: 94, Fig. 62:1; Fig. 62:2, unprovenanced (said to be from the Ordos region) has the same composition.

361 Nikulina 1994: Pl. II:134, lower left, dead prey over the predator's shoulders, but with the lion's tail raised; Aruz, Graff, and Takic (eds) 2014: 310, No. 182A, second row, left, Sanctuary of Apollo, Sacred Way deposit, Delphi Archaeological Museum, inv. 9796; combined with (from the same plaque) Nikulina: Pl. II:136, upper right, dead prey upside-down and rigid along the predator's back, lion's tail between its hind legs; Aruz, Graff, and Takic (eds) 2014: 310, No. 182A, third row, right; and, on a companion plaque not shown in Nikulina 1994, Aruz, Graff, and Takic (eds) 2014: 310, No. 182B, third row, left, Delphi Archaeological Museum, inv. 9797.

362 Smith 1981: 32, Fig. 10 (drawing), Hierakonpolis (Egypt), carved stone palette depicting a lion attacking a man fallen on the battlefield; the composition is closely related to Collon 1995: 159, Fig. 128, Nimrud (Iraq), Palace of Ashurnasirpal II, 'Phoenician style' carved ivory inlaid with lapis lazuli and carnelian, gilded, *c.* 9th-7th centuries BC, with a décor of a lioness attacking a prone (Nubian?) boy, her far foreleg wrapped around the boy's shoulders; British Museum 00032505001 (see also <https://www.bmimages.com/preview.asp?image=00032505001>, viewed 3 January 2019); one of a pair: both plaques of the pair are shown in Aruz, Graff, and Takic (eds) 2014: 151, No. 50 and Fig. 3.45; Young *et al.* 1981: Pl. 22:c-f, Phrygian site of Gordion (Turkey), tumulus P:107, small wood sculptures of lions, *c.* 700 BC. Later examples follow below.

363 Schiltz 1994: 307, Fig. 229, providing a date of *c.* 3rd-2nd centuries BC (Oxus); Boardman 2000: 171, Fig. 5.37a-c

The complexity of Xiongnu dead-prey predation is generally lost in non-Xiongnu adaptations, whether of non-Chinese or Chinese production. On these, the prey is generally shown hanging (often stiffly) beneath the mouth of the predator.[364] The body of the prey may be replaced by depiction of only the head or by an abstract cipher[365] (as on Figure 21), a reduction that also occurs in the context of (presumably) live prey on bronze harness fittings from Luristan.[366] In addition, the bodies of tiger and prey in non-Xiongnu eastern examples tend to be static or rigid, and the tiger's tail is commonly shown as hanging straight down behind the hind legs. Han examples include a gilded bronze plaque from Pingshuo 平朔 (Shanxi), representing the dead prey as an indistinct curl, but with the tiger's tail drawn forward between its hind legs[367] (Figure 21). In this context, the limp prey draped over the tiger's shoulders, together with the tight composition and the style of execution, on the carved wood comb found in a Han tomb at Shuihudi 睡虎地 (Yunmeng 雲夢, Hubei) M47:93[368] all suggest that the comb represents an imported Xiongnu product (Figure 34).

More complex Han compositions are not necessarily more explicit. For instance, a stone bas relief from Jiawang (Tongshan, Xuzhou Municipality, Jiangsu)[369] makes use of a single type of animal (with a horse- or donkey-like head and feline or canine paws), repeated in different positions (Figure 35). Three of these are grouped to each side of the two central animals (of the same type), shown with entwined necks. One of the three is shown lunging toward another; both the latter and a third, more peripheral, animal turn away from this lunge. This arrangement suggests a live-prey predation model, with lunging predator and two prey,[370]

(Taxila), for which I follow the dating of Colledge 1986: 15. For Ionian examples, see Nikulina 1994: Pl. II:162, lentoid seal, *c.* first half 4th century BC, British Museum BM 91.6-25.3; Pl. II-166, lentoid seal, *c.* late 5th-first half 4th centuries BC, Bibliothèque Nationale (Paris). The convention also occurs at Pazyryk, on a carved wood plaque of a tiger alone: Rudenko 1970: 164, Fig. 84 (kurgan 4, bridle ornament). Note that the stag-prey on the Oxus plaque, very small in comparison to the lion, is held out between the lion's front paws. This loosening of the typical steppe iconography makes it difficult to ascertain whether the prey is alive or dead. Note that Oscar White Muscarella has repeatedly raised questions about the provenance and authenticity of the Oxus treasure, summarized and rebutted in Curtis 2004.

364 Non-Chinese examples include: a find from Guoxianyaozi 崞縣窯子 (Liangcheng 涼城, Inner Mongolia; Tian Guangjin and Guo Suxin 1986: 94, Fig. 62:3); examples from Ningxia such as Yanglang (Guyuan; Ningxia 1993: 32, Fig. 18:8 [IIIM4:82]; 33, Fig. 19:12 [IM12:5], 16 [IIIM3:65]); Pingyang 平洋 (Tailai 泰來, Heilongjiang; Heilongjiang 1990: Pl. 40:2 [M188:26]). Further non-Chinese examples evidencing heavy Xiongnu influence include: Shihuigou 石灰溝 (Yijinhuoluo Banner 伊金霍洛旗, Inner Mongolia; Yikezhaomeng 1992: 92, Fig. 1:5 [silver]); Nianfangqu 碾房渠 (Dongsheng 東勝 Municipality, Inner Mongolia; Yikezhaomeng 1991: 406, Fig. 2 [gold]). The common static manner of depicting the prey appears to reflect the influence of Xiongnu-attributed sculpture of deer *couchant*, as in Tian Guangjin and Guo Suxin 1986: Pl. 104, 109, Sujigou 速機溝 (Jungar Banner, Inner Mongolia); Pl. 108, Yulongtai 玉隆太 (Jungar Banner, Inner Mongolia). Static depiction of the full body of the prey beneath the tiger's jaws may perhaps have been used in some cases of live-prey predation: the depiction on the Majiayuan 馬家塬 (Zhangjiachuan 張家川, Gansu) M15:3 gold foil piece is ambiguous and could derive from live- or dead-prey versions (Gansu 2014: 046, top; 047, dated by excavators to the Warring States).

365 Reduced to a head: Pingyang (Tailai, Heilongjiang) M188:26 (Heilongjiang 1990: Pl. 40:2); reduced to an indistinct mass: Maoqinggou (Liangcheng, Inner Mongolia) M74:5 and perhaps M5:6-1,2 (Tian Guangjin and Guo Suxin 1986: 281, Fig. 45:2, 1, respectively).

366 Amiet 1976: Pl. 129, 131, showing the head of the prey flanked by heraldically-positioned predators; similarly, on Pl. 128, a human head is substituted for the animal master, flanked by heraldic animals.

367 Pingshuo 1987: 12, Fig. 32, 6M50:8, gilded bronze; tomb *c.* 24 AD, per Psarras 2015.

368 Hubei 1986: 515, Fig. 38.5 (*c.* 173 BC, per Psarras 2015). Despite the occurrence of Chinese-produced gold plaques of live-prey predation (where, additionally, the prey bites the predator) at the Xiongnu site of Xigoupan (Jungar Banner, Inner Mongolia; Tian Guangjin and Guo Suxin 1986: Pl. 63, M2:26, 27), few other examples of Chinese-manufactured steppe-type objects are now documented on non-Chinese sites. We may most reasonably conclude that such imitations instead served a Chinese market (see Psarras in preparation).

369 Jiangsu 1959: Pl. 71, Fig. 91.

370 Two prey appear on a gold foil live-prey predation plaque from the non-Chinese site of Majiayuan (Zhangjiachuan, Gansu) M20MS:8 (Gansu 2014: 045).

rather than two predators. On the main prey, as well as on one of the two entwined animals in the center of the composition, the animal's tail is drawn between the hind legs. Despite the ambiguity of the composition, Xiongnu influence is clear in the combination of predation with the complex positioning of the tail.

A second version of dead-prey predation appears in Xiongnu art, as on gold plaques from Aluchaideng (Hanggin Banner, Inner Mongolia)[371] (Figure 36). In these, the body of the dead prey forms only the background for feeding tigers. The same composition occurs on a turquoise-inlaid gold plaque from Tillia-tepe tomb 4[372] and a carved wood saddle arch from Pazyryk kurgan 5,[373] on which the heads and forefeet of tigers executed in the round are attached to the edge of a semi-circular plaque with a décor of an elk *couchant*. While Aluchaideng remains difficult to date beyond the Late Warring States-Han, Xinzhuangtou (Yixian, Hebei) XZHM30:35,[374] a gold plaque with a similar composition, in reasonably Xiongnu style, and featuring the tail of one predator drawn forward between its hind legs, indicates Chinese knowledge of the composition by the late 4th-3rd centuries BC.

The composition also occurs in Han imitations, as on a carved jade plaque from the tomb of the Marquis of Haihun (Xinjian [Nanchang Municipality, Jiangxi]),[375] on which, however, the prey (a boar) seems to be alive. Similarly, a complex, less directly related composition appears on a gold garment hook from Sanlidun 三里墩 (Lianshui 漣水, Jiangsu)[376] (Figure 37). The Sanlidun piece reverses steppe norms, representing the dead (?) prey by a large head, rather than either the full body, as in the Aluchaideng plaques, or the small head below the mouth of the predator, in the case of the Yanglang-related version. Although the prey's head dominates the piece because of its relative size, the influence of the Aluchaideng-type variant is clear in the surrounding of that head by a dragon's body (reinforced by serpents).

The same change in compositional emphasis occurs on an earthenware model well (*jing* 井) with relief décor from Shaogou 燒溝 (Luoyang Municipality, Henan) M1028A:14,[377] which combines live- and dead-prey predation on the longer sides, with the animal master depicted on at least one short side (Figure 38, the animal master is visible on the left). In this case, although the prey (a deer) seems to be alive, it is compositionally insignificant, like the Aluchaideng yaks; emphasis is instead placed on the several monstrous animals attacking it from three sides. Again as on the Aluchaideng plaques, the heads and forefeet of the predators are accentuated at the expense of the rest of their bodies. The Aluchaideng composition is more regular, less animated than that of Shaogou M1028A:14, but its influence, rendered as live-prey predation, is undeniable.

As with the animal master or tree of life iconography, Han interpretations of predation are often complicated in flat or low-relief work by the separation of elements of the composition, a tendency established in Eastern Zhou animal master-related scenes (as Figures 4, 7). Such spatially-loose treatment stands in direct contrast to décors with a long Chinese tradition,

371 Tian Guangjin and Guo Suxin 1986: 345, Fig. 2:4.
372 Sarianidi 1985: Pl. 122, M4: 36.
373 Rudenko 1970: Pl. 165a. Parzinger *et al.* 2008: 17 dates Pazyryk kurgan 5 to *c.* 250 BC.
374 Hebei 1996, Vol. 2: Col. Pl. 27, Pl. 143:1; cf., also Col. Pl. 28, Pl. 143:2, XZHM30:33.
375 Jiangxi 2016: 157, bottom.
376 Nanjing 1973: 83, Fig. 4:7, *c.* 70 BC, per Psarras 2015.
377 Zhongguo kexueyuan 1959: 129, Fig. 61.

such as the various interlaces and meanders, which during much of the Bronze Age tend to be dense and tightly interconnected. By the time of the Han, this looseness largely defines Chinese figural décor as a whole, even when it is obscured by surface enrichment, achieved through inlay, gilding, or the superimposition of ornamental motifs extraneous to the composition.[378] While all of these are also used in the art of some steppe cultures – particularly in Sarmatian work or on pieces from Tillia-tepe[379] – even in the more successful Chinese versions,[380] the principal composition almost always lacks the tension underlying even similarly ornate steppe versions. It is rare to find Han compositions in flat or low relief characterized not by individual elements in juxtaposition, but by entwined elements on multiple, overlapping visual planes, as on one panel of the stone bas reliefs from Yangzishan 羊子山 (Chengdu Municipality, Sichuan) M1[381] (Figure 22) or the bas relief décor of animals in mountains on a bronze *lian* in the Freer Gallery of Art (Smithsonian Institution, Washington, DC).[382] This kind of spatial complexity, in itself, therefore suggests additional foreign influence.

Han compositional norms can make it difficult to distinguish between animal combat, animal predation, and animals beneath the tree of life. The problem is readily visible on stamped bricks from Luoyang (Henan), which may in fact combine iconographies, as in the loose composition of live-prey predation beside the tree of life on one brick.[383] In addition, Han versions may truncate the iconography, depicting more than one predator and no prey, as in the procession of tiger and bird on a bronze tray from Guangzhou (Guangdong) M5054:18.[384] Similarly, the primary (feline) predator may be replaced by the bird, in contrast with steppe compositions, in which the bird typically constitutes a secondary predator, as on the Dyrestuj (Burjatija [Russia]) multiple-predator predation plaque[385] (Figure 32). In these Han versions, the bird attacks the prey, as on a stone relief from Zhangxu 張圩 (Suining 睢寧, Xuzhou Municipality, Jiangsu)[386] (Figure 39), in which the bird hovers over a horse, its beak aimed at the horse's neck. This reductive principle is perhaps most pronounced on hollow bricks from Luoyang, on which predation is implied between two predators, tiger and bird (*enroulé*), separated by a floral frieze and geometric motifs[387] (Figure 40).

[378] As on the Dingzhou (Hebei) tubular fitting: Zhonghua 1973: Pl. 85.

[379] *L'Or* 1995; Sarianidi 1985. The appearance of turquoise-inlaid goldwork in Springs and Autumns-era Qin (e.g., Li 2004: 104, Pl. 35; 106, Pl. 37, all Yuandingshan [Lixian, Gansu] 98LDM2 sword fittings; Zhongguo 1993: Pl. 99, iron-bladed shortsword; Pl. 100, duck-shaped garment hooks; Pl. 101, *taotie*-type fittings, all Yimen 益門 [Baoji 寶鷄 Municipality, Shaanxi] M2, Late Springs-Autumns), implies its use by contemporaneous non-Chinese peoples, raising the possibility that this type of embellishment originated in the Far Eastern steppe.

[380] E.g., Nanjing 2013: front cover; 39, Fig. 23:5, Dayunshan (Xuyi, Jiangsu) M2:31, weight, bronze inlaid with gold, silver, turquoise, carnelian.

[381] Zhongguo meishu 1988: 86-87, Pl. 102, second row, center, right side of the stone (massed horse-drawn carriages).

[382] Watson 1974: No. 45; also Watson 1995: 91, Fig. 159.

[383] Huang Minglan 1986: 28-29.

[384] Guangzhoushi 1981, Vol. 1: 437, Fig. 272.

[385] Rudenko 1969: Pl. XXXVIII:1.

[386] Xuzhou 1985: Pl. 254.

[387] Zhou Dao, Lü Pin, and Tang Wenxing 1985: Pl. 3; see also Luoyang 1990: 65, Figs 7, 8.

The Bird Head

Esther Jacobson has suggested iconographic equivalence between the antlers of the deer-prey and the tree of life in steppe art from the Scythians through the Xiongnu,[388] manifested in the use of bird heads as terminal points on antlers and in the transposition of antlers to the feline predator[389] (Figures 41, 42). This amalgamation is undoubtedly reflected in the antlered birds on register 2 of the *c.* later-sixth century BC Liulige (Huixian, Henan) M59:23 bronze *hu*[390] (Figure 10). The motif is utilized extensively in Chu and culturally-related states from the Late Springs and Autumns through the Warring States.[391] As an independent image, it appears on a bronze sculptural element from Tengzhou (Shandong), dated to the Middle Springs-Autumns (*c.* 7th-early 6th centuries BC), in the form of antlers with bird-shaped attachments throughout.[392] It is retained in the Han as the crested bird of Mancheng (Hebei) M2:3032[393] (Figure 43) and, in attenuated form, in the use of bird heads as decorative reinforcement, as on the Wu family shrines and other sites in Jiaxiang and Yanggu (Shandong).[394] Steppe derivation is clear and may likewise be seen on Late Warring States[395] and Han Chinese imitations of steppe work. The latter include plaques, exemplified by gold predation iconography plaques from Shizishan (Xuzhou Municipality, Jiangsu), on which bird heads appear both on the antlers of the deer-

388 Jacobson 1984. Scythian examples include: Galanina and Gratch 1987: Pl. 70, Ilicevskij [Crimea], gold quiver cover; Scythian manufacture with Greek influence, *c.* first half 5th century BC; Pl. 101, Ak-Mečet' [Crimea], gold appliqué; Scythian manufacture, *c.* first half 5th century BC; Pl. 82, Nymphea [Crimea] kurgan 17, gold plaque; Scythian production, *c.* mid-fifth century BC; note the bird head at the end of the tail of the winged lion. For the Altai, examples include pieces from Katanda (Rudenko 1970: Pl. 140e, wood plaque), Berel' (Rudenko 1970: Pl. 142d, carved wood deer mask), and Pazyryk (Rudenko 1970: 262-263, Fig. 129-131, tattoos of the master of Pazyryk kurgan 2).

389 Aluchaideng (Hanggin Banner, Inner Mongolia), gold plaque inlaid with turquoise and red stones (Tian Guangjin and Guo Suxin 1986: Pl. 69:4, Col. Pl. 16:1); see also Xigoupan (Jungar Banner, Inner Mongolia) M2:60, gold foil appliqué (Tian Guangjin and Guo Suxin 1986: 345, Fig. 2:1; 356, Fig. 4:3), and Noyon uul (Rudenko 1969: Pl. XLII; also visible Pl. XLI; Trever 1932: Pl. 9:2). Non-Chinese examples occur in a datable Chinese context in Hebei 1996, Vol. 2: Col. Pl. 26:2, Xinzhuangtou (Yixian, Hebei) XZHM30:105, turquoise-inlaid gold sword chape; Col. Pl. 30:3, Xinzhuangtou XZHM30:24; Pl. 145:5, XZHM30:23; Pl. 146:1, XZHM30:24, both gold semi-spherical appliqués, *c.* late 4th-3rd centuries BC.

390 Guo Baojun 1959: Pl. 93. On register 2 of the same piece, an antlered bird with snakes is depicted in heraldic mirror image on each side of a (snake?-) crested animal master. Cf., also the handles in the form of an antlered beast on a Late Springs-Autumns *gui* in the Palace Museum (Beijing; Gugong 1999: 238, Pl. 232).

391 As in Hubei 1989, Vol. 2: Pl. 83, tomb of the Marquis Yi of Zeng (Leigudun [Suizhou Municipality, Hubei]) E37 (bronze sculpture). Note that a horned (crested) bird occurs on pieces from Sanxingdui 三星堆 (Guanghan 廣漢 Municipality, Sichuan), *c.* 1200 BC, such as Bagley (ed.) 2001: 150, No. 50, Sanxingdui K2(3):193-1 fragment; Fig. 50.1, vessel lid (Guimet [Paris] MA1612), attributed to Changsha (Hunan); Fig. 50.2, Hejiacun 賀家村 (Qishan 岐山, Shaanxi) *jia* 斝; Fig. 50.33, Sanxingdui K2(3):23 fragment (all bronze); Jay Xu (Bronze at Sanxingdui, in Bagley [ed.] 2001: 59) describes the motif as common in the Middle Yangzi region and suggests that it may have been exported westward. See the essentially contemporaneous Late Shang/Early Western Zhou (i.e., *c.* 11th century BC) bronzes from Shigushan 石鼓山 (Baoji 寶雞 Municipality, Shaanxi): Shaanxi 2016: 33, Fig. 59 (M4:804, *gui*); 34, Fig. 60 (M4:804, lid), bronze (rubbings). Nonetheless, there seems to be no continuity between these and the Eastern Zhou examples. The latter, even if recalling or even reviving the past, nonetheless constitute new conceptions.

392 So 1995: 20, Fig. 12.

393 Zhongguo shehui kexueyuan 1980, Vol. 1: 267, Fig. 179; Vol. 2: Col. Pl. 25, Pl. 182, M2:3032, cups on stand; gilded bronze, inlaid turquoise, jade rings.

394 Liu Xingzhen and Yue Fengxia 1991: 75, 81 (Front shrine); 92-93, 100 (Left shrine); 124-126, 133-135 (Rear shrine), Wu Family shrines (Jiaxiang, Shandong); Liaocheng 1989: 54, Fig. 11, Balimiao (Yanggu, Shandong) M1; Zhu Xilu 1992: 77, Fig. 104, Hualin (Jiaxiang, Shandong); 38, Fig. 45, Songshan (Jiaxiang, Shandong) M1.

395 E.g., Shaanxi 2003a: 6, Fig. 5; 8, Fig. 10:1, Beikang 北康 (Xi'an Municipality Northern Suburbs, Shaanxi) 99SXLM34:21, ceramic mold. Published as Warring States; in my view, Late Warring States through comparison of Shaanxi 2003a: 11, Fig. 21:6, 99SXLM34:4, earthenware *fou* to Xianyang 2005: 260, Fig. 206:5 (M257); 262, Fig. 209:1 (M97), all, Renjiazui 任家嘴 (Xianyang Municipality, Shaanxi). For discussion, see Psarras in preparation.

prey, but also as fill around the predation image,[396] as well as freer-form renditions, such as on lacquered boxes from Beishantou (Chaohu Municipality, Anhui).[397]

Less obviously, the application of bird heads to predators is transposed in Han work to the attachment of multiple human heads on sphinx (a composite predator), as in the eight secondary heads forming a fan-like crown over the primary head of the sphinx on a carved stone panel from Shilipu (Xuzhou Municipality, Jiangsu)[398] (Figure 44) or the multiple heads on the tail of a sphinx on a stone bas relief from the tomb of Lord Feng (Tanghe [Nanyang Municipality, Henan])[399] (Figure 45).

[396] Lin (ed.) 2012: 84-85, 188-191, No. 82.
[397] Anhui 2007: 112, Fig. 80:2, BM1:37; 113, Fig. 81, BM1:29.
[398] Xuzhou 1985: Pl. 25.
[399] Nanyang 1980: 244, Fig. 8:2.

II: Decorative Elements

Chapter 6

Fantastic Elements

Foreign influence on Han art far exceeds these three central iconographies of the animal master, the tree of life, and animal predation, particularly in regard to minor, decorative animal and plant motifs. Some of these, such as the sphinx and the griffin, parallel the animal master and related iconographies in age and origin, and were first incorporated into Chinese art at much the same time. Many minor motifs, however, become widespread only during the Han, when they are integral to scenes of paradise.

Among the assorted winged animals common in Han scenes of paradise figure the sphinx, a human-headed lion (as in Figure 44, center), and the griffin, most commonly combining the body of a lion with the head and wings of an eagle.[400] These forms developed throughout Egypt, the Near East, and the Aegean from as early as the 4th millennium BC,[401] remaining popular through the Hellenistic age in these territories, as well as the Western steppe[402] and Bactria. By the Late Classical and Hellenistic periods, Greek variants may be distinguished from the Achaemenid, although the two are often blended: Greek work is associated with lanky bodies and naturalistic features (Figure 46); Achaemenid, with heavy-set, monumental bodies with wide, square jaws. Greek griffins typically have naturalistic wings and a markedly-scalloped crest;[403] Achaemenid, rounded wings, a short, fairly uniform crest, and horns terminating in spheres or circles.[404] Significantly, both Greek and Persian characteristics appear in the Altai[405]

[400] The term 'griffin' is often used quite loosely, but is properly distinguished from the chimaera, which combines the lion's head with the winged body of a goat or deer.

[401] Crowley 1989: 40-44, traces the sphinx from *c.* third-millennium BC Egypt, *c.* late nineteenth-century BC Syria (with wings), through *c.* late sixteenth-century BC Crete, and the griffin throughout the Near East and Aegean from *c.* the 4th millennium BC through the early-middle 2nd millennium BC, in multiple guises, with the crested form emerging in *c.* early-middle second-millennium BC Mitanni (northern Syria, southeastern Turkey; Crowley 1989: 46-51).

[402] E.g., Greek-produced or inspired work on *c.* fourth-century BC Scythian sites: Galanina and Gratch 1987: Pl. 150-154, Tol'staja Mogila (Dnepropetrovsk), gold scabbard; Greco-Scythian manufacture; Pl. 179, Kul'-Oba, Kerč', gold bracelet; Greek manufacture; Pl. 245, Tri Brata (Three Brothers), Crimea, Greek-influenced enameled gold temple pendants.

[403] *Inter alia*, Ionian examples, *c.* first half 4th century BC: Nikulina 1994: Pl. II:161, chalcedony lentoid seal. The griffin on theTillia-tepe M5:8 chalcedony seal (Sarianidi 1985: Pl. 74) closely echoes Ionian work and may indeed be an heirloom import. Note that Nikulina 1994: Pl. II:280 (rock crystal seal) combines a Greek sphinx with Achaemenid-type wings. For the webbed crest as a 'Greek type,' see also Pfrommer 1993: 61; 61, Fig. 45-I, silver rhyton, Tuch el-Karamus [Egypt], *c.* late 4th-first half 3rd centuries BC. The convention also appears on Achaemenid renderings (Nikulina 1994: Pl. III:437, agate cylinder seal, *c.* 5th-4th centuries BC), as well as on some griffins from Pazyryk (Rudenko 1970: Pl. 135 and Pl. 170 [drawing of reconstruction], kurgan 1, felt appliqué saddle blanket; Pl. 81b, kurgan 1, wood bridle ornaments; Pl. 86a, b, kurgan 1, wood harness ornaments, the latter noted by Pfrommer 1993: 61, Fig. 45h).

[404] *Inter alia*, Curtis and Tallis 2005: 84, No. 46, originally Palace G, Persepolis (Marvdasht, Fars [Iran]), stone relief, *c.* 359/358-338/337 BC; Nikulina 1994: Pl. II:278, agate lentoid seal, *c.* first half 4th century BC.

[405] Pazyryk figures are generally characterized by extreme stylization and lankiness. Within this context, however, the sphinx on the felt appliqué hanging from Pazyryk kurgan 5 (Rudenko 1970: Pl. 173, detail) has a Near Eastern appearance. In contrast, Pazyryk griffins may incorporate more Greek features, such as a moderately-webbed crest, together with a wing that is more Achaemenid in overall shape, but formed of more naturalistic, individually-drawn feathers (Rudenko 1970: Pl. 168B, kurgan 2 felt appliqué saddle blanket), or more Achaemenid features, as a square head with pronounced, squared jaw, a flat, short crest, and a rounded, (apparently) undifferentiated wing (Rudenko 1970: Pl. 169A, kurgan 1 felt appliqué saddle blanket). Greek precedent for wings of the same shape, with individually-drawn feathers, is provided by a gold brooch reportedly from Patras (Greece; Williams and Ogden 1994: 71, No. 24, *c.* 340-320 BC). By way of comparison, the griffin predator of the felt appliqué hanging or carpet from Noyon uul kurgan 6 (Rudenko 1969: Pl. XLI, XLV), however, bears neither the webbed crest nor the high haunches of the 'Greek' form, and

and the Far Eastern steppe.[406] For instance, the winged and horned tigers on stamped copper plaques from Pazyryk kurgan 2 (Figure 47),[407] on the live-prey predation plaques in the Siberian Collection of Peter the Great,[408] and on the Xiongnu headdress from Aluchaideng (Hanggin Banner, Inner Mongolia)[409] (Figure 48) are all markedly Achaemenid. The winged tiger on the Aluchaideng headdress, in particular, very closely resembles those of the Pazyryk kurgan 2 plaques. In contrast, Xianbei winged horses recognizably derive from the Hellenic.[410]

Pre-Han Chinese examples are rare, largely limited to sculptures of a winged and eagle-clawed feline from the tomb of King Cuo of Zhongshan.[411] These are extremely Achaemenid in the shape of the animal's body and head, including the square jaw with bared teeth.[412] The spade-shaped nose, however, is a stylistic characteristic shared with a griffin/chimaera from the Oxus treasure.[413] This last detail suggests that Achaemenid influence reached Warring States China via Bactria. Creatures of the same type, with the same form of snout and horns, appear on a gilded wood and horn torque (set on a copper [?] ring) from Pazyryk kurgan 2[414] (Figure 49), which I interpret as reflecting the influence of pieces like the Oxus griffin/chimaera. In this context, contact with the Altai may have reinforced the heavily-Achaemenid Chinese adaptation of the form, but seems unlikely to have been the main point of transmission. These conventions were maintained, albeit in softened form, during the Han, as in the winged lions forming the feet of a *zun* from Huzhuang 胡莊 (Yizheng 儀征, Jiangsu).[415] Bactrian influence is also visible in some Han fantastic beasts that do not demonstrate Achaemenid stylistic characteristics, as in the sphinx with a double torso on the stone relief from Shilipu (Xuzhou Municipality, Jiangsu)[416] (Figure 44) and the second

more closely resembles Achaemenid-associated variants. In contrast, a winged lion on the embroidered cloth from the same kurgan displays a greyhound-like body (Rudenko 1969: Pl. LXVII:1). At Tillia-tepe, the griffin on a chalcedony seal from tomb 5 (Sarianidi 1985: Pl. 74, M5:8) directly echoes Ionian work and may indeed be an heirloom import.

406 In the case of the winged tiger of Pingyang (Tailai, Heilongjiang) M188:26, an adaptation of the Xiongnu dead-prey predation iconography (Heilongjiang 1990: Pl. 40:2), the 'wings' appear to be a variation of musculature. Otherwise, winged animals in northern non-Chinese cultures are largely limited to Xianbei winged horses, as on gilded bronze plaques from Laoheshen 老河深 (Yushu 榆樹, Jilin) M56:3, 37, M105:16-1,2, M105:21-1, 2 (Jilin 1987: Pl. 33:1, 2; Pl. 34:1, 2; Pl. 35:9, 10, respectively) and Zhalainuoer 扎賚諾爾 (Hulunbuir [Hulunbei'er] 呼倫貝爾 Municipality, Inner Mongolia) M1 in bronze (Zheng Long 1961: 17, Fig. 4:1).

407 Rudenko 1970: 102, Fig. 46.

408 Even though the modeling of the horse is more Greek than Achaemenid. Pfrommer 1993: 59, Fig. 44 (State Hermitage Museum 1727-1/6, gold).

409 Tian Guangjin and Guo Suxin 1986: 344, Fig. 1:4 (gold).

410 As on gilded bronze plaques from Laoheshen (Yushu, Jilin) and Zhalainuoer (Hulunbuir Municipality, Inner Mongolia, as noted above (Jilin 1987: Pl. 33:1, 2; Pl. 34:1, 2; Pl. 35:9, 10; Zheng Long 1961: 17, Fig. 4:1). In these cases, Greek influence is likely to have reached the Xianbei through the Xiongnu, a culture characterized by a marked degree of Hellenism (Psarras forthcoming).

411 Hebei 1995, Vol. 1: 143, Fig. 51 (XK:58); Vol. 2: Col. Pl. 16:1 (DK:35), 2 (XK:58), bronze, silver inlay: two pairs are reported, DK:35-36, XK:58-59. Note that the winged dragons from the same tomb are in a style not readily identifiable as deriving from either Persian or Greek influence: Hebei 1995, Vol. 1: 120, Fig. 39B; Vol. 2: Col. Pl. 7; Pl. 79, XK:15, the vertical handles (or flanges) on the bronze *fanghu* XK:15; and Vol. 1: 139, Fig. 49A; Vol. 2: Col. Pl. 14, as the sculptural base of the tray DK:33, bronze, silver and gold inlay. The Achaemenid head, jaw, and prominent teeth also occur on a Warring States gold tiger from Fengxiang 鳳翔 (Shaanxi; Liu Yang [ed.] 2012: 105, No. 39).

412 Cf., Curtis and Tallis 2005: 121, No. 118, gold rhyton, reputedly from Hamadan (Iran) 1321; 194, No. 301, bronze weight, Susa acropolis.

413 Collon 1995: 187, Fig. 150; Curtis and Tallis 2005: 148, No. 194 (British Museum 123924). See also <https://www.britishmuseum.org/research/collection_online/collection_object_details.aspx?objectId=282239&partId=1&searchText=123924>, viewed 3 January 2019.

414 Rudenko 1970: 107, Fig. 50 [reconstruction, drawing]; Pl. 68D, E.

415 Xu (ed.) 2017: 108-109, No. 35.

416 Xuzhou 1985: Pl. 25.

stone of the Left Wu family shrine[417] (Figure 50, lower right). These examples further recall the double-headed horse ridden by the deity on a series of gold Kushan coins minted under Kanishka,[418] which may serve as either as an immediate or as an additional source for the motif.

Less obviously, a Near Eastern origin with Bactrian transmission seems likely for the sphinx with the forelegs of a deer on a stone from the Left Wu shrine (Jiaxiang, Shandong)[419] (Figure 50, second beast from the lower right). A similar hybrid (a sphinx with the rear legs of a deer) occurs on a Near Eastern-derived gold scabbard from the Scythian tomb of Kelermes ([Kuban,] Krasnodar [Russia]) kurgan 1 (*c.* late 7th-early 6th centuries BC).[420] The same scabbard depicts a griffin with the forelegs of a deer, later repeated on the griffin from the Oxus Treasure, as well as on an appliqué from Pazyryk kurgan 2.[421] In this context, it is possible that the sphinx-deer from the Left Wu family shrine also derives from Bactria. More commonly, however, Han sphinxes[422] demonstrate Altaian influence (cf., Figure 51).[423]

Indeed, an Altaian connection is most common in Han versions of Achaemenid-style fantastic beasts, suggesting a path of transmission different from that of the pieces from the tomb of King Cuo of Zhongshan. For instance, stone bas reliefs from Shuanggou (Suining, Xuzhou Municipality, Jiangsu)[424] (Figure 52, bottom), Dongjiazhuang 董家莊 (Anqiu 安丘, Shandong),[425] and Yi'nan (Shandong)[426] all make use of the heavy bodies and powerful heads characteristic of Achaemenid art, combined with a stylistic execution highly reminiscent of Pazyryk (Figure 47).[427] Notably, the Dongjiazhuang and Yi'nan stones carry a border décor of continuous triangles in a continuation of Bronze Age Chinese tradition. However, the motif is also used as a border at Pazyryk, such as on the Achaemenized lion-head frieze on a felt wall-hanging from Pazyryk kurgan 1.[428] Thus, when it occurs at Dongjiazhuang and Yi'nan in combination with the Achaemenized-Pazyryk style of fantastic beasts, it may also reflect Pazyryk influence, readily accepted in a Chinese context.

Finally, in a further example, the Hellenistic influence visible in the lanky bodies and lean musculature of the winged felines on stone bas reliefs from Taishang 臺上 (Tongshan 銅山,

---

[417] Liu Xingzhen and Yue Fengxia 1991: 92-93.

[418] Rosenfield 1993: Pl. VII:132-133, whom Rosenfield identifies with the Zoroastrian Mozdooano (Rosenfield 1993: 82-83). Consensus now places Kanishka's accession at AD 127; for recent discussions, see especially Jongeward and Cribb 2014: 3, with references.

[419] Liu Xingzhen and Yue Fengxia 1991: 92-93, upper right.

[420] Galanina and Gratch 1987: Pl. 35.

[421] Collon 1995: 187, Fig. 150; Curtis and Tallis 2005: 148, No. 194, Oxus gold griffin/chimaera, British Museum 123924; Rudenko 1953: 128, Fig. 74, on which the head of the griffin is very Achaemenid.

[422] E.g., Jinguyuan 金谷園 (Luoyang Municipality, Henan); *c.* 14 AD, per Psarras 2015: Luoyang 1985: 170, Fig. 20 (photograph); 165, Fig. 5:1 (drawing), wall paintings. Variants include a Shilipu (Xuzhou Municipality, Jiangsu) stone bas relief, one sphinx with a non-Chinese face around which radiate eight small heads, and another with a double human torso rising from its feline chest (Xuzhou 1985: Pl. 25), reproduced here as Figure 44. The latter is repeated in the Left Wu family shrine (Jiaxiang, Shandong): Liu Xingzhen and Yue Fengxia 1991: 92-93, upper right.

[423] As in Rudenko 1953: 280, Fig. 163, kurgan 1.

[424] Jiangsu 1959: Pl. 67, Fig. 86 (bottom).

[425] Shandong 1982: Pl. 537. Also cf., Powers 1991:121, Fig. 60.

[426] Nanjing 1956: Pl. 52. Also cf., Powers 1991:120, Fig. 59.

[427] Rudenko 1970:102, Figs 45-46, kurgan 2, copper plaques; Pl. 169A, kurgan 1, felt appliqué on a saddle blanket.

[428] Rudenko 1970: Pl. 148a.

Xuzhou Municipality, Jiangsu)[429] (Figure 53), Maocun 茅村 (Xuzhou Municipality, Jiangsu),[430] and Liuquan 柳泉 (Xuzhou Municipality, Jiangsu),[431] may also reflect Altaian influence. Elongation is often characteristic of Han depiction of animals, at least in part as an extension of Warring States taste. Perhaps sharing this characteristic with the Altai facilitated Han adoption of Pazyryk style.

Similarly, Achaemenid influence on Han art may at times have been received through the steppe, as is the case in the rendering of the fantastic beasts on lacquered boxes from Beishantou (Chaohu Municipality, Anhui).[432] Although Achaemenid in flavor, the Beishantou boxes follow a composition widespread in the Far Eastern steppe: mirror-image horses with inverted hindquarters, antlers, and both tails and antlers ending in bird heads, combined with the striated musculature generally representative of cultures located more to the west within the Far Eastern steppe (Tuva, the Altai, parts of Xinjiang and Ningxia).[433] Indeed, the Beishantou combination of composition and musculature corresponds most closely to Daodunzi (Tongxin, Ningxia) M19:9-10 (without antlers; Figure 54) and related pieces of somewhat differing style (with antlers).[434] The presence in a Beikang (Xi'an Municipality Northern Suburbs, Shaanxi)[435] Chinese tomb of a ceramic mold featuring a related composition confirms that this image was known in China at least by the Late Warring States.

429 Xuzhou 1985: Pl. 176.

430 Jiangsu 1959: Pl. 6, Fig. 3:2 (center right).

431 Jiangsu 1959: Pl. 78-79 top, Figs 101-103.

432 Anhui 2007: 112, Fig. 80:2 (BM1:37); 113, Fig. 81 (BM1:29); Col. Pl. 50:4 (BM1:29), 5 (BM1:37), 6 (BM1:37).

433 Kenk 1986: 112, Fig. 8:4, Sagly-Baži (Tuva) II, kurgan 13, bone; Polos'mak 1994: 46, Fig. 44; 47, Fig. 48, Ak-Alaxa (Altai) I, felt; Xinjiang 1981: Pl. 8:4, Alagou 阿拉溝 (Hejing 和静, Xinjiang), gold foil; Ningxia 1988b: 344, Fig. 9:13 (M19:9, shown upside down); Pl. 15:5 (M19:10); both, gilded bronze. Note that this marking is not characteristic of Xiongnu work; although the site yielded some Xiongnu plaques, I do not consider Daodunzi to be Xiongnu. For discussion, see Psarras in preparation.

434 Including Hebei 1996, Vol. 1: 724, Fig. 419:2, Xinzhuangtou (Yixian, Hebei) XZHM30:43, silver plaque; Griessmaser 1936: 26-27, No. 18, gilded bronze. Both of these examples may well be Chinese-produced, but follow steppe norms (see Psarras in preparation). Cf., the Xiongnu antlered tiger: Tian Guangjin and Guo Suxin 1986: Col. Pl. 16:1, Aluchaideng (Hanggin Banner, Inner Mongolia), gold inlaid with turquoise and red stones.

435 Shaanxi 2003a: 6, Fig. 5; 8, Fig. 10:1, 99SXLM34:21.

Chapter 7

Plant Motifs

In contrast to early Chinese art, plant motifs have a long history in art from Egypt as early as the late 4th millennium BC and from the Near East and the Aegean by *c.* the 2nd millennium BC, becoming popular from *c.* the 4th century BC and thereafter in Greece and in regions where a strong Greek influence was felt. Species are generally difficult to identify with certainty, even at times in the case of plants as well-known as the lotus and papyrus, and the exchange of intercultural influences is so intricate that identification of an absolute origin may be impossible. In China, plant décors seem to emerge in the Eastern Zhou, remaining rare until the Han, when they are incorporated into scenes of paradise.

The earliest motif appears to be a broad-petaled quatrefoil rosette with small points in the center of the outer edge, a form attested continuously from approximately the Late Springs-Autumns, ubiquitously during the Han (Figure 55).[436] It is followed around the Middle-Late Warring States (*c.* late 4th century BC) by a heart shape identifiable as the Greek ivy leaf (Figures 56), incorporated only rarely into Chinese bronze work, as on a mirror from Changsha (Hunan).[437]

Although I can find no single Western prototype for the Zhou quatrefoil[438] and no earlier Chinese precedent, the form is in context in the West and not in China; this strongly suggests that it developed in China as the result of Western influence, rather than through reproduction of a Western prototype. Rosettes of various types are common in the Near East and the Aegean, again from an early date.[439] They are, of course, extremely common in Late Classical and Hellenistic Greek work. On most of these the outer edge of the petal is rounded or slightly incurving at the center, like a broad heart (ivy leaf).[440] A relatively broad petal with a pointed

[436] E.g., Zhongguo qingtongqi 1995: 110: Pl. 124, openwork bronze harness ornament, Jinsheng (Taiyuan Municipality, Shanxi), Late Springs-Autumns; Hebei 1979: 4, Fig. 6, silver ornament from the tomb of King Cuo of Zhongshan; Bian Chengxiu 1972: 45, Fig. 5, bronze harness ornament, Fenshuiling (Changzhi Municipality, Shanxi) M126, Middle Warring States; Hebei 1962: 626, Fig. 21:5, circular bronze ornament, Baijia 百家 (Handan 邯鄲, Hebei) M3:64, Middle Warring States. To cite only a few Han examples: Xianyang 1979: 132, Fig. 10:2, Maquan (Xianyang Municipality, Shaanxi) M1:91, gold foil appliqué on a lacquer *guan*, *c.* 67 AD (per Psarras 2015); Guo Yong 1963: 5, Fig. 3, bronze plate supporting a ring handle; p. 6, Fig. 5, relief décor on a bronze *zun* (produced in 26 BC), both Youyu 右玉 (Shanxi); Shandong 1985: 251, Fig. 25:6, King of Qi 齊 (Linzi 臨淄 [Zibo 淄博 Municipality, Shandong]) burial goods pits K3:68-2 (d. 132 BC, per Psarras 2015), bronze peg/hook from a lacquered *lian* toiletries box. In some versions, the petals are elongated toward the center, as on fittings from the Mancheng M2:4024 *lian* toiletries box (Zhongguo shehui kexueyuan 1980, Vol. 1: 305, Fig. 206:2, 5, bronze, gold and silver inlay).

[437] Bagley (ed.) 2001: 223, Fig. 74.2, Changsha Municipality (Hunan).

[438] Pfrommer 1993: 61, Fig. 45B, describes the form as a 'quatrefoil ivy blossom.'

[439] For example, on *c.* mid-second millennium BC 'Atchana ware' painted pottery (Mitanni, southern Turkey-northern Syria), as in Collon 1995: 113, Fig. 91; Aruz, Benzel, and Evans (eds) 2008: 198, No. 119, prefer the term 'Nuzi ware.' For discussion, see Collon 1995: 112, which suggests development of these décors from Egyptian sources. See also Crowley 1989: 84-90; 440-442, Figs 210-228; Boardman 2000: 79-80.

[440] For late Hellenistic examples, see Pfrommer 1993: 33, Fig. 29, outer petals, Qast il-Faraun (Petra [Jordan]), *c.* late 1st century BC-early 1st century AD; 35, Fig. 32, fragment, Temple of the Lion-Griffins (Petra), AD 27 *ante quem*; 53, Fig. 41A, inner petals, gold plaque, Bactrian?, *c.* 1st century BC; pp. 134-135, No. 13 (alternating with daisies).

edge does sometimes occur, from the Late Cycladic I (*c.* 1625-1525 BC) through Neo-Assyrian (*c.* 8th century BC) and Late Hellenistic work (i.e., *c.* 2nd-1st centuries BC).[441]

During the Han, ornaments (fittings or appliqués) with the Zhou quatrefoil are found in non-Chinese territory, including south Siberia (Burjatija)[442] and Mongolia.[443] Because the form is so common in Han China, it is easy to assume that items bearing the décor were Han products; nonetheless some, if not all, may have been produced locally. For instance, non-Chinese-type cloth boots from Noyon uul (Batsumber, Tuv [Mongolia]) kurgan 6,[444] birch bark appliqués from Burkhan tolgoi (Khuag-Undur, Bulgan [Mongolia]) tomb 76,[445] and Tillia-tepe tomb 2 gold-foil ornaments[446] carry the motif, but seem unlikely to have been imported, either because of the medium (for the Mongolian sites) or the manner of production (for Tillia-tepe). This conclusion is further supported by the gold foil quatrefoil appliqués, again in the form of the Zhou quatrefoil, from Duurlig nars (Bayan-Adarga, Khenty [Mongolia]) tomb 2, generally believed to date to the Han era.[447] In this case, as part of the décor nailed to a coffin, they are placed in the center of the rhomboids formed by a diagonal latticework of gold strips. This composition occurs on figural work from Commagene (Turkey, *c.* 1st century BC), Parthian Hatra (Iraq, *c.* 2nd century AD), and roughly-contemporaneous northern India, representing decorative patterns on garments or headdresses.[448] Its use at Duurlig nars is in keeping with this convention,[449] with the substitution of the Zhou quatrefoil for the circles or rosettes with elongated petals seen at Hatra. By extension, the Duurlig nars coffin ornaments, if not locally produced, would more likely have been imported from areas west of China than from China. In this context, the occurrence of the trellis-and-rosette composition (with the jagged zigzags common in Chinese bronze décor and a rosette with ivy-like leaves) on a bronze mirror in

441 E.g., Aruz, Benzel, and Evans (eds) 2008: 424, No. 278A, B, Thera (Akrotiri [Greece]), faience, *c.* 1625-1525 BC; Parrot 1961: 266, Figs 341, Khorsabad (Iraq), 342, Til Barsip ([Tell Ahmar,] Syria), both 8th century BC wall paintings; Pfrommer 1993: 110-111, No. 1; Pl. 1, partially-gilded silver bowl, 'Hellenized Near East,' *c.* 2nd century BC, trefoil; 116-117, No. 4; Pl. 2, partially-gilded silver bowl, 'Hellenized Near East,' *c.* 1st century BC, ivy calyx quatrefoil.

442 Rudenko 1969: Pl. XXXII:3, 5, Pad' Sudži and Ivolga (Burjatija [Russia]).

443 Rudenko 1969: Pl. XXXIII:4-5, Noyon uul kurgan 1 finials; Eregzen 2011:71, No. 054, Takhiltyn khotgor (Mankhan, Khovd [Mongolia]) M64, iron coffin appliqué; 221, Nos 325-326, Noyon uul kurgan 20, gilded bronze umbrella rib finials. Cf., the *mingqi* 明器*(funerary models)* lead bow-ends from the provision Han tomb of Fangwanggang (Chaohu Municipality, Anhui) FM1 (Anhui 2007: 48, Fig. 30:1-4; Col. Pl. 18:1), dated by excavators to the Middle Western Han.

444 Rudenko 1969: 138, Fig. 34a.

445 Eregzen 2011: 71, No. 055.

446 Sarianidi 1985: Pl. 101, M2:21.

447 Eregzen 2011: 69, No. 052.

448 Rosenfield 1993: Fig. 16 (two views), headdress on the head (Sikri sandstone sculpture fragment) of a man, identified by Rosenfield as 'Indo-Scythian' (not specifically dated); Yamuna River find (Mathura Museum No. 2122); Fig. 141, stone sculpture of the Parthian Princess Washfari, AD 137, tunic; Hatra (Iraq Museum [Baghdad] No. 56752); Fig. 154, stone frieze of Mithridates I Kallinikos (King of Commagene [Turkey], r. *c.* 100-70 BC) meeting Heracles, hierothesion of Arsamaeia-on-the-Nymphaios (Turkey), tunic (following the dates proposed by Olbrycht 2009); Ghirshman 1962: 89, Fig. 100, marble sculpture of Uthal, King of Hatra, tunic and headdress, *c.* 2nd century AD; Hatra temple III (Mosul Museum [Iraq]); 91, Fig. 102, head of a Parthian king (stone sculpture fragment), *c.* 2nd century AD, headdress (Iraq Museum); 95, Fig. 106, limestone sculpture of Ubal, daughter of Jabal (Parthian princess), tunic; *c.* 2nd century AD, Hatra temple IV (Iraq Museum). In these examples, the lattice generally consists of lines of circles/discs. The term 'Indo-Scythian' refers to 'Scythians' (i.e., steppe peoples) in northern India, broadly *c.* 2nd century BC-1st century AD; for an introductory discussion with references, see <http://www.iranicaonline.org/articles/indo-scythian-dynasty-1>, viewed May 2016.

449 The composition seems likely to represent a diagonal version of the quatrefoil rosettes inside a square grid, as on a carved stone threshold in the Southwestern Palace of Sennacherib (Nineveh), *c.* 700 BC, on which the grid again consists of circles: Collon 1995: 140, Fig. 114. The square grid with similar quatrefoil rosettes is maintained on the Pazyryk kurgan 5 knotted carpet (Charrière 1979: Pl. 199).

the Museum of Far Eastern Antiquities (Stockholm; *c.* 4th-early 3rd centuries BC)[450] implies a similar date for the development of this décor, but does not demonstrate a Chinese origin. The Stockholm mirror and the Duurlig nars coffin ornaments thus illustrate the interplay of cultural exchange over considerable distance and time.

Like the quatrefoil rosette, the heart-shaped leaf or petal identifiable as the Greek ivy becomes widespread in Chinese art only during the Han (as on Figure 57). Its use in Han work primarily as the foliage or flowers of trees (Figure 58, lower center)[451] echoes Indian convention,[452] suggesting Indian transmission to the Han. However, the motif is compatible with the small, near-heart shape described by a single spiral that is used to form rosette-clusters on the lid of a Late Springs-Autumns copper-inlaid bronze *hu* from the Arthur M. Sackler collection.[453] This form parallels the larger near-heart shape consisting of two open spirals (the curled end being the globes of the heart) used in place of the old zigzag or triangle motif on the neck of another Sackler *hu*, also dated to *c.* Late Springs-Autumns.[454] These near-hearts in turn seem the natural extension of softer variants of the Bronze Age zigzag vessel décor, seen as early as an Early Western Zhou *hu* in the Palace Museum (Beijing),[455] as well as on Late Springs-Autumns and Early Warring States pieces in the Sackler collection, where the line resembles a broad leaf shape[456] or a heart-like form[457] (see also Figure 62, lower belly). The smallest heart-like form is close to the ivy in outline; it remains in use as a geometric motif during the Han[458] (Figure 59). Whether the softened zigzag resulted from foreign influence is unclear; its development, however, may have facilitated later adoption of the ivy leaf.

In Western art, the ivy leaf appears both with and without vine, stem, or branches. Despite general association with Greek art, earlier examples may also be found, such as heart shapes on gold jewelry from the tomb of Khnemet, funerary complex of Amenemhat II (Dahshur [Egypt]), dynasty XII, *c.* 1981-1802 BC.[459] Early Greek-manufactured pieces include a mid-sixth century BC East Greek terracotta amphora[460] (cf., Figure 56), followed by adoption in Persia[461]

450 Watson 1995: 44, fig 83, lower right.
451 As on stone bas reliefs from the Wu family shrines, as a bud, combined with the lotus flower (Liu Xingzhen and Yue Fengxia 1991: 79, Front shrine) and as tree foliage on stone bas reliefs from Zengjiabao 曾家包 (Chengdu Municipality, Sichuan) M1 (*c.* 65 AD, per Psarras 2015; Chengdu 1981: 27, Fig. 5, on the tree to the upper left of the small building shown on the lower right of the stone). Also, by extension, as heart-shaped saucers on a bronze lamp from Luobowan 羅泊灣 (Gui 貴 xian, Guangxi; Zhongguo qingtongqi 1998: 118, Pl. 116).
452 The ivy leaf appears as tree foliage in *c.* second-century BC Mathura (Errington, Cribb, and Claringbull [eds] 1992: 44, symbol chart 1), as well as in Kushan bas reliefs (e.g., Rosenfield 1993: Fig. 81, no provenance, stone bas relief depicting the Temptation of Sakyamuni). It is also used as an ornamental motif on clothing, for example on a stone statue of Kanishka from Surkh Kotal (Afghanistan; Rosenfield 1993: Fig. 120 = Fussman 1983: Pl. 11, with a date of *c.* 78-180 AD, adopting AD 78 as year 1 of Kanishka's reign).
453 So 1995: 256-257, No. 44, bronze inlaid with copper.
454 So 1995: 252-254, No. 43, bronze inlaid with copper and gold.
455 Gugong 1999: 154, Pl. 137.
456 As on So 1995: 302-305, No. 58, elliptical, lidded vessel, *c.* 6th century BC.
457 So 1995: 252-254, No. 43, *c.* late 6th-early 5th centuries BC; 255, Fig. 43.1, *c.* early 5th century BC *hu*.
458 As on So 1995: 302-305, No. 58. This small, heart-like spiral sometimes appears in Early Western Zhou work as the depiction of animals' ears, as at Rujiazhuang 茹家莊 (Baoji Municipality, Shaanxi; Lu and Hu 1988, Vol. 1:344, Fig. 238:3 [BRM1A:190, jade tiger]; Vol. 2: Col. Pl. 20 [BRM1A:18, bronze *ying* 罃]), but does not seem otherwise to have been widely adopted. Qin and Han examples of the heart-spiral include Shaanxi 2004:397, Fig. 329 (hollow brick, Qin Palace 2 [Xianyang Municipality, Shaanxi] XYNIIT76[4]:25); 487, Fig. 398 (hollow brick, Qin Palace 3 XYNIIIJ5:4); Zhou Dao *et al.* 1985: Pl. 204 (Zhengzhou [Henan] Han stamped brick), as in (here) Figure 60.
459 Aruz, Benzel, and Evans (eds) 2008: 102, Fig. 33.
460 Trofimova 2007: 82, No. 5, Berezan (Ukraine), *c.* 550-540 BC.
461 Pfrommer 1993: 38.

and northern India. The motif is common particularly from the 4th century BC onward[462] and is ubiquitous at Tillia-tepe.[463] Whether introduction of the ivy in China occurred by the Late Springs-Autumns/Early Warring States remains open to question; certainly, it must have been part of a wide range of western floral motifs which emerge in Chinese art during the second half of the Warring States.

A second form of rosette appears in the tomb of King Cuo of Zhongshan ([Sanji,] Pingshan, Hebei), with the multiple wide petals with the incurving edge of Greek versions.[464] The occurrence of this form together with the same type of rosette with pointed petals[465] suggests that the standard Greek form was received and then modified. The Greek form with incurving petals continues through the Han era in Noyon uul (Batsumber, Tuv [Mongolia]) kurgan 25 as a fitting (axle ornament?), probably an import (Figure 60),[466] as well as at Tillia-tepe.[467] This multi-petaled rosette (with pointed petals) also occurs, perhaps rarely, in Han work (Figure 28, upper left).[468] In this context, it is difficult to know if the rosette with multiple, broad, pointed petals on the girdle of a yaksi from the Upper Monastery at Nathu (Pakistan; *c.* 1st-2nd centuries AD), represents continuity of an unidentified Greco-Persian prototype shared with Eastern Zhou China or, instead, Chinese influence.[469]

Finally, a gilded bronze *hu* from Nanyaozhuang 南窯莊 (Xuyi, Jiangsu), dated to the Middle-Late Warring States, offers the example of small cinqfoil rosettes with moderately-narrow, fairly short, pointed petals which seems to have no immediate counterpart in the published archaeological record.[470] On this piece, the cinqfoils form an open netting attached to the vessel so that it seems to float over the upper portion of the jar. In different form, technically complex but compositionally simpler, this piece echoes the floral traceries of the contemporaneous Hellenistic world (Figure 61), including on such pieces as the Greek-produced gold gorytus in

[462] *Inter alia*: Galanina and Gratch 1987: Pl. 157-160, Scythian tomb at Soloxa (Zaporož'e [Ukraine]), gilded silver vase, *c.* first half 4th century BC; Pfrommer 1993:37, Fig. 35d, Thessaloniki (Macedonia [Greece]), bracelet (detail only), *c.* second quarter 3rd century BC.

[463] Including Sarianidi 1985: Pl. 48-50 (M6:4), 62 (M2:19).

[464] Hebei 1995, Vol. 2: Col. Pl. 17:2: Pl. 97:5, BDD:42, 43, appliqués, gilded bronze with silver inlay.

[465] Hebei 1995, Vol. 1: 239, Fig. 102:14 (GSH:99), 15-16 (GSH:100), 17-18 (GSH:104), 19 (GSH:103); Vol. 2: Pl. 179:2 (GSH:104), 3 (GSH:103), all jade. A similar composition appears on a circular jade box from the Han tomb of Beishantou (Chaohu Municipality, Anhui) BM1:1 (Anhui 2007: Col. Pl. 67), dated by excavators to the Early Western Han.

[466] Rudenko 1969: Pl. XXXIII:5 (M25:22). Noyon uul M6 and the Kondrate'ev kurgan (on the same site) provide multiple examples of Greek floral motifs in the woven and embroidered textiles, as Rudenko 1969: 160, Fig. 71; Pl. LIII-LVII, LXV-LXVII (kurgan 6); 164, Fig. 75; Pl. LXIX (Kondrat'ev).

[467] Sarianidi 1985: Pl. 43, M1:4.

[468] Such as Yaozhuang (Hanjiang, Yangzhou Municipality, Jiangsu) M101:190 (Yangzhou 1988: 38, Fig. 30:1, reproduced here as Figure 28), in silver foil on the lid of a *lian* toiletries box, each petal accentuated with a tear-drop carnelian inlay. Because of the inlay, the Yaozhuang rosette undoubtedly reflects the influence of work such as a turquoise-inlaid gold rosette from Tillia-tepe M1:4 (Sarianidi 1985: Pl. 43). The same type of inlay, with very small, widely-spaced stones, occurs at times on other Han productions, such as the Mancheng M1:1068 dragon-shaped axle fitting (Zhongguo shehui kexueyuan 1980, Vol. 1: 188, Fig. 129:1, gilded bronze, carnelian and turquoise inlay [termed *mingqi*]; Zhongguo qingtongqi 1998: 155: Pl. 152, gilded bronze) or the paradise landscapes on a tubular carriage fitting from Sanpanshan 三盤山 (Dingzhou 定州 Municipality, Hebei) M122 (Zhongguo qingtongqi 1998: 154, Pl. 151, gilded bronze); Wu Hung 1984: 39, dates the site to *c.* 90 BC.

[469] Chandra 1979: Fig. 35; dating follows John Hubert Marshall, *The Buddhist Art of Gandhara: the Story of the Early School, its Birth, Growth and Decline*, (New Delhi: Oriental Books Reprint Corporation, 1980 [1960, 1st edition]): 47 (not seen), cited by Assomull 2013 and Litvinsky 2005.

[470] Zhongguo meishu 1992: 99, Pl. 114. The openwork of the floral net is similar to the masses of small snake-like meanders common on openwork bronzes from the tomb of the Marquis Yi of Zeng (Leigudun [Suizhou Municipality, Hubei]: e.g., Zhongguo meishu 1992: 64-65, Pl. 76-78, *zun-pan* 尊盤); however, the Leigudun openwork is extremely dense.

the Scythian tomb at Čertomlyk (Dnepropetrovsk, Ukraine).[471] Such work seems to have had little impact on Chinese work before the Han.[472] However, the apparent rarity of floral décors during the Eastern Zhou may be true of bronze, but not of more ephemeral media.

This possibility is underscored by embroidered garments from the Chu tomb of Mashan (Jiangling, Jingzhou Municipality, Hubei) M1 (*c.* late 4th century BC).[473] While the décor on Mashan brocades is generally geometric and derives from Chinese bronze traditions,[474] the embroideries incorporate a large number of floral motifs in a composition that implies the familiarity of Chinese artisans with contemporaneous Hellenistic floral scrolls or traceries. The latter, developed around the 4th century BC,[475] became popular in the Hellenistic period in all regions where Greek influence was pronounced or Greek work imported (Persia, Bactria, India, the Western steppe)[476] (cf., Figure 61). Chinese adoption of the composition, together with its floral elements, seems to have taken place virtually contemporaneously with this spread of Hellenism. Indeed, its use at Mashan may be seen as a freer version of Bronze Age interlace, a variant of the broad-band interlace common on Warring States vessels[477] (Figure 62). This is particularly visible on N2, on which exotic birds are depicted by means of exotic floral scrolling (Figure 63). The compatibility of the Hellenistic floral interlace or scroll with Zhou bronze design in turn raises the possibility that the rounded curves of some otherwise standard Zhou bronze décors reflect earlier foreign influence. These rounded décors appear as early as the Early Western Zhou openwork bronze shortsword scabbards from Liulihe 琉璃河 (Fangshan 房山, Beijing),[478] followed by Middle Western Zhou examples such as on bronze *you* from Tunxi 屯溪 (Huangshan Municipality 黃山, Anhui).[479] Especially where combined with the shortsword, this pattern seems likely to reflect the influence of northern non-Chinese

[471] Trofimova 2007: 28, Fig. 3.4, *c.* 350-325 BC.

[472] The décor of a *hu* from Xiaotianxi 小田溪 (Fuling 涪陵, Sichuan; Zhongguo meishu 1992: 139, Pl. 160; Sichuan 1974: 67, Fig. 6, M3:23, silver-inlaid bronze, Middle-Late Warring States) includes a register of open, heart-like double spirals at the base of the belly, below a décor of open, intersecting spirals. The overall pattern may generally be related to the Chinese meander, which appears on the vessel foot, but its loose curves also recall Hellenistic vegetal scrolls or traceries.

[473] Another example may possibly be the Chinese embroidery from Pazyryk kurgan 5 (Rudenko 1970: 175-177, Figs 89-91; Gryaznov 1969: Pl. 129-130; Zhongguo shehui kexueyuan 1980, Vol. 1: 310, Fig. 212:1, detail), similar to Mashan pieces (Hubei 1985: Fig. 46 [insert after p. 58], N7; 62, Fig. 49, N22). Although Pazyryk kurgan 5 may postdate Mashan, other Pazyryk-culture sites may not.

[474] This is especially easy to see in the reconstructions on Hubei 1985: 42-44, Figs 34-36; 48-49, Figs 39-40.

[475] Pfrommer (1993: 27) identifies the origin of the floral scroll as Late Classical Macedonian, transmitted to Greece specifically at the time of Alexander the Great, i.e., *c.* late 4th century BC.

[476] As visible in Greek-produced Scythian goldwork: *inter alia*, Galanina and Gratch 1987: Pl. 118-121, Tolstaja mogila (Dnepropetrovsk [Ukraine]), gold pectoral; *c.* 4th century BC; Pl. 135, Dejev (Xerson [Ukraine]), gold headdress plaques; on the Sanci Stupa II stone bas reliefs, *c.* second half 1st century BC (Ray 1975: Pl. 56); embroidered wool fragments from the Xiongnu Noyon uul kurgan 6 (Rudenko 1969: 164, Fig. 75; Pl. LXV-LXVIII), whose blend of Achaemenid (e.g., the lion on Rudenko 1969: Pl. LXVII:2) with predominantly Greek imagery makes a Bactrian production likely. Additionally, some Han influence may be inferred from the long-haired *xian* immortal kneeling on a flower (Rudenko 1969: Pl. LXVII:3). Another such figure (Rudenko 1969: Pl. LXV:1), however, appears to be a Greek putti (no long hair). Additional examples below.

[477] Hubei 1985: 58, Fig. 45 (N2); cf., Zhongguo meishu 1992: 118, Pl. 136, Wangshan (Jiangling, Jingzhou Municipality, Hubei), bronze *zun* with silver and gold inlay, Middle-Late Warring States; Bagley (ed.) 2001: 223, Fig. 74.1, lid of lacquer box from Baoshan 包山 (Jingmen 荊門 Municipality, Hubei) M2, *c.* later 4th century BC (third quarter 4th century, before 316 BC, per Thote 2001); Hubei 1985: Col. Pl. 29:2, Mashan (Jiangling, Jingzhou Municipality, Hubei) M1:8-2 lacquer bowl; Col. Pl. 30:1, Mashan M1:17-14, lacquer *lian*.

[478] Beijing 1995: Pl. 70:1 (M52:28), 2 (M253:47), 3 (M253:47), echoed in simpler form by largely contemporaneous examples of the same form from Zhuyuangou 竹園溝 (Baoji Municipality, Shaanxi): Lu Liancheng and Hu Zhisheng 1988, Vol. 2: Pl. 110:5 (BZM19:59).

[479] Rawson 1990, Vol. IIA: 117, Fig. 164.

cultures. While this curved line remains in use for the remainder of the Bronze Age,[480] the more typical angular interlace remains largely dominant until the Middle-Late Springs-Autumns and Warring States. It therefore seems likely that foreign influence incorporated from various sources throughout the Bronze Age, subsequently reinforced by Hellenistic contact, ultimately facilitated reception of the western influences visible in the Mashan embroideries.

While the floral motifs on the Mashan embroideries are generally Hellenistic, transmission of some individual flower shapes is likely to have been reinforced by contact with steppe cultures. Of particular interest are a number of motifs which, although appearing on the Mashan embroideries, do not (at present) seem to have been used on Eastern Zhou bronzes: four-point stars, simple bud-forms, various types of fleur-de-lis, scrolling leaf forms (as in a cross between acanthus and palmette[481]), together with a kidney (asymmetrical) or tear (symmetrical) shape, sometimes paired with a circle, on N2 (Figure 63);[482] with trefoils and small papyrus fans on N7 (Figure 64);[483] lotus forms as buds on N9 (Figure 65);[484] lotus blossoms on N10.[485]

For these, the origins are well-documented: the four-pointed stars have Neo-Assyrian precedent, carried through to Tillia-tepe;[486] the scrolling acanthus is typically Hellenistic (Figure 61), again continuing through Tillia-tepe.[487] The two different trefoils on Mashan N7[488] are similarly identifiable (Figure 64): one, as essentially a three-petaled version of the older Zhou quatrefoil rosette; and the other, a more tulip-like shape, readily comparable to Hellenistic work.[489] The related fleur-de-lis, common in Hellenistic and related work, appears to derive from mid-second millennium BC Cretan and Mycenaean variants[490] of the palmette

---

480 Rawson 1990, Vol. IIA: 114, Fig. 161, the Song *hu* (bronze), Late Western Zhou; Zhongguo meishu 1992: 9, Pl. 11, Shangma (Houma, Shanxi) *hu*, Middle Springs-Autumns; 85, Pl. 99, tomb of King Cuo of Zhongshan ([Sanji,] Pingshan, Hebei) gold- and silver-inlaid bronze tray stand (DK:33), *c.* 309 BC (=Hebei 1995, Vol. 2: Col. Pl. 14); 118, Pl. 136, Wangshan (Jiangling, Jingzhou Municipality, Hubei) silver- and gold-inlaid bronze *zun*, Middle-Late Warring States. Rawson 1990, Vol. IIA: 113-114, notes that this rounded interlace was 'infrequently used till the... Eastern Zhou period.'

481 The palmette may represent a combination of lotus and papyrus or other plants (cf., Kantor 1999). Note that Boardman 1994: 36, Fig. 2.22, considers forms with a rounded (rather than elongated) profile as characteristically Greek. Note that the papyrus motif may be drawn as a semi-circular fan shape enclosing multiple vertical striations, as on the Narmer palette (Kom el-Ahmar [Hierakonpolis, Egypt]; *c.* 3200-2980 BC, per Smith 1981: 33), but may also be more triangular, like a lotus (e.g., Smith 1981: 126, Fig. 119, Weserkaf Temple [Saqqara, Egypt], relief; Dynasty V, *c.* 2565-2420 BC). The two forms may therefore be difficult to differentiate.

482 Hubei 1985: 58, Fig. 45 (N2).

483 Hubei 1985: 64, Fig. 51.

484 Hubei 1985: Col. Pl. 28:3 (photo, clearer than the Pl. 28:4 drawing).

485 Hubei 1985: Col. Pl. 28:2 (drawing, clearer than the Pl. 28:1 photograph). The more blossom-like lotus occurs in some Indian versions, as on a Mathura carved pillar, *c.* first half 1st century BC (Ray 1975: Pl. 64).

486 Neo-Assyrian examples include wall paintings from Khorsabad (Iraq) and Til Barsip (Tell Ahmar [Syria]), where they are enclosed by a circle surrounded by four small fleur-de-lis which resemble tear-shapes pointing outward: Parrot 1961: 266, Figs 341 (Khorsabad), 342 (Til Barsip). For Tillia-tepe: Sarianidi 1985: Pl. 7, M3:14, gold foil.

487 Cook 1997: 174, notes the acanthus in Late Classical Greece; Pfrommer 1993: 28, 31, discusses acanthus variants. Examples include: Pfrommer 1993: 30, Fig. 26, interior of a silver kylix, *c.* late 4th-early 3rd centuries BC; 126, No. 9, silver bowl, *c.* late 2nd-early 1st centuries BC; Collon 1995: 187, Fig. 150; Curtis and Tallis 2005: 148, No. 194, Oxus gold griffin/chimaera, British Museum 123924; Colledge 1977: Pl. 24a, Aïrtam (Uzbekistan), *c.* 2nd century AD, Parthian Buddhist reliefs; Ray 1975: Pl. 85, 92, Sanci Stupa II, *c.* second half 1st century BC; Sarianidi 1985: Pl. 158-159, Tillia-tepe M4:8 shortsword hilt and pommel with a somewhat rounded half-acanthus; the Metropolitan Museum of Art, Roman marble pilaster (acc. no. 10.210.28a-c), *c.* first half 1st century AD, with S-form acanthus scrolling (<https://www.metmuseum.org/toah/works-of-art/10.210.28/>, viewed 4 January 2019).

488 Hubei 1985: Col. Pl. 22:1; Col. Pl. 24:1, both, three-petaled quatrefoil; Col. Pl. 24:2, more tulip-like trefoil.

489 Pfrommer 1993: 30, Fig. 26, silver kylix, *c.* late 4th-early 3rd centuries BC.

490 Crowley 1989: 434, Fig. 184, Mycenaean pottery décor details, *c.* 1310-1190 BC, which Crowley identifies as palmettes; 435, Fig. 190, discoid seal, Crete?, *c.* 18th century BC; 435, Fig. 192, Mycenaean gold jewelry, *c.* 1550-1460 BC, both identified as papyrus.

or the papyrus. It subsequently appears in Neo-Assyrian work, followed by Persian and Greek through Tillia-tepe; examples may occasionally be found in Late Warring States and Han-era non-Chinese cultures in western China.[491] Finally, the papyrus (generally, a smooth-edged fan), like the lotus (typically with an irregular upper edge in profile),[492] is well-known as Egyptian (as early as the late 4th-3rd millennia BC), but both became so popular throughout the Near East and the Aegean that they come to constitute what Janice Crowley terms 'international' motifs.[493]

As the data now stands, the Eastern steppe, including the Altai, seems an unlikely source for most floral motifs. However, the Pazyryk culture makes greater use of floral forms[494] than do non-Chinese cultures farther east, including the lotus,[495] the palmette,[496] the fleur-de-lis, scrolling leaf forms, and (from Šibe) floral volutes, all of which reflect the Achaemenid and Greek influences readily visible in the culture. Elsewhere, floral motifs are generally limited to simple rosettes (particularly in Xiongnu and Xianbei art)[497] and, sporadically, the fleur-de-lis (among both the western non-Chinese and the Xiongnu).[498] Again, these forms reflect

[491] Parrot 1961: 266, Fig. 341, the Neo-Assyrian (*c.* 8th century BC) Khorsabad (Iraq) wall paintings; Reeder (ed.) 1999: 263, No. 126, Oxuz kurgan (Nyžnyj Siroxozy, Xerson [Ukraine]), gold plaque, *c.* 325 BC, where the form is identified as lotuses; 300, 302 (detail), No. 154, Soboleva mogila (Dnepropetrovsk [Ukraine]), floral frieze, gold gorytus plaques, *c.* 350-325 BC; Sarianidi 1985: 87, No. 34 (Cat. III,8); 237, 8.Ill.34, M3, gold appliqués; Dai Yingxin and Sun Jiaxiang 1983: 25, Fig. 4:3, Nalin'gaotu (Shenmu, Shaanxi), gold appliqué (Late Warring States-Han); Tian Guangjin and Guo Suxin 1986: 380, Fig. 3, Xigoupan (Jungar Banner, Inner Mongolia) M4:2, 3, gold appliqués (Han). See also below, footnote 500.

[492] Smith 1981: 33, Fig. 13, Narmer palette (carved schist); Crowley 1989: 77, for use in Mesopotamia (Syria) in the late 20th century BC; 78, in Crete in the Old Palace Period, *c.* 1550-1460 BC; Collon 1995: 140, Fig. 114, Neo-Assyrian Southwest Palace of Sennacherib, *c.* 700 BC.

[493] Crowley 1989: 295, 297, 298.

[494] Rudenko 1970, from Pazyryk: lotus columns (Pl. 47, kurgan 1, saddle pendants, felt and leather), scrolling leaf forms (Pl. 67F, kurgan 2, belt), lotus and palmette (e.g., Pl. 77, kurgan 1, wood psalia; Pl. 79, kurgan 1, wood bridle with psalia), lotus and related fleur-de-lis (Pl. 148B, C, kurgan 2, felt carpet), fleur-de-lis (Pl. 154, kurgan 5, felt hanging), a simple rosette (Pl. 97C, iron, 98D, wood; both, kurgan 3, psalia), and from Šibe: floral volutes (Pl. 139A, horn saddle arch).

[495] For the lotus column, see: Curtis and Tallis 2005: 84, No. 46, Persepolis stone relief, reign of Artaxerxes III (359/358-338/337 BC), continuing at Tillia-tepe (Sarianidi 1985: Pl. 81-84, M3:1, gold ornaments).

[496] Bands of alternating lotus and palmette have precedents in Middle Assyria, as on the upper frieze of a wall painting (reconstructed) in the Kar-tukulti-Ninurta palace (Tulul ul Aqar, Salah al-Din Governorate [Iraq]), *c.* 1243-1207 BC (Aruz, Benzel, and Evans [eds] 2008: 207, Fig. 68), followed later by (*inter alia*) Greek red-figured ceramics, *c.* first half 4th century BC (e.g., Trofimova 2007: 254-255, No. 151, lidded lekanis, *c.* 370-360 BC; 256-257, No. 152, calyx-krater, *c.* early 4th century BC; both, Yuz Oba kurgan VI [Kerč', Crimea]), and Greek work including the gold gorytus from the Scythian kurgan of Čertomlyk (Dnepropetrovsk [Ukraine]), *c.* 350-325 BC (Trofimova 2007: 28, Fig. 3.4).

[497] Two variants of the rosette occur consistently in northern non-Chinese material from the Han era (or perhaps, in some cases, the Late Warring States): one with broad petals, occurring in areas associated with Xiongnu culture (especially Inner Mongolia, Ningxia); the other with thin petals, occurring in areas associated with the Xianbei (especially eastern Inner Mongolia, Heilongjiang): *inter alia*, Tian Guangjin and Guo Suxin 1986: 369, Fig. 3:11, Yulongtai 玉隆太 (Jungar Banner, Inner Mongolia), Xiongnu; Cheng Daohong 1982: 21, Fig. 4:6 (unidentified tomb), 9 (Yimin Bus Station 伊敏車站 [Hulunbuir Municipality, Inner Mongolia] M1:2, silver), Xianbei. The form is most commonly used singly on bronze appliqué ornaments. A Greek source for the Xiongnu motif seems likely, given the history of the form. In the Western steppe, a version essentially identical to the Xiongnu variant is described by Nebelsick as derived from 'Mediterranean and Near Eastern architectural decoration' (Nebelsick 2012: 458; 459, Fig. 6.1, Berestnjaxi [Kaniv] kurgan 4, *c.* mid-fifth century BC; Fig. 6.2, Berestnjaxi kurgan 5, *c.* late 5th century BC; Fig. 6.3, Jablonivka kurgan 1-2, *c.* late 6th-early 5th centuries BC; Fig. 6.4, Ostniažka, date not provided [all, Ukraine]). This appears later, by extension, at Tillia-tepe (Sarianidi 1985: Pl. 1, M4:12; individual rosettes in stamped gold with a narrow perpendicular rim, pierced for threading). Pazyryk examples are noted above. The form would then have passed from the Xiongnu to the Xianbei. See Psarras in preparation.

[498] The fleur-de-lis appears only rarely, as on appliqués from the non-Xiongnu, non-Chinese site of Majiayuan (Zhangjiachuan, Gansu), Late Warring States (Gansu 2014: 97, top [M14:62], bottom [M14:55-4]; 108, bottom [M16:75]), and Nalin'gaotu (Shenmu, Shaanxi), Late Warring States-Han (Dai Yingxin and Sun Jiaxiang 1981: 25, Fig. 4:3, silver foil). Pfrommer 1993: 61, Fig. 45c, d provides examples of the fleur-de-lis grouped into cross-like quatrefoils from

the transmission of Hellenistic influence across the steppe. All were certainly in contact with contemporaneous China, meaning at least the Late Warring States and Han. The massed compositions of Hellenistic art, however, are absent from the greater Eastern steppe (including the Altai). In this context, although the floral scroll must have reached China via Bactria or India, reinforcing influence for specific floral forms could well have reached China from the steppe.

Transmission through the same dual sources, Hellenized sedentary cultures and the steppe, is also likely in the case of the tear/kidney used as a near-floral in the Mashan embroidery[499] N2 (Figure 63). As in Western convention, the form appears on N2 in various arrangements. One of these, a central circle framed by four outward-pointing tears, has Neo-Assyrian precedents.[500] The tear-circle combination further yields a complex series of variants, some made more floral by the attachment of the tears to the central circle. In one such case, with inward-pointing tears, functions as a rosette on the Hellenic gold ear studs from the 'Pyre' grave in the Taman Peninsula (Krasnodar [Russia]), *c.* 350-300 BC.[501] The basic form continues in use through the Han in cultures marked by Hellenistic influence: as, for instance, on an embroidered strip from Han-era Sampula ([Shanpula 山普拉,] Lop [Luopu 洛浦], Xinjiang),[502] or on gold semispherical appliqués with a filigree décor of three inward-pointing tears around a central circle from the tomb of the King of Nanyue (Xianggangshan [Guangzhou Municipality, Guangdong]).[503] These Han-era pieces, clearly deriving from the same sources reflected in the Mashan embroideries, illustrate the longevity of the motif outside of China, as well as its reintroduction to China during the Han.

At the same time, use of the tear/kidney as an independent shape is widespread across the steppe, where it is often used to indicate musculature, sometimes with inlay. Examples occur as early as *c.* the 7th century BC at Aržan 2 (Tuva),[504] followed later by the Altai, Sarmatians, steppe-inspired pieces at Tillia-tepe, and the Far Eastern steppe.[505] It likewise appears

Pazyryk and Noyon uul (respectively). The motif later occurs in Kushan art as a decorative element on clothing and weaponry (Rosenfield 1993: Fig. 1a; Fig. 2a, upper right). Variations of the motif also occur as gold appliqué ornaments from Tillia-tepe M3:8 (Sarianidi 1985: Pl. 34), as well as on gold foil ornaments from the Xiongnu site of Xigoupan (Jungar Banner, Inner Mongolia) M4 (Tian Guangjin and Guo Suxin 1986: 380, Fig. 3, top). A trefoil whose outer petals are more horizontal appears on an embroidered wool carpet/hanging from Noyon uul kurgan 6 (Rudenko 1969: 160, Fig. 71), which, from the large number of Hellenistic motifs included, may well be of Bactrian manufacture. The date of Majiayuan is often given as *c.* 5th-3rd centuries BC; I have followed Gansu 2008: 28, which specifies the Late Warring States.

499 Hubei 1985: 81, Fig. 66, wood bodies with cloth garments; 67, Fig. 55 (N19).

500 E.g., wall paintings from Khorsabad (Iraq), dated to the reign of Sargon II (721-705 BC) and Til Barsip (Tell Ahmar [Syria]), also *c.* 8th century BC, in the form of a circle enclosing a four-pointed star and surrounded by four small fleur-de-lis resembling outward-pointed tears: Parrot 1961: 266, Fig. 341 (Khorsabad), 342 (Til Barsip).

501 Williams and Ogden 1994: 172, No. 109.

502 Xinjiang 2001: 170, No. 324.

503 Guangzhou 1991, Vol. 1: 121, Fig. 81:9; Vol. 2: Col. Pl. 19:3, C112; Lin (ed.) 2012: 283, No. 158, noting the difficulty of knowing where the pieces were produced.

504 Aržan (Tuva) kurgan 2 provides an early steppe example: Čugunov, Parzinger, and Nagler (eds) 2010: Pl. 72:1, top center (No. 5-54); Pl. 110:6 (No. 22-3), both grave 5, burial 2, gold, *c.* 7th century BC. The kidney/tear shape occurs as surface ornamentation without inlay on a bone plaque from Sagly-Baži (Tuva): Kenk 1986: 112, Fig. 8:4, Sagly-Baži II, kurgan 13, *c.* 7th-3rd centuries BC; see also Gryaznov 1969: Pl. 52.

505 For Pazyryk, see Rudenko 1953: 273, Fig. 156; Rudenko 1970: 230, Fig. 108, kurgan 1 (painted and partially tinned leather appliqué from a saddle blanket), where the shape is used as musculature on an elk in a life-prey predation scene; on p. 128, Fig. 74, kurgan 2, it is used as reinforcement less immediately recognizable as musculature on the forequarters of a composite griffin. On bronze pieces from the non-Chinese north, the kidney-tear retains the form of an inlay-cell, but with no remaining trace of inlay: Tian Guangjin and Guo Suxin 1986: 76, Fig. 44:1 (Xichagou [Xifeng,

somewhat sporadically as musculature in Achaemenid work, as on a bronze weight in the form of a lion *couchant* from Susa,[506] as well as on highly-Achaemenized, steppe-influenced work such as the griffin ornament from the Oxus Treasure (*c.* 5th-3rd centuries BC).[507] In these cases, the convention seems likely to derive from steppe influence. Given steppe influence on China, it is likely that this source supplemented the Hellenistic, perhaps in the case of the less floral arrangements of the tear/kidney on Mashan N2.

Finally, the tear/kidney as an independent shape serves to form the godroons executed in relief on Neo-Assyrian and, later, Achaemenid and related vessels, such as a gold embossed bowl from the Oxus Treasure.[508] Godrooned, circular, lidded boxes (in the form of flattened spheres) are known sporadically in Chinese tombs from the Late Warring States and Han,[509] whether as imports or local imitations of Persian norms. Apart from the 'garlic-top' of narrow-necked Qin *hu* and related vessel forms,[510] which must be an adaptation of the same godroon convention, the tear/kidney in relief appears to have exercised minimal influence in China, either during the Eastern Zhou or the Han.

The Han made widespread use of the floral motifs adopted during the Eastern Zhou, including those of the Mashan embroideries, frequently with continued reinforcement through foreign contact. Among the most common images are the tears-and-circle[511] and the fleur-de-lis[512] (Figure 12, upper right). The Zhou quatrefoil[513] is ubiquitous, as are variants such as the cruciform quatrefoil, seen on a bronze harness ornament from Baijia (Handan, Hebei) M3:64

Liaoning], mixed non-Chinese site; likely Xiongnu production), 2 (Inner Mongolia, E-1045; likely Xianbei production), 3-4 (unattributed). As inlay on Sarmatian pieces, see *L'Or* 1995: 51, No. 58, Siberian Collection of Peter the Great, *c.* 2nd century BC, phalera; gold, turquoise with inlay cells of several shapes; 97, No. 121, Sladkovski (Rostov [Russia]) kurgan 14, M1, *c.* late 1st-early 2nd centuries AD (correcting the original designation of BC, which seems to be an error); Greek or Hellenized, gold, turquoise, glass paste. The kidney-tear is extremely frequent on Tillia-tepe (*inter alia*, Sarianidi 1985: Pl. 62, M2:19; Pl. 157, M4:8). At the same time, in all of these cultures, a small, straight tear is used simultaneously and is far more common than the kidney-tear form: Tian Guangjin and Guo Suxin 1986: 83, Fig. 51:1 (unprovenanced; possibly Xiongnu-influenced Xianbei).

506 Curtis and Tallis 2005: 194, No. 301.

507 British Museum ANE 123924, gold: *inter alia*, Collon 1995: 187, Fig. 150; Schiltz 1994: 307, Fig. 227, which Schiltz dates to *c.* 5th-4th centuries BC. Note that the tuft on the griffin's tail is essentially heart (ivy)-shaped.

508 *Inter alia*, Curtis and Tallis 2005: 112, No. 97, gold; 113, No. 100, Oxus Treasure, gold; 114-115, Nos 101-103, silver. For Assyrian carinated bowls, see Curtis 2008: 244-245.

509 For a presentation of parallel pieces found in Warring States and Early Western Han Chinese tombs, see Nickel 2012, Li Ling 2014. For recent illustrations, see Xu (ed.) 2017: 164-166, No. 75, Dayunshan (Xuyi, Jiansu). Examples of Gandharan pyxis are made in a similar form (Pal 1986: 157, No. S32, Taxila, grey schist, *c.* 1st century BC; Errington, Cribb, and Claringbull [eds] 1992: 186-187, No. 186, Gandhara, steatite, *c.* early-mid 1st century AD); the Taxila bowl carries an incised décor of repeating lanceolate petals over the body and lid, in parallel to the godroons on the examples from China, raising the possibility of a connection with the Chinese pieces. A miniaturized variant is attested in silver with gold floral inlay in Tillia-tepe M1:30 (Sarianidi 1985: Pl. 146).

510 Zhongguo qingtongqi 1998: 3: Pl. 3, Taerpo 塔兒坡 (Xianyang Municipality, Shaanxi) *bianhu*; 6, Pl. 6, Shuihudi (Yunmeng, Hubei) M9 *hu*; 7, Pl. 7, Changling 長陵 (Xianyang Municipality, Shaanxi) carriage pit *hu*, all bronze.

511 Zhou Dao, Lü Pin, and Tang Wenxing 1985: Pl. 38, Zhengzhou (Henan), stamped brick.

512 Han examples of the fleur-de-lis include the stone bas reliefs from the Wang Deyuan tomb (Suide, Shaanxi), where it is shown growing beneath the plant-throne of the Queen Mother of the West and King Father of the East and is carried by immortals to the rabbit concocting the elixir of immortality (Shaanxi 1959: 14-16, Figs 1-5), as in (here) Figure 12.

513 Han examples include: Xianyang 1979: 132, Fig. 10:2, Maquan (Xianyang Municipality, Shaanxi) M1:91, gold foil appliqué on a lacquer *guan* M1:91; Guo Yong 1963: 5, Fig. 3 (bronze plaque supporting a ring handle); 6, Fig. 5 (relief décor on a bronze *zun*), Youyu (Shanxi); Shandong 1985: 251, Fig. 25:6, King of Qi (Linzi, [Zibo Municipality, Shandong]) burial goods pit K3:68-2, cap on tubular fittings.

(*c.* Middle Warring States)[514] and repeated (in combination with the tears-and-circle) on the Mancheng (Hebei) M2:4024 lacquer *lian*.[515]

The tear/kidney as an independent motif is frequently applied to stamped bricks during the Qin[516] and Han[517] (Figure 59), as well as appearing in work obviously deriving from steppe convention, as in the tear-shaped turquoise or carnelian inlay on Mancheng M1:4090,[518] a gilded bronze fitting in the image of a bear. The same source of influence is clear in the row of elongated tears/kidneys that accentuate the breast and throat of the winged dragon forming the base of a stand for chime stones from Dayunshan (Xuyi, Jiangsu) M1, despite the dragon's Achaemenized horns.[519] The massed tears nonetheless illustrate the difficulty of distinguishing between the source of a motif assessed in isolation, since massed tears are also used as a floral swag on Mashan N2 (Figure 63). Even in cases where Han application of the tear/kidney closely echoes the Achaemenid godroon, as in the rows of tears, alternately pointing up or down, on another Mancheng fitting M1:4091[520] or on the stems of the double-cup stand, Mancheng M2:3032[521] (Figure 43), steppe use of the tear/kidney as reinforcement or musculature may well have played a role. For instance, the single tear filling the upper portion of the legs of a lacquer *ding* from Bojishan (Tianqi, Xuzhou Municipality, Jiangsu) M5[522] fits the norms for both Achaemenid and steppe conventions, in a Han context.

At the same time, Han floral motifs may include some which were in use in the Hellenized world, but seemingly not adopted at that time by Late Warring States China. However, if floral décor was indeed more readily adopted in Eastern Zhou textiles, the perishability of the material record makes it difficult to assess the situation. One such case may be the 'daisy' rosette, known from a *c.* fourth-century BC Greek gorytus from the Scythian 'Five Brothers' kurgan 8 (Elizavetovskaja, Ušakovskij, Rostov).[523] Distribution of the daisy follows throughout Hellenized eastern regions: on the sandal of a Hellenistic marble sculpture at Aï Khanoum,[524] on silver bowls which Pfrommer identifies as probably of Parthian make,[525] and in India as early as the Shunga period (*c.* 200-50 BC).[526] Such wide use around China would have provided multiple sources for its adoption from the Late Warring States through the Han. Although I have found no Warring States examples, the daisy, drawn with stem and leaves, appears on

514 Hebei 1962: 626, Fig. 21:5, bronze openwork harness ornament.

515 Zhongguo shehui kexueyuan 1980, Vol. 1: 305, Fig. 206, gold- and silver-inlaid bronze fittings.

516 Shaanxi 2004: 491, Fig. 403, Qin Palace 3 (Xianyang Municipality, Shaanxi) XYNIIIT102(3):4, with a principle décor of live-prey animal predation.

517 Zhou Dao, Lü Pin, and Tang Wenxing 1985: Pl. 204-205, Zhengzhou (Henan). When used on bricks, the tear/kidney is often marked inside with stripes or dots.

518 Zhongguo shehui kexueyuan 1980, Vol. 1: 92, Fig. 62:1.

519 Xu (ed.) 2017: cover, 64-65, No. 4, silver-inlaid bronze. Note, however, that horns with (near-)spherical tips also occur in Middle Western Zhou representations, as on the Zhui *gui* (Zhongguo 1976: Pl. 44). The source of the convention on this *gui* is unclear; I assume that its appearance may have facilitated the subsequent absorption of Achaemenid stylistic tendencies. For a later example, Rudenko 1953: 133, Fig. 179, Pazyryk kurgan 2 torque (gilded wood on a copper [?] ring), here Figure 50. In some cases, the horns appear to have merged with the representation of ears, as on Rudenko 1953: 129, Fig. 75, Pazyryk kurgan 2 copper plaques, reproduced here as Figure 48.

520 Zhongguo shehui kexueyuan 1980, Vol. 1: 92, Fig. 62:3, gilded and silvered bronze inlaid with carnelian, turquoise, and white jade.

521 Zhongguo shehui kexueyuan 1980, Vol. 1: 267, Fig. 179, gilded bronze inlaid with turquoise.

522 Xu (ed.) 2017: 102, No. 31.

523 *Minami Rosia* 1991: 60, No. 31, gold.

524 Picikjan 1991: Pl. 45.

525 Pfrommer 1993: 134-140, Nos 13-16, *c.* 1st century BC.

526 Poster 1986: 94, No. 23, Kaushambi (Uttar [India]).

a stamped brick from Sanjie 三界 (Pengzhou, Sichuan),[527] as well as a stone bas relief from Jiunüdun (Suining, Xuzhou Municipality, Jiangsu)[528] (Figure 68) and a fragment of a bronze money tree from Guijiayuanzi (Zhaotong Municipality, Yunnan).[529] A coneflower-like rosette (characterized by a domed center, surrounded by downward-pointing petals) appears on the same Parthian and Shunga prototypes noted for the daisy, as well as on the Jiunüdun and Guijiayuanzi examples, also cited. Although the form is likely to be Greek-derived, in the absence of earlier Eastern examples, it is unclear whether or not the coneflower would have been available to Chinese artisans before the Han.

Similarly, the peony-like, multi-petaled rosette on the painted ceiling of Dahuting (Mixian, Henan) M2[530] (Figure 66) and on stone bas reliefs at Songshan (Jiaxiang, Shandong) M2[531] seems not to have been used in the Warring States. It is nonetheless an old form, occurring in the tomb of Tutankhamun (reigned *c.* 1332-1323 BC), where it is identified by Helene J. Kantor as a water lily.[532] The motif appears in Neo-Assyrian work,[533] although it is likely to have been adopted in the Near East at an earlier date through contact with Egypt.[534] It subsequently occurs in Hellenistic[535] and, later still, Kushan[536] art. It must have reached Xinjiang at an early date, perhaps in the second half of the 2nd millennium BC, if the dating of Aidinghu 艾丁湖 (Turfan [Tulufan] 吐魯番)[537] may be accepted. It remains attested in the region through the 3rd century AD.[538] From this, we may again conclude that multiple sources are likely to have been available to China even before the Han.

In other cases, forms or conventions absorbed by the Han were new developments, quickly transmitted and adopted. For instance, the lotus and papyrus are used as foliage or flowers on trees in several Han depictions, from the Wu family shrines (Jiaxiang, Shandong; Figure 67) and Balimiao (Yanggu, Shandong) M1[539] to the somewhat attenuated form seen at a number of sites in Xuzhou (Jiangsu), including Baishan (Peixian), Zhangxu (Suining), and Peixian.[540] Although this use of the papyrus has a long history, occurring for instance in *c.* 2000-1700 BC

---

527 Zhongguo meishu 1988: 167, Pl. 206.

528 Xuzhou 1985: Pl. 129.

529 Yunnan1962: 398, Fig. 6:7, *c.* 65 AD, per Psarras 2015.

530 An Jinhuai and Wang Yugang 1972: Pl. 7:6.

531 Zhu Xilu 1992: 47-49, Figs 56-60; 58-60, Figs 74, 75, 77. See also Chongqing 1998: 83, Fig. 7, Linfei Plant (Wushan, Chongqing Municipality, Sichuan), gilded bronze plaque, dated Eastern Han.

532 Kantor 1955: 140, Fig. IV.36.

533 Wu Guo 2009: 111, Fig. 6, Nimrud, tomb of Mulishu-Mukannishat-Ninua, wife of Assurnasirpal II (884–824 BC.), gold headdress.

534 Cf., Aruz, Benzel, and Evans (eds) 2008.

535 Pfrommer 1993: 32, Fig. 28A.

536 Rosenfield 1993: Pl. 3c (detail of belt pattern on a stone sculpture); Fussman 1983: 31, Fig. 9 (left).

537 Yang Jianhua 2004: 156, Fig. 77:5.

538 Yang Jianhua 2004: 156, Fig. 77:1, Yanghai 洋海 (Turfan), *c.* 9th-8th centuries BC; Fig. 77:4, Alagou 阿拉溝 (Hejing 和靖), *c.* 4th-3rd century BC; Fig. 77:5. Wu Guo 2009: 111, Fig. 6, notes the relationship of the rosettes from Aidinghu, Yanghai, and (Jiaohe 交河) Goubei 溝北 (Turfan; *c.*3rd century BC-3rd century AD) with a Neo-Assyrian prototype (the headdress of Mulishu-Mukannishat-Ninua, noted above). If Aidinghu, in particular, is correctly dated, a specifically Neo-Assyrian (*c.* 900-612 BC) source would be too late to serve as prototype. This rosette further appears on a culturally and chronologically unattributed bronze plaque from Inner Mongolia (Tian Guangjin and Guo Suxin 1986: 85, Fig. 53:2). Note that because of its longevity, the form itself cannot establish dating.

539 Liu Xingzhen and Yue Fengxia 1991: 41 (Wu Liang shrine), 79 (Front shrine), 112, top (Left shrine), Wu family shrines (Jiaxiang, Shandong); Liaocheng 1989: 54, Fig. 11, bottom, Balimiao (Yanggu, Shandong) M1.

540 Xuzhou 1985: Pl. 262, 254, 263, respectively.

at Mari (Syria),[541] it was, much later, integrated into northern Indian and Kushan art.[542] A Han-era transmission to China from these regions is likely. Notably, the Han share the northern Indian depiction of the fan-shaped lotus with straight (rather than the usual incurving) sides, again suggesting a northern Indian origin for the Han image. An Indian origin for the form is also likely for a variant of this style of lotus, used as foliage on the twisted tree of a stone bas relief from Haining (Zhejiang),[543] as well as on the Front Wu family shrine (Figure 67), recalling northern Indian images of multiple triangular chattras (umbrellas).[544]

The twisted tree on the Haining or Front Wu family shrine relief is undoubtedly of Greek derivation, developed as part of Greek naturalism. When it may have been adopted in the East is unclear; an example with entwined branches crowned by birds figures on a silver bowl, perhaps *c.* 250 BC-100 AD, is said to have been preserved in Tibet.[545] Entwined branches likewise appear on trees on the north Indian stone shrines of Jetavana (Sanci, *c.* 1st century BC),[546] while trees with twisted trunks are depicted on several Xiongnu bronze or gold plaques, including examples from the Siberian Collection of Peter the Great[547] and Xichagou (Xifeng Municipality, Liaoning)[548] (Figure 17). In these cases, the steppe renditions undoubtedly reflect Greek influence. Independently of this, entwined branches are implied in Xiongnu and Xiongnu-derived Xianbei plaques where the antlers of a deer standing beneath trees become tangled with the branches.[549] In China, trees with twisted trunks appear as early as a Bojishan (Tianqi, Xuzhou Municipality, Jiangsu) XBM3:67 mirror,[550] *c.* 154 BC. Nonetheless, it is the tree with entwined branches that becomes emblematic in Han work, with examples including stone reliefs from Zengjiabao (Chengdu Municipality, Sichuan) M1 (Figure 58, lower right)[551] and Zhangxu (Suining, Xuzhou Municipality, Jiangsu).[552]

Another tree was undoubtedly transmitted to the Han via the steppe, in this case ultimately deriving from a form occurring in Mesopotamia in the Mitannian period, *c.* 1500-1200 BC, classified by Janice Crowley as one version of the 'volute tree.'[553] This tree appears, surmounted by a bird, as a thin gold ornament originally part of a headdress from Issyk (Semirečʼe

541 Crowley 1989: 80-81, generalized as an Asian, but not an Aegean, practice.

542 E.g., Errington, Cribb, and Claringbull (eds) 1992: 44, symbol chart 1, *c.* 2nd century BC Mathura; Rosenfield 1993: Fig. 81, no provenance, stone bas relief.

543 Jiaxing 1983: 17, Fig. 47.

544 Cf., Errington, Cribb, and Claringbull (eds) 1992: 44, symbol chart 9, from a stone pillar base at Amaravati (Andhra [India]), *c.* 2nd century AD.

545 Colledge 1977: Pl. 466.

546 Meister, Dhaky, and Deva (eds) 1988: Pl. 1.

547 Gold inlaid with turquoise, coral, black stone or glass, these mirror-image plaques bear the décor of mounted hunters pursuing a boar. For photograph, see Schiltz 1994: 242-243, Fig. 178. This piece is customarily dated to *c.* 5th-3rd centuries BC and attributed to an unknown culture in western Siberia. For additional discussion, see Psarras forthcoming. The inlay work on these plaques corresponds to *c.* 2nd century BC-2nd century AD decorative conventions common among the Xiongnu, the Sarmatians, and at Tillia-tepe, with precedents of a different style provided by an Achaemenized gold armlet from the treasure of the Oxus (Collon 1995: 186, Fig. 149).

548 Tian Guangjin and Guo Suxin 1986: 73, Fig. 39:2; 96, Fig. 64:4, 6.

549 Tian Guangjin and Guo Suxin 1986: 79, Fig. 46:3, 4 (unprovenanced); and, identical, Lijiataozi 李家套子 (Tongxin, Ningxia): Ningxia 1988a: 19, Fig. 6:2.

550 Xuzhou 1997: 12, Fig. 18; Li Yinde and Meng Qiang 1997: 23, Fig. 1; back cover (color photo). An essentially identical mirror in the collection of the Freer Gallery (Smithsonian Institution, Washington, DC) is published in Deydier 1980: 99, Pl. 75.

551 Chengdu 1981: 27, Fig. 5.

552 Xuzhou 1985: Pl. 254.

553 Crowley 1989: 429, Fig. 154a, b (cylinder seals); 430, Fig. 156 (faience); Crowley 1989: 129, identifies the volute tree as popular in 'Syria and Assyria,' but not in the Aegean.

[Kazakhstan]).[554] It occurs as well on a Xiongnu bronze plaque from Xichagou (Xifeng Municipality, Liaoning),[555] as well as on Xianbei plaques where it functions both as tree and deer antlers.[556] A further Xiongnu-related example is provided by a wool felt appliqué hanging or carpet from Noyon Uul (Mongolia) M6,[557] pointing to continuous use of the motif in the steppe. The form, which appears frequently in Han art, with examples including Zengjiabao (Chengdu Municipality, Sichuan) M1[558] (Figure 58, upper center), the Front Wu shrine (Jiaxiang, Shandong),[559] and in more angular form, Jiunüdun (Suining, Xuzhou Municipality, Jiangsu)[560] (Figure 68), thus appears likely to have been received from the steppe.

Despite this deep assimilation of primarily Hellenistic motifs, the type of floral work attested by the Mashan embroideries does not characterize Han work. Han scenes of paradise, for all their floral aspect, depend primarily on the depiction of the whole plant: the daisy with stem and leaves (Figures 8, 68), the tree with blossoms (Figure 67), and the like (Figure 23). In Han approximations of the floral scroll[561] (Figures 13, 27), a vegetal meander tends to be associated, not with blossom motifs, but with animals which, compositionally, serve the same purpose (as on Figure 12, upper left; 13). Elements of this transformation are already visible particularly on Mashan N9, utilizing both floral and animal components (Figure 65). The Han version nonetheless represents an original creation, combining reworked floral forms and the Hellenistic floral scroll with the Chinese meander and the predominance of the animal characteristic of steppe art. Ultimately, this synthesis typifies Han art.

[554] Akišev 1978: 219 (drawing). In this report, Akišev proposes a date of *c.* 5th century BC, but the date is modified to *c.* 5th-4th centuries BC in Akišev 1983.
[555] Tian Guangjin and Guo Suxin 1986: 96, Fig. 64:4.
[556] Tian Guangjin and Guo Suxin 1986: 72, Fig. 38:3.
[557] Rudenko 1969: 146, Fig. 48 (drawing); Pl. XXXIX, XLI (photographs).
[558] Chengdu 1981: 27, Fig. 5.
[559] Liu Xingzhen and Yue Fengxia 1991: 75, second register, far right.
[560] Xuzhou 1985: Pl. 129.
[561] Contrast Rawson 2012: 30.

Conclusion

The contribution of Buddhist imagery to Han art is, naturally, readily visible; the same is true for Han-produced imitations of steppe exotica,[562] which follow or adapt steppe compositions in highly sinicized style. At the same time, such examples represent only a small portion of the foreign influence absorbed by the Han and an equally small portion of all influence received from India, Bactria, and the steppe. Indeed, Han art, like that of the Eastern Zhou, offers ample evidence of extensive influence from multiple foreign cultures in areas far beyond religious symbolism and exotica. In contrast to the post-Han era, when imported objects occur quite frequently in the archaeological record, few such imports have been identified for the Han and pre-imperial period. As long as lacunae in the archaeological record persist over large areas of Central Asia and, most notably, the Far Eastern steppe over the 1st millennium BC, we may never be able to reconstruct specific paths of transmission. Nonetheless, a wide range of décors occur in Chinese art for which not only is there no Chinese precedent, but which are well-known in non-Chinese cultures as far removed as Greece and the Near East.

In general terms, many of the foreign elements widely adopted by the Han were available during the Eastern Zhou, in both northern and southern states, albeit with fewer variations and in a context naturally dominated by Bronze Age norms. Further, foreign influence involved not only specific motifs and set iconographies (the animal master, the tree of life, animal predation), but compositional and stylistic elements deriving from the West, as much as from the steppe. Steppe influence far exceeds sinicized exoticism or, indeed, the animal predation iconography, introducing or reinforcing the intensive use of animal forms and a style of execution far freer and more naturalistic (in its stylization) than the Chinese norm. In a different context, freer and more naturalistic execution also characterizes Hellenistic influence. At the same time, the animal master, the tree of life, and floral designs, less typical of steppe-produced work, represent western developments and require transmission to China by cultures other than the steppe.

The initial pre-imperial adoption of foreign iconographies and motifs is significant as more than precedent for the Han, not least because the images in question were used diffferently in Han and pre-Han art. Two periods of the Eastern Zhou show intense adoption of foreign elements: near the Middle-Late Springs and Autumns, and again near the Middle-Late Warring States. The three major iconographies, together with influence reflected in the creation of early florals (such as the Zhou quatrefoil), appear in the Springs-Autumns, with increasing use thereafter. Secondarily, a host of floral motifs, rarely used in China, were adopted toward the Middle Warring States, by which time animal predation and related iconographies seem to have been used more frequently than the animal master or tree of life. This shift in focus may correspond to increasingly close contact with steppe cultures (not today specifically identifiable). It also appears to me that, although all of these elements were incorporated into the Han iconography of paradise, they played a different role during the Eastern Zhou. For instance, the way the animal master iconography came to be adapted particularly in southern

[562] *Inter alia*, Xu (ed.) 2017: 158, No. 69, Dayunshan (Xuyi, Jiangsu) M9; 159, No. 70, Tianqishan 天齊山 (Xuzhou Municipality, Jiangsu), both gold buckle sets.

China suggests that it was used to illustrate local social or ritual concerns. It remains difficult to suggest what these might be.

More significantly, it seems to me too great a coincidence that the animal master, in particular, with its vast and complex religious significance outside of China, should have incorporated some (albeit unknown) religious value in Eastern Zhou China, as well. It therefore appears that the Eastern Zhou must have understood that this foreign iconography carried religious significance of some kind, a conclusion further supported by its use in turn as the basis of (pre-Buddhist) Han religious iconography. This chain of association suggests that, however the animal master may have been transmitted, it was accompanied by some type of explanation, hence by some type of personal contact.

In contrast, the increasing popularity of predation and other animal forms, executed in the new, more naturalistic style, gives the impression of fulfilling evolving aesthetic requirements, without any of the religious meaning which presumably accompanied these images in the steppe. The greater Middle-Late Warring States use of floral motifs seems to follow the same visual logic. We may even speculate either that Middle-Late Warring States steppe cultures made use of floral motifs to an extent not seen during the Han period, or that Late Eastern Zhou China came to be in relatively close contact with Hellenistic Bactria or with northern India.

In fact, these two periods of intensive foreign contact in the Middle-Late Springs-Autumns and Middle-Late Warring States parallel largely contemporaneous developments in Greece and the Near East. Since these regions, with their long history of interaction, were also the source of most of the décors introduced into China during the Eastern Zhou, this coincidence may not be fortuitous. In approximately the 7th century BC, Greek art became transformed through an 'Orientalization,' in which Near Eastern (Figure 2) and Egyptian influence was incorporated to create a new Greek art[563] (Figure 69); in the late 4th century BC, Greek (including Macedonian) art spread across Central Asia and northern India with the political conquests of Alexander the Great. This Hellenism reiterated the Persian influence which earlier had spread through much the same territory, presumably with Achaemenid imperial expansion in the later 6th century BC. (It is important to bear in mind, however, that, as illustrated by the Greek era of Orientalization, intercultural exchange is not dependent on conquest.) In this context and despite the distance, it appears that these more Western cultural movements affected China, largely at the same time. In Eastern Zhou China, however, Greek and Near Eastern influence was absorbed more cautiously; the 'occidentalization' of Chinese art came to fruition only during the Han. Nonetheless, because Bactria, India, and the Far Eastern steppe all retained Achaemenid and Hellenistic influence into the Christian era, such influence could be – and seemingly was – introduced and reintroduced to the Han in different forms. At a time when the social structures dictating the artistic conventions of the Chinese Bronze Age had been transformed, the Han were free to create a new visual culture. This they did with reference both to the Chinese past and to foreign influence, previously-sinicized and newly-absorbed.

The result is a creation so natural that, on the surface, virtually all Han imagery seems autochthonous.

563 See Dezsö and Vér 2013, with extensive bibliography; Aruz, Graff, and Takic (eds) 2014: 248-329.

Maps

Map 1: Overview of the Mediterranean through China. Basic map, Data © 2015 Google, INEGI: www.google.com/maps/d/viewer?mid=1b5d4wz5Dta1TnPPgClglI7YqheY&hl=en&ll=25.99755013846791%2C31.201170000000047&z=2, to which I have added further detail (locations approximate). See also the map provided by Dyson 1963 for locations in the Ancient Near East.

Map 2: Modern Chinese Provinces. Map based on Anon., *Zhonghua renmin gongheguo fensheng dituji* (Shanghai: Ditu, 1984).

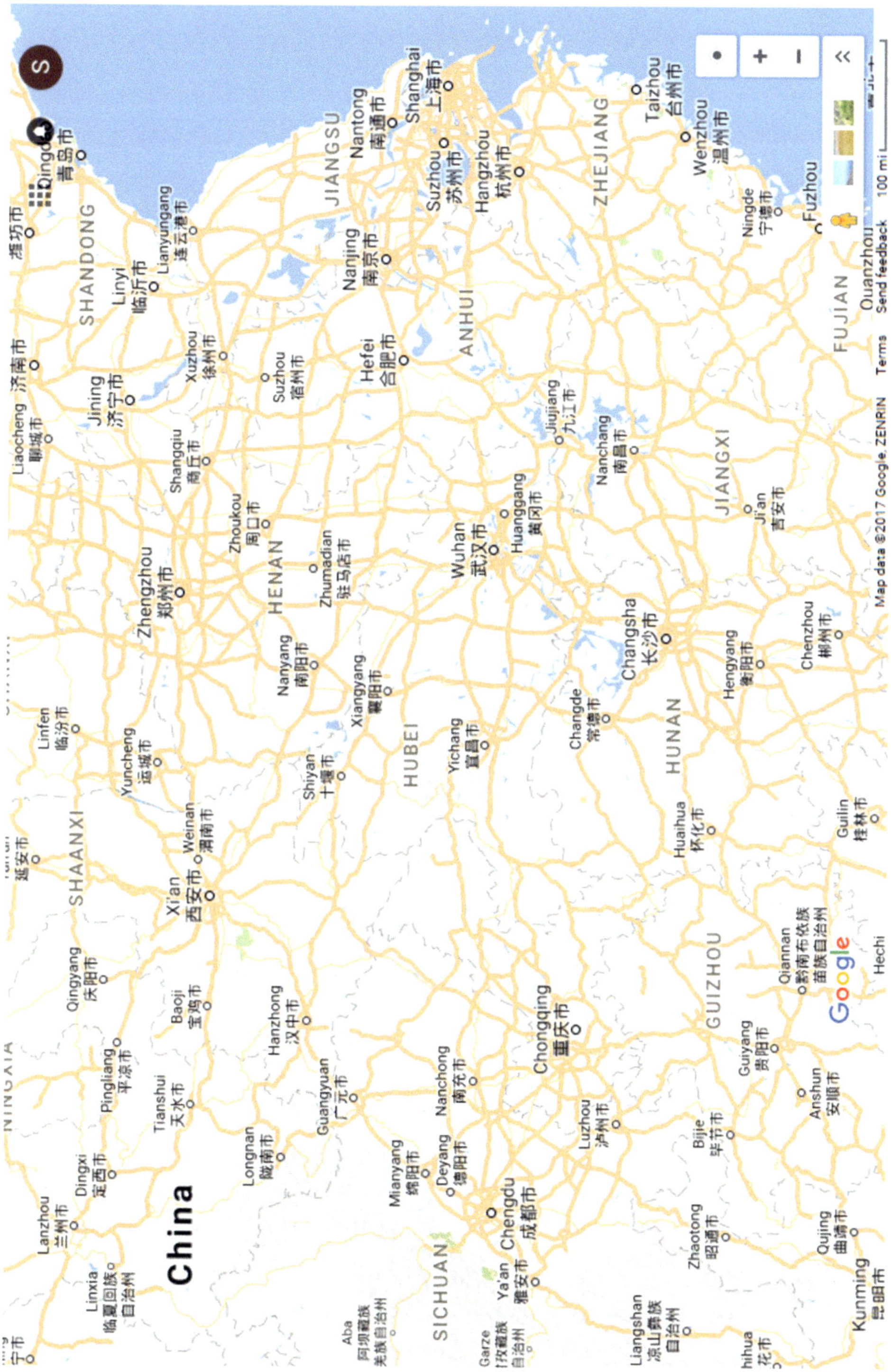

Map 3: Selected Chinese Cities. Data (c) 2017 Google, ZENRIN.www.google.com/maps/@31.2612752,107.7069026,6z

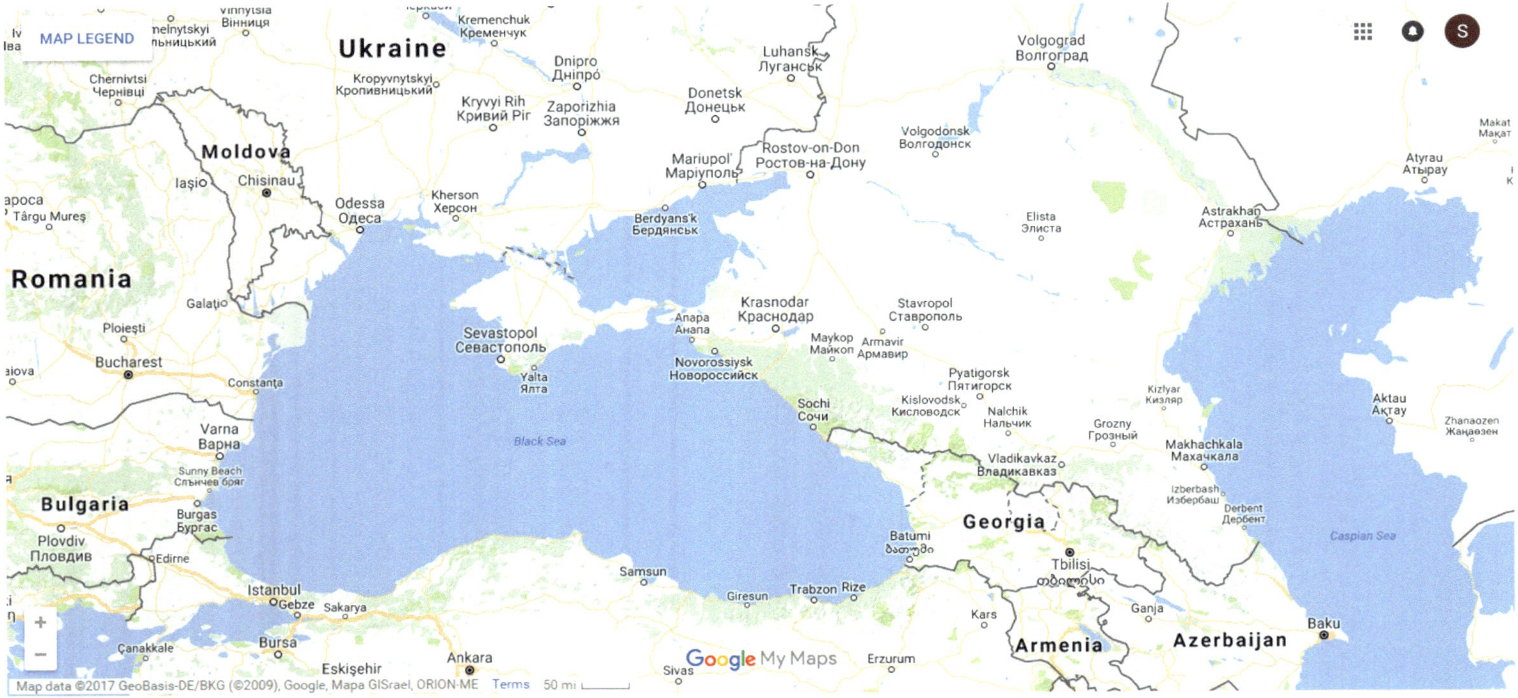

Map 4: Selected Scythian and Sarmatian Sites. Map data © 2017 GeoBasis-DE/BKG (© 2009), Google, Mapa GISrael, ORION-ME: www.google.com/maps/d/viewer?mid=14mzjozMpbNpj7XYQS260Fg_nxks&hl=en_US&ll=44.77793600000002%2C34.18945299999996&z=6

Figures

Figure 1. Mawangdui (Changsha Municipality, Hunan) M1 black lacquered coffin. Hunan 1973, Vol. 1: Fig. 17 (insert after p. 16), detail.

Figure 2. Northwestern Iran bronze vase, *c.* 10th-8th centuries BC. The Metropolitan Museum of Art. Purchase, Joseph Pulitzer Bequest, 1964. Accession Number 64.257.1a, b. www.metmuseum.org/art/collection/search/325693.

Figure 3. Cyprus, hematite cylinder seal, c. 14th century BC. The Metropolitan Museum of Art. Gift of Nanette B. Kelekian, in memory of Charles Dikran and Beatrice Kelekian, 1999. Accession number 1999.325.223. www.metmuseum.org/art/collection/search/327819.

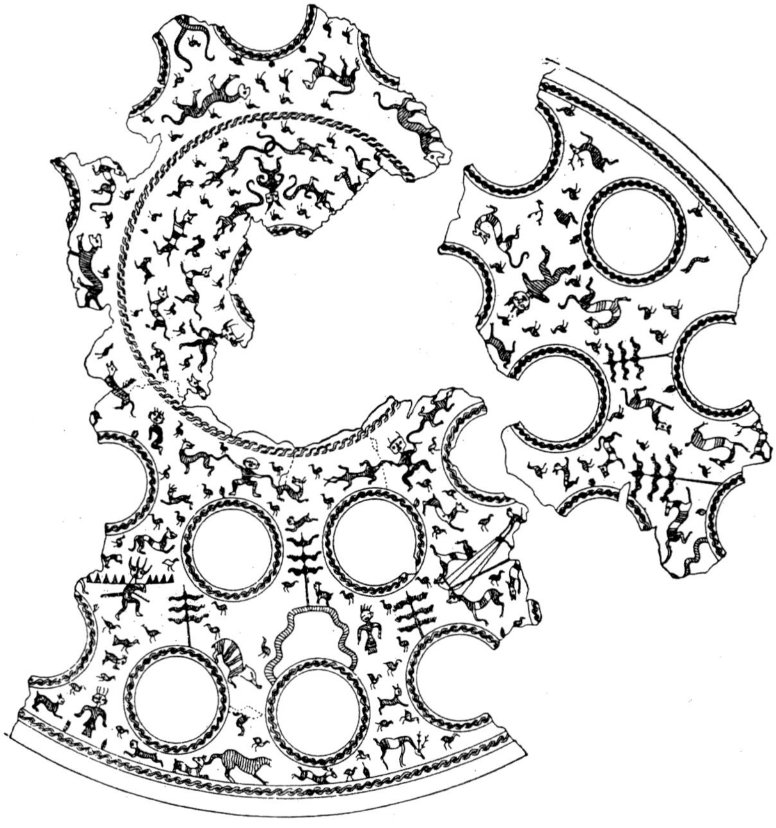

Figure 4. Gaozhuang (Huaiyin Municipality, Jiangsu) M1:114-2 incised bronze fragment. Huaiyin 1988: 209, Fig. 22.

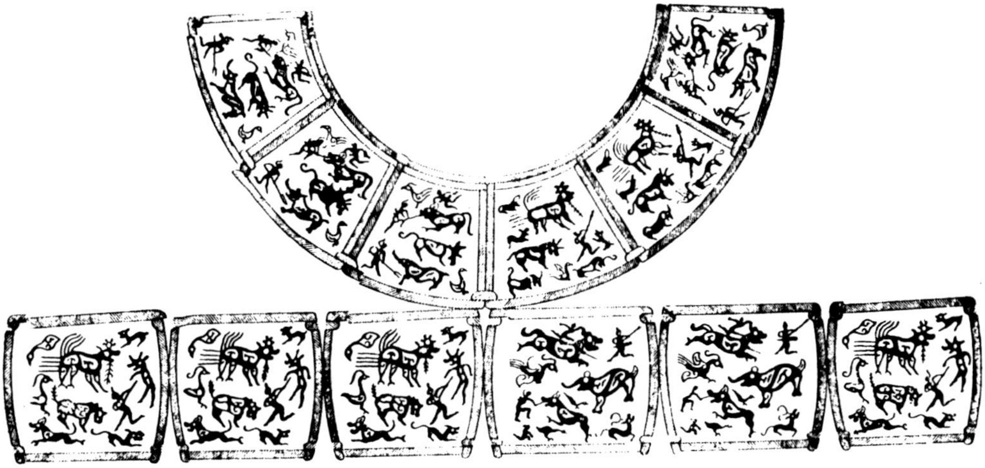

Figure 5. Jiagezhuang (Tangshan Municipality, Hebei) M5 copper-inlaid bronze *hu*. An Zhimin 1953: 86, Fig. 11.

Figure 6. Mancheng (Hebei) M2:3004 partially-silvered bronze *boshanlu* incense burner. Zhongguo shehui kexueyuan 1980, Vol. 1: 257, Fig. 171.

Figure 7. Gaozhuang (Huaiyin Municipality, Jiangsu) M1:0137 incised bronze fragment. Huaiyin 1988: 204, Fig. 17.

Figure 8. Nanyang (Henan) stamped brick. Nanyang 1990: Pl. 181.

Figure 9. Nimrud carved stone (gypsum alabaster), Neo-Assyrian, *c.* 883-859 BC. The Metropolitan Museum of Art. Gift of John D. Rockefeller Jr., 1932. Accession number 32.143.3. www.metmuseum.org/art/collection/search/322610.

Figure 10. Liulige (Huixian, Henan) *hu* M59:23 (bronze). Guo Baojun 1959: Pl. 93.

Figure 11. Hanjiaqu (Yishui, Shandong) stone bas relief. Zhongguo meishu 1988: 45, Pl. 54.

Figure 12. Hejiagou (Suide, Shaanxi) stone bas relief. Shaanxi 1959: 39, Pl. 28.

Figure 13. Yanjiacha (Suide, Shaanxi) stone bas relief. Zhongguo meishu 1988: 67, Pl. 79.

Figure 14. Xindu (Sichuan) stamped brick. Zhongguo meishu 1988: 173, Pl. 216.

Figure 15. Songshan (Jiaxiang, Shandong) stone bas relief. Zhongguo meishu 1988: 2, Pl. 2.

Figure 16. Yingzhuang (Nanyang Municipality, Henan) stone bas relief. Wang and Shan 1990: Pl. 248.

Figure 17. Daodunzi (Tongxin, Ningxia) M10:33 Xiongnu bronze plaque. Ningxia 1988B: 345, Fig. 10:6.

Figure 18. Suide (Shaanxi) stone bas relief. Shaanxi 1959: 109, Fig. 111-112.

Figure 19. Maquan (Xianyang Municipality, Shaanxi) lacquered *lian* toiletries box. Xianyang 1979: 133, Fig. 11, especially Fig. 11:1, 4, 7, 8.

Figure 20. Greek or Boeotian calyx-krater, red figure terra cotta, *c.* early 4th century BC. The Metropolitan Museum of Art. Rogers Fund 1957. Accession number 57.11.3. www.metmuseum.org/art/collection/search/254930.

Figure 21. Pingshuo (Shanxi) 6M50:8 gilded bronze plaque. Pingshuo 1987: 12, Fig. 32.

Figure 22. Yangzishan (Chengdu Municipality, Sichuan) M1 stone bas relief. Zhongguo meishu 1988: 86-87, Pl. 102, detail.

Figure 23. Jiunüdun (Suining, Xuzhou Municipality, Jiangsu) stone bas relief. Jiangsu 1959: Pl. 23, Fig. 27.

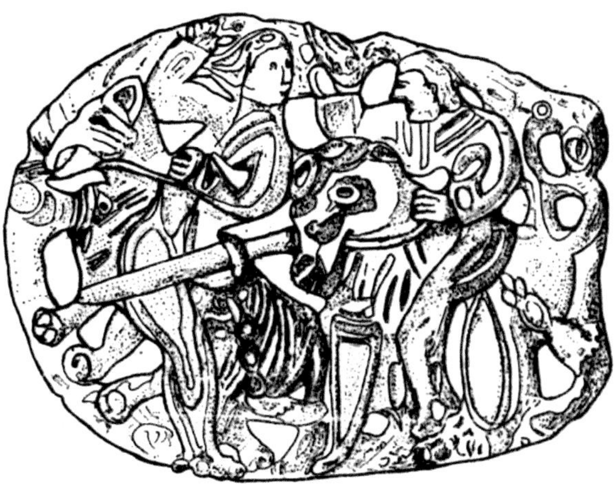

Figure 24. Xichagou (Xifeng, Liaoning) Xiongnu bronze plaque. Tian and Guo 1986: 73, Fig. 39:2.

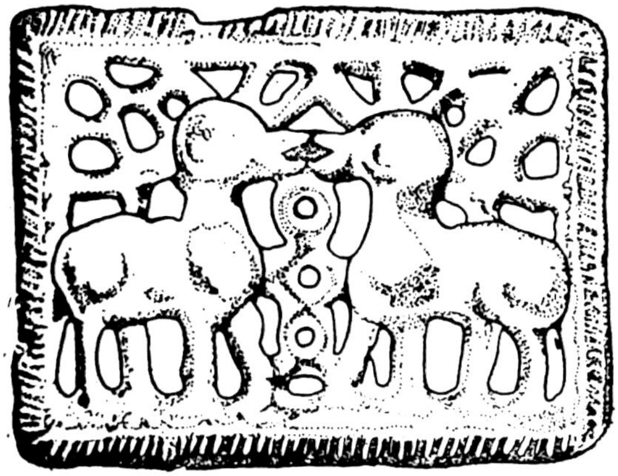

Figure 25. Erlanhugou 二蘭虎溝 (Qahar [Chaha'er] Right Rear Banner 察哈爾右翼後旗, Inner Mongolia) Xianbei bronze plaque. Tian and Guo 1986: 79, Fig. 46:1.

Figure 26. Liulige (Huixian, Henan) M76:85 bronze *hu*. Guo Baojun 1959: Pl. 103:1.

Figure 27. Mancheng (Hebei) M1:2250 gilded bronze harness ornament. Zhongguo shehui kexueyuan 1980, Vol. 1: 201, Fig. 136:1.

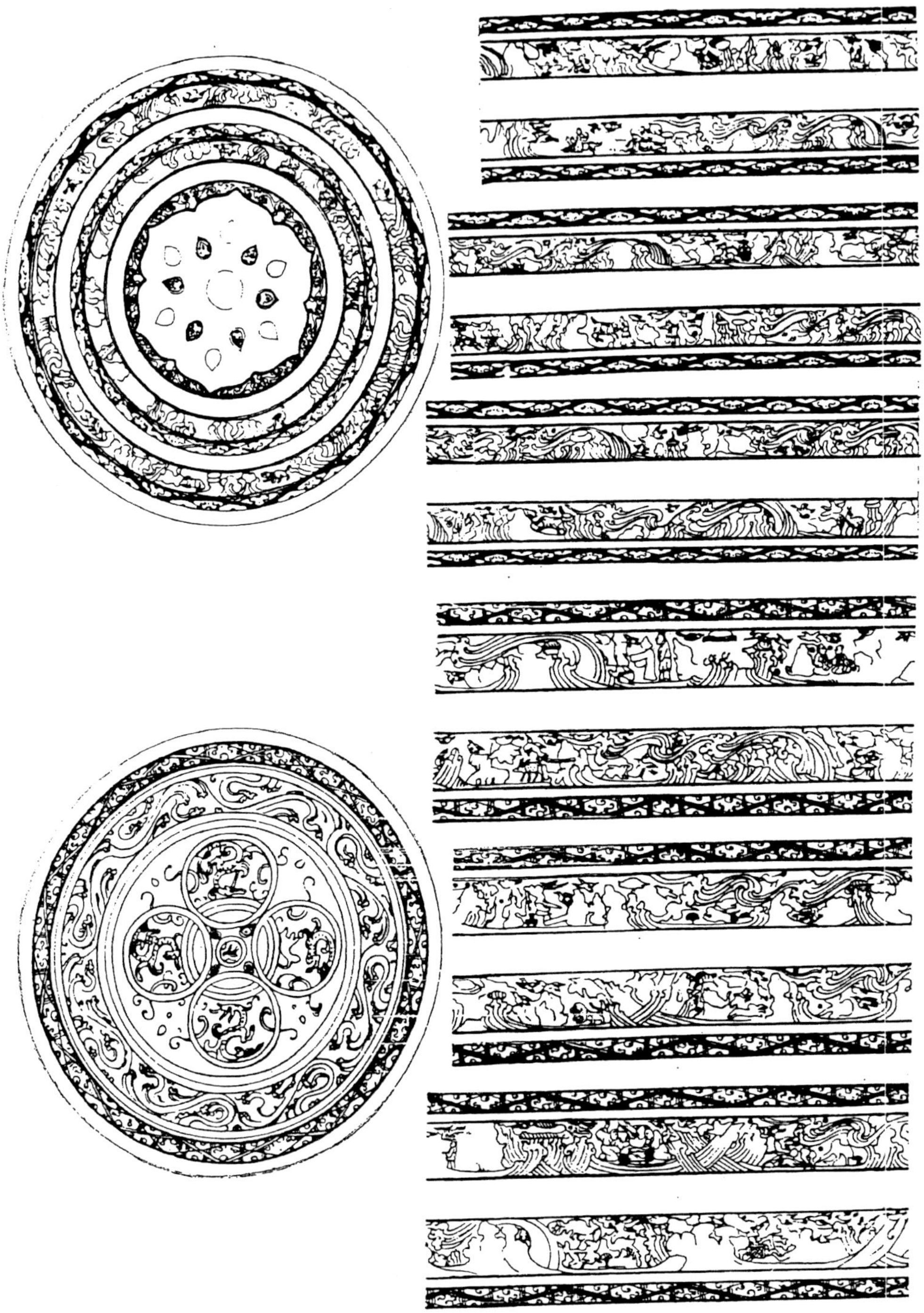

Figure 28. Yaozhuang (Hanjiang, Yangzhou Municipality, Jiangsu) M101:190 lacquered *lian* with silver fittings and carnelian inlay. Yangzhou 1988: 38, Fig. 30.

Figure 29. Qinglongshan (Peixian, Xuzhou Municipality, Jiangsu) stone bas relief. Nanjing 1984: 25, Fig. 8.

Figure 30. Noyon uul (Batsumber, Tuv [Mongolia]) M6:254 silver plaque. Rudenko 1962: Pl. XXXVII:3.

Figure 31. Western Iran bronze beaker, Iron Age II (*c.* 10th-9th centuries BC). The Metropolitan Museum of Art. Purchase, Joseph Pulitzer Bequest, 1948. Accession number 48.178.1. www.metmuseum.org/art/collection/search/324053, additional image 4.

Figure 32. Dyrestuj (Burjatija [Russia]) bronze plaque. Rudenko 1969: Pl. XXXVIII:1.

Figure 33. Unprovenanced ("Ordos") Xiongnu bronze plaque. Tian and Guo 1986: 94, Fig. 62:2.

Figure 34. Shuihudi (Yunmeng, Hubei) M47:93 carved wood comb. Hubei 1986: 515, Fig. 38.5.

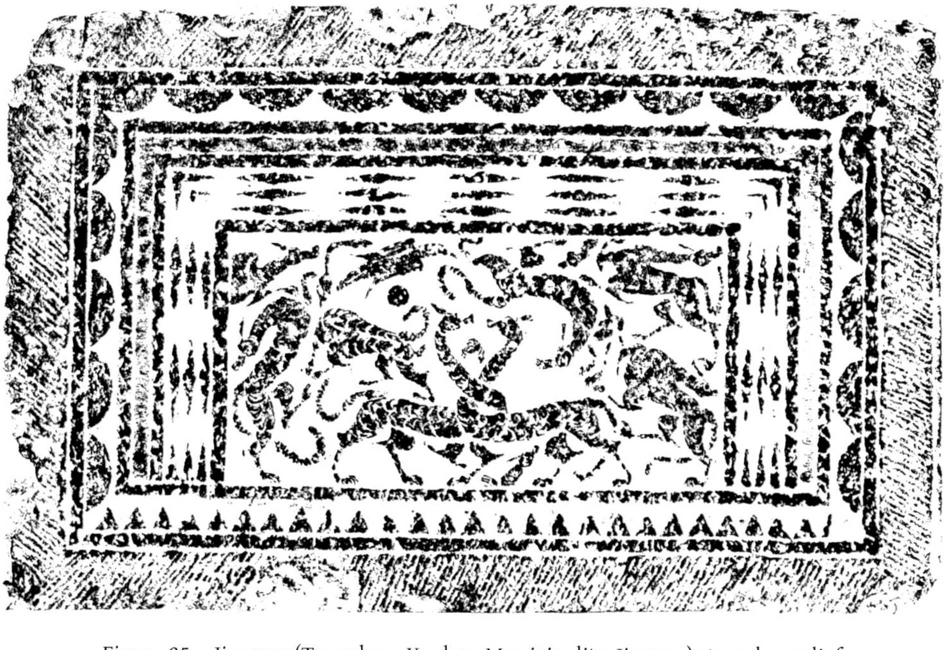

Figure 35. Jiawang (Tongshan, Xuzhou Municipality, Jiangsu) stone bas relief. Jiangsu 1959: Pl. 71, Fig. 91.

Figure 36. Aluchaideng (Hanggin Banner, Inner Mongolia) Xiongnu gold plaque. Tian and Guo 1986: 345, fig. 2:4.

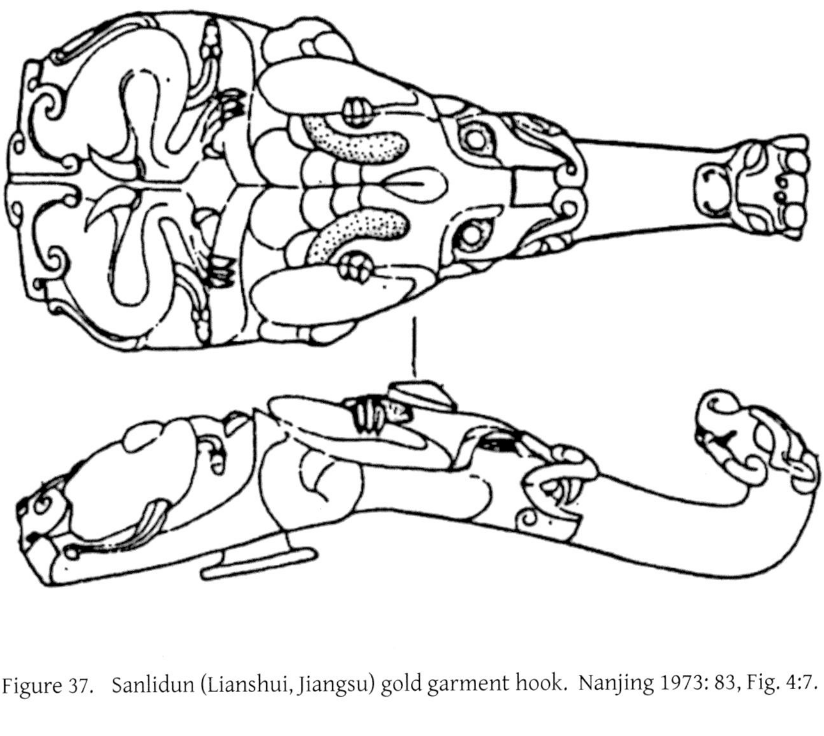

Figure 37. Sanlidun (Lianshui, Jiangsu) gold garment hook. Nanjing 1973: 83, Fig. 4:7.

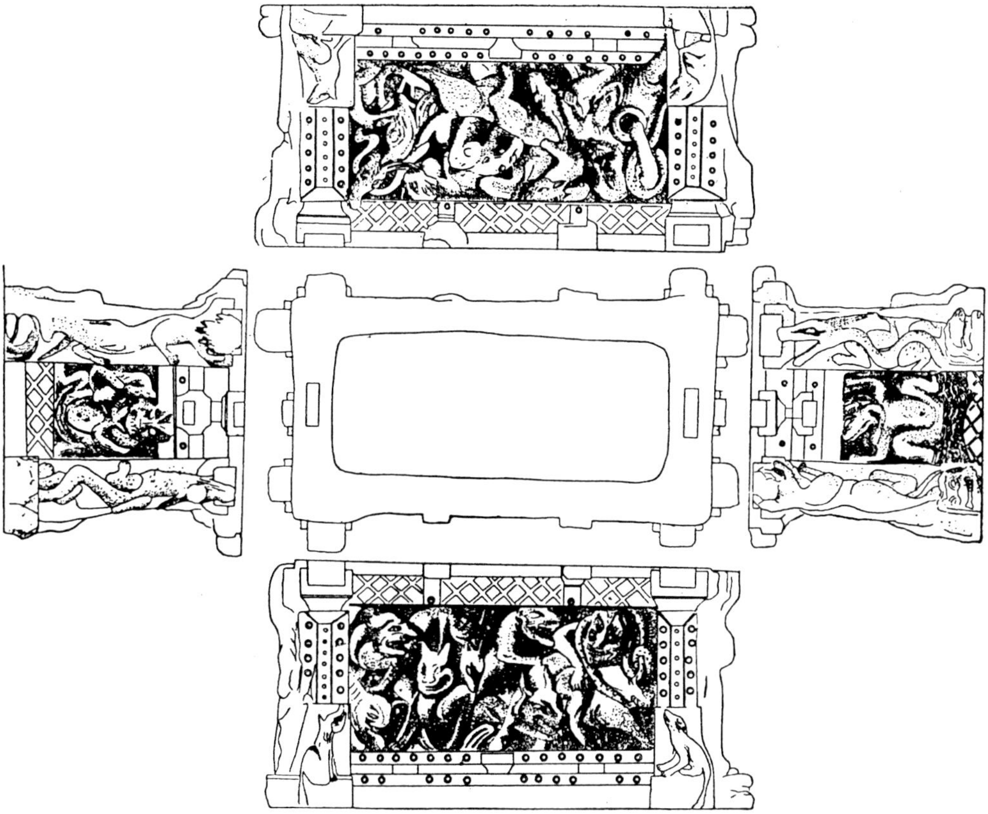

Figure 38. Shaogou (Luoyang Municipality, Henan) M1028A:14 earthenware model well. Zhongguo kexueyuan 1959: 129, Fig. 61.

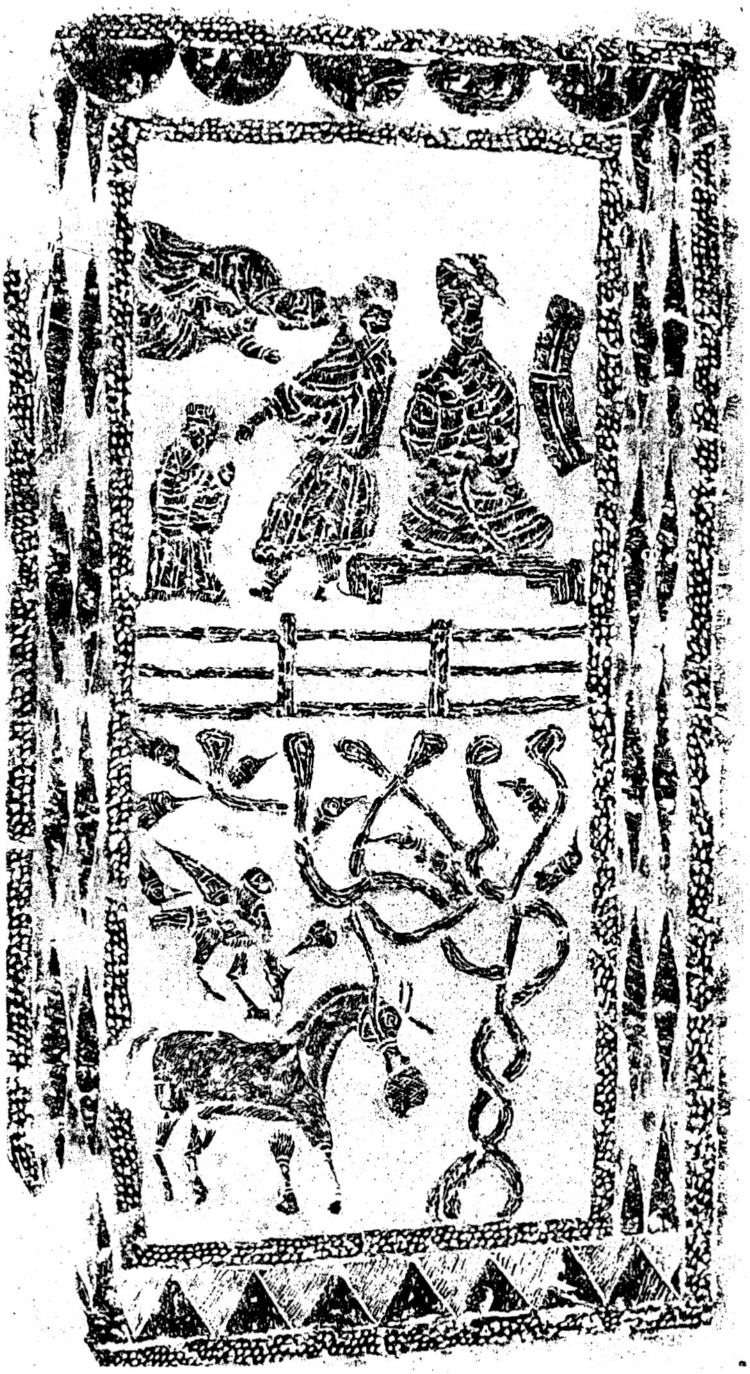

Figure 39. Zhangxu (Suining, Xuzhou Municipality, Jiangsu) stone bas relief. Xuzhou 1985: Pl. 254.

Figure 40. Luoyang (Henan) hollow brick. Zhou Dao, Lü Pin, and Tang Wenxing 1985: Pl. 3, detail, left-hand page.

Figure 41. Aluchaideng (Hanggin Banner, Inner Mongolia) Xiongnu gold plaque, inlaid with turquoise and red stone. Tian and Guo 1986: Col. Pl. 16:1, right.

Figure 42. Thracian silver goblet, *c.* 4th century BC. The Metropolitan Museum of Art. Rogers Fund, 1947. Accession number 47.100.88. www.metmuseum.org/art/collection/search/324029.

Figure 43. Mancheng (Hebei) M2:3032 gilded bronze double cup stand, inlaid with turquoise, jade rings. Zhongguo shehui kexueyuan 1980, Vol. 2: Col. Pl. 25.

Figure 44. Shilipu (Xuzhou Municipality, Jiangsu) stone bas relief. Xuzhou 1985: Pl. 25.

Figure 45. Tomb of Lord Feng or his consort (Tanghe [Nanyang Municipality, Henan]) stone bas relief. Nanyang 1980: 244, Fig. 8:2.

Figure 46. Greek situla, South Italian, Apulian, attributed to the Lycurgus Painter; red figure terracotta, *c*. 360-340 BC. The Metropolitan Museum of Art. Fletcher Fund, 1956. Accession number 56.171.64. www.metmuseum.org/art/collection/search/254923.

Figure 47. Pazyryk kurgan 2 copper plaque. Rudenko 1953: 129, Fig. 75.

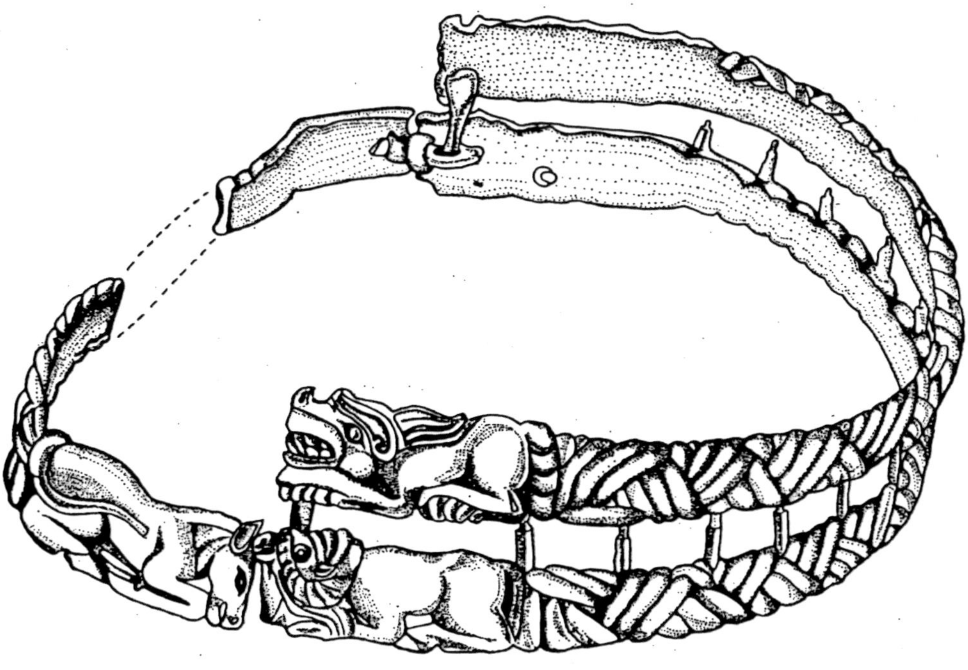

Figure 48. Aluchaideng (Hanggin Banner, Inner Mongolia) Xiongnu gold headdress. Tian and Guo 1986: 344, Fig. 1:4.

Figure 49. Pazyryk kurgan 2 torque, gilded wood and horn on a copper ring (reconstruction). Rudenko 1953: 133, Fig. 79.

Figure 50. Left Wu Family Shrine (Jiaxiang, Shandong) stone 2 (bas relief). Liu and Yue 1991: 92-93, detail.

Figure 51. Pazyryk kurgan 1 leather appliqués on a felt saddle blanket. Rudenko 1953: 280, Fig. 163.

Figure 52. Shuanggou (Suining, Xuzhou Municipality, Jiangsu) stone bas relief. Jiangsu 1959: Pl. 67, Fig. 86 (bottom).

Figure 53. Taishang (Tongshan, Xuzhou Municipality, Jiangsu) stone bas relief. Xuzhou 1985: Pl. 176.

Figure 54. Daodunzi (Tongxin Ningxia) M19:9 gilded bronze plaque. Ningxia 1988B: 344, Fig. 9:13 (originally published upside down).

Figure 55. Pad' Sudži (Burjatija) bronze appliqué. Rudenko 1962: Pl. XXXII:3.

Figure 56. Archaic Greek or Cretan black-figured terracotta hydria (water jar), attributed to the Eagle Painter, *c.* 520-510 BC. The Metropolitan Museum of Art. Fletcher Fund, 1964. Accession number 64.11.1. www.metmuseum.org/art/collection/search/255157.

Figure 57. Zhengzhou (Henan) hollow brick.
Zhou Dao, Lü Pin, and Tang Wenxing 1985: Pl. 206.

Figure 58. Zengjiabao (Chengdu Municipality, Sichuan) M1 stone bas relief. Chengdu 1981: 27, Fig. 5.

Figure 59. Zhengzhou (Henan) stamped brick. Zhou Dao, Lü Pin, and Tang Wenxing 1985: Pl. 204.

Figure 60. Noyon uul (Batsumber, Tuv [Mongolia]) M25:22 bronze fitting. Rudenko 1962: Pl. XXXIII:2.

Figure 61. Stag rhyton, gilded silver inlaid with garnet and glass, inscribed in Aramaic (or Persian?); Near Eastern (Parthian), *c.* 50 BC- AD 50. J. Paul Getty Museum, accession number 86.AM.753. Digital image courtesy of the Getty's Open Content Program. www.getty.edu/art/collection/objects/12859/unknown-maker-stag-rhyton-near-eastern-parthian-about-50-bc-ad-50/.

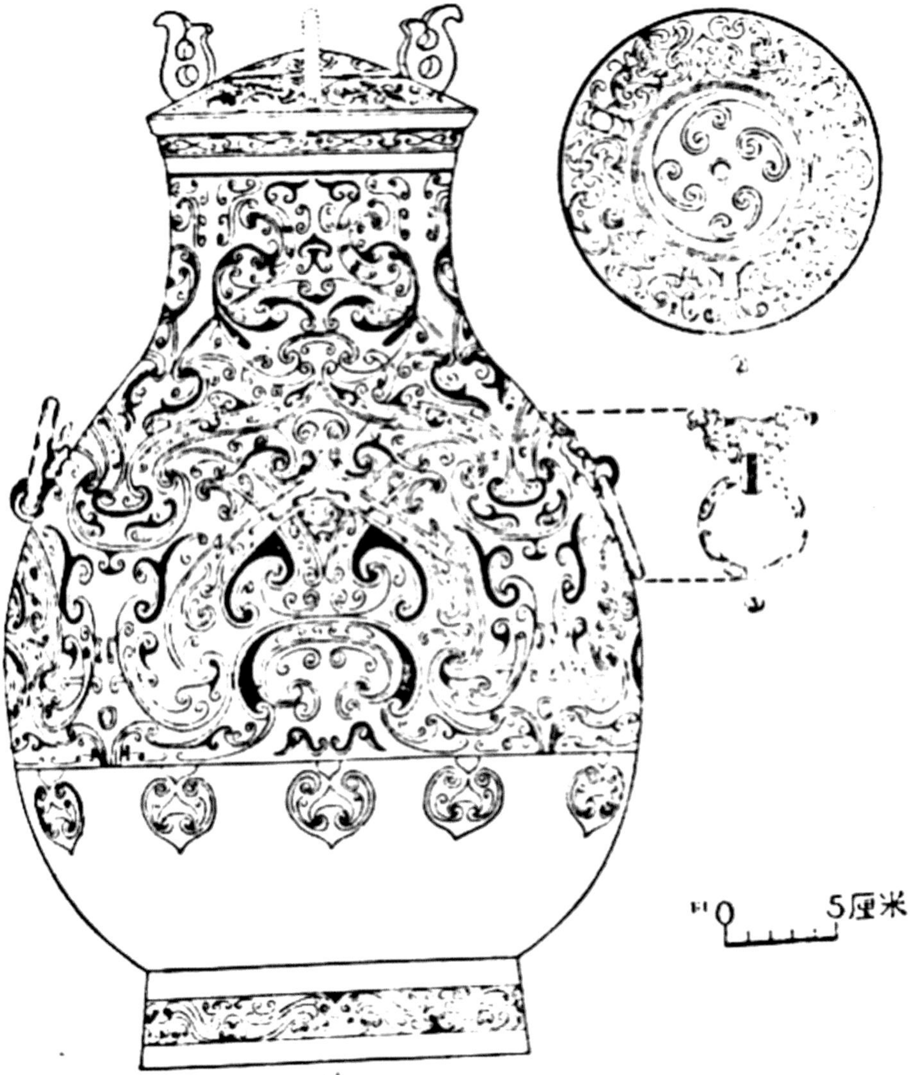

Figure 62. Xiaotianxi (Fuling, Sichuan) M3:23 silver-inlaid bronze, *c*. Middle-Late Warring States; Sichuan 1974: 67, Fig. 6.

Figure 63. Mashan (Jiangling, Jingzhou Municipality, Hubei) M1, N2, embroidered silk. Hubei 1985: 58, Fig. 45.

Figure 64. Mashan (Jiangling, Jingzhou Municipality, Hubei) M1, N7, embroidered silk. Hubei 1985: Fig. 46 (insert after p. 58), reproduced here upside-down relative to the original publication.

Figure 65. Mashan (Jiangling, Jingzhou Municipality, Hubei) M1, N9, embroidered silk. Hubei 1985: Col. Pl. 28:3.

Figure 66. Dahuting (Mixian, Henan) M2 painted ceiling. An and Wang 1972: Pl. 7:6, detail.

Figure 67. Wu family Front shrine (Jiaxiang, Shandong) stone bas relief. Liu and Yue 1991: 79.

Figure 68. Jiunüdun (Suining, Xuzhou Municipality, Jiangsu) stone bas relief. Xuzhou 1985: Pl. 129.

Figure 69. Ionian (East Greek) terracotta oinochoe, *c.* 625 BC. J. Paul Getty Museum, accession number 81.AE.83. Digital image courtesy of the Getty's Open Content Program. www.getty.edu/art/collection/objects/9694/unknown-maker-oinochoe-east-greek-milesian-about-625-bc/?dz=#b3db43215e0d0d3426 2b91ab6e8cb573761827cb.

Selected References

Akišev, K. 1978. *Kurgan Issyk: iskusstvo sakov v Kazaxstana*. Moscow: Iskusstvo.

Akišev, K. 1983. *Drevnee zoloto Kazaxstana.* Almaty: Oner.

Amiet, P. 1976. *Les antiquités du Luristan. Collection David-Weill.* Paris: Boccard.

An Jinhuai 安金槐 and Wang Yugang 王与刚1972. Mixian Dahuting Handai huaxiangshi mu he bihua mu 密县打虎亭汉代画像石墓和壁画墓. *WW* 1972.10: 49-62, Pl. 6-7.

An Zhimin 安志敏1953. Hebeisheng Tangshanshi Jiagezhuang fajue baogao 河北省唐山市賈各莊发掘報告. *KGXB* 1953.1-2: 57-116, Pl. 1-24.

Anhui 1978. Anhuisheng wenwu gongzuodui 安徽省文物工作队, Fuyang diqu bowuguan 阜阳地区博物馆, Fuyangxian wenhuaju 阜阳县文化局. Fuyang Shuanggudui Xi Han Ruyin hou mu fajue jianbao 阜阳雙古堆西汉汝阴侯墓发掘简报. *WW* 1978.8: 12-31.

Anhui 2007. Anhuisheng wenwu kaogu yanjiusuo 安徽省文物考古研究所, Chaohushi wenwu guanlisuo 巢湖市文物管理所. *Chaohu Hanmu* 巢湖漢墓. Beijing: Wenwu.

Artamonov, M. I. 1973. *Sokrovišča Sakov.* Moscow: Iskusstvo.

Aruz, J., K. Benzel, and J. M. Evans (eds) 2008. *Beyond Babylon: Art, Trade, and Diplomacy in the Second Millennium BC.* New York: Metropolitan Museum of Art.

Aruz, J., S. B. Graff, and Y. Rakic (eds) 2013. *Cultures in Contact: From Mesopotamia to the Mediterranean in the Second Millennium BC.* (The Metropolitan Museum of Art Symposia) New York: The Metropolitan Museum of Art.

Aruz, J., S. B. Graff, and Y. Takic (eds) 2014. *Assyria to Iberia at the Dawn of the Classical Age*. New York: The Metropolitan Museum of Art.

Assomull, R. V. 2013. The Classical Influence on the Representation of Women in the Art of Buddhist Gandhara. Unpublished Senior Honors Thesis, Brandeis University. <https://bir.brandeis.edu/bitstream/handle/10192/25310/AssomullThesis2013.pdf?>, viewed 27 December 2018 (cached).

Bagley, R. 1995. *Shang Ritual Bronzes in the Arthur M. Sackler Collections* (Ancient Chinese Bronzes in the Arthur M. Sackler Collections, Vol. 1) New York: Harry N, Abrams.

Bagley, R. (ed.) 2001. *Ancient Sichuan: Treasures from a Lost Civilization*. N.p.: Seattle Art Museum and Princeton University Press.

Barnard, N. 1973. *The Ch'u Silk Manuscript: Translation and Commentary.* (Studies on the Ch'u Silk Manuscript Part 2, Supplement 1) Canberra: Australian National University (Department of Far Eastern History, Research School of Pacific Studies, Institute of Advanced Studies).

Beijing 1995. Beijing shi wenwu yanjiusuo 北京市文物研究所. *Liulihe Xi Zhou Yanguo mudi 1973-1977* 琉璃河西周燕国墓地 1973-1977. Beijing: Wenwu.

Bernard, P. 1987. Les nomades conquérants de l'empire gréco-bactrien. Réflexions sur leur identité ethnique et culturelle. *Comptes-rendus des séances de l'Académie des Inscriptions et Belles-Lettres*, 131e année, No. 4: 758-768.

Bernard, P. 1996. The Greek Kingdoms of Central Asia, in Harmatta 1996: 96-126.

Bian Chengxiu 邊成修 1972. Shanxi Changzhi Fenshuiling 126-hao mu fajue jianbao 山西長治分水岭126 号墓发掘简报. *WW* 1972.4: 38-46.

Boardman, J. 1994. *The Diffusion of Classical Art in Antiquity* (A.W. Mellon Lectures in the Fine Arts, 1993; Bollingen Series, XXXV, 42) Princeton: Princeton University Press.

Boardman, J. 1995. *Athenian Black Figure Vases*. London: Thames and Hudson (reprint; 1st edition, 1974; corrected edition, 1991).

Boardman, J. 2000. *Persia and the West: An Archaeological Investigation of the Genesis of Achaemenid Persian Art*. London: Thames and Hudson.

Bulling, A. 1966-1967. Three Popular Motives in the Art of the Eastern Han Period. *Archives of Asian Art* 20: 25-53.

Bulling, A. 1967-1968. Historical Plays in the Art of the Han Period. *Archives of Asian Art* 21: 20-38.

Bunker, E. C. 1983-1985. The Steppe Connection. *Early China* 9-10: 70-76.

Bushnell, L. 2008. The Wild Goat-and-Tree Icon and its Special Significance for Ancient Cyprus, in G. Papantoniou, (ed.) *POCA 2005 Postgraduate Cypriot Archaeology. Proceedings of the Fifth Annual Meeting of Young Researchers in Cypriot Archaeology. Department of Classics, Trinity College, Dublin, 21-22 October 2005*: 65-76. Oxford: British Archaeological Reports/Archaeopress.

Chandra, R. G. 1979. *Indo-Greek Jewellery*. New Dehli: Abhinav Publications.

Charrière, G. 1979. *Scythian Art: Crafts of the Early Eurasian Nomads*. New York: Alpine Fine Arts Collection, Ltd.

Cheng Daohong 程道宏1982. Yiminhe diqude Xianbei mu 伊敏 河地区的鲜卑墓. *NMGWWKG* 2: 18-23.

Cheng *et al*. 1992. Cheng Linquan 程林泉, Han Guohe 韓国河, Yang Junkai 楊軍凱, and Wu Chun 吳春. Xi'an shi Weiyang qu fangdi chankaifa gongsi Hanmu fajue jianbao 西安市未央区房地產开发公司汉墓发掘简报. *KGYWW* 1992.5: 25-32.

Chengdu 1981. Chengdu shi wenwu guanlichu 成都市文物管理处. Sichuan Chengdu Zengjiabao Dong Han huaxiang zhuan shi mu 四川成都曾家包东汉画像磚石墓. *WW* 1981.10: 25-32, Pl. 4.

Chernykh, E. N. 1992. *Ancient Metallurgy in the U.S.S.R.: The Early Metal Age*. S. Wright (trans.) Cambridge: Cambridge University Press.

Childs-Johnson, E. 1995. The Ghost Head Mask and Metamorphic Shang Imagery. *Early China* 20: 79-92.

Chongqing 1988. Chongqing Wushanxian wenwu guanlisuo 重庆巫山县文物管理所, Zhongguo shehui kexueyuan kaogu yanjiusuo Sanxia gongzuodui 中国社会科学院考古研究所三峡工作队. Chongqing Wushanxian Dong Han liujin tong paishide faxian yu yanjiu 重庆巫山县东汉鎏金铜牌饰的发现与研究. *KG* 1998.12: 77-86.

Chongqing 1992. Chongqing shi wenhuaju 重庆市文化局, Chongqing shi bowuguan重庆市博物馆, Xu Wenbin徐文彬, Tan Yao譚遙, Gong Tingwan龔廷萬, and Wang Xinnan王新南 (eds) *Sichuan Handai shique*四川汉代石闕. Beijing: Wenwu.

Colledge, M. A. R. 1977. *Parthian Art*. Ithaca, N. Y.: Cornell University Press.

Colledge, M. A. R. 1986. *The Parthian Period* (Iconography of Religions XIV, 3) Leiden: E. J. Brill.

Collon, D. 1987. *First Impressions: Cylinder Seals in the Ancient Near East*. Chicago: University of Chicago Press.

Collon, D. 1995. *Ancient Near Eastern Art*. Los Angeles: University of California Press.

Cook, R. M. 1997. *Painted Greek Pottery*. London and New York: Routledge (3rd edition; 1st, 1960).

Craven, R. C. 1991. *Indian Art*. London: Thames and Hudson (reprint of 1976 edition).

Crowley, J. 1989. *The Aegean and the East: An Investigation into the Transference of Artistic Motifs between the Aegean, Egypt, and the Near East in the Bronze Age*. Jonsered: Paul Åstroms.

Čugunov, K., H. Parzinger, and A. Nagler (eds) 2010. *Der skythenzeitliche Fürstenkurgan Aržan 2 in Tuva*. Mainz: Philipp von Zabern.

Curtis, J. 2004. The Oxus Treasure in the British Museum. *Ancient Civilizations from Scythia to Siberia* 10: 293-338.

Curtis, J. 2008. Observations on Selected Metal Objects from the Nimrud Tombs, in J. E. Curtis, H. McCall, D. Collon, and L. al-Gailani Werr (eds) *New Light on Nimrud. Proceedings of the Nimrud Conference 11th-13th March 2002*: 243-253. London: British Institute for the Study of Iraq and The British Museum.

Curtis, J. and N. Tallis (eds) 2005. *Forgotten Empire: The World of Ancient Persia*. Berkeley and Los Angeles: University of California Press.

Dai Yingxin 戴應新 and Sun Jiaxiang 孫嘉祥 1983. Shaanxi Shenmuxian chutu Xiongnu wenwu 陕西神木县出土匈奴文物. *WW* 1983.12: 23-30, Pl. 4-5.

Davydova, A. and S. Minyaev 2008. *The Xiongnu Decorative Bronzes: New Discoveries in Russia. Xudožestvennaja bronza Sjunnu: novye otkrytija v Rossii* (The Archaeological Sites of the Xiongnu, Vol. 6) St. Petersburg: Gamas.

Deydier, C. 1980. *Chinese Bronzes*. J. Seligman (trans.) New York: Rizzoli.

Dezsö, T. and Á. Vér 2013. Assyrians and Greeks: The Nature of Contacts in the 9th-7th Centuries BC. *Acta Antiqua Hungarica* 53: 325-359.

Dingxian 1973. Dingxian bowuguan 定县博物馆. Hebei Dingxian 43-hao Hanmu fajue jianbao 河北定县 43号汉墓发掘简报. *WW* 1973.11: 8-20, Pl. 1-4.

Du Jinpeng 杜金鹏 1994. Lun Linqu Zhufeng Longshan wenhua yu guanshi ji qi xiangguan wenti 论临朐朱封龍山文化玉冠饰及其相关问题. *KG* 1994.1: 55-65.

Dumézil, G. 1978. *Romans de Scythie et d'alentours*. Paris: Payot.

Eregzen, G. (ed.) 2011. *Xünnügijn öv/Treasures of the Xiongnu*. Ulaanbaatar: Institute of Archaeology, Mongolian Academy of Sciences; National Museum of Mongolia.

Erickson, S. N. 1995. Money Trees of the Eastern Han Dynasty. *BMFEA* 66: 5-115.

Errington, E., J. Cribb, and M. Claringbull (eds) 1992. *The Crossroads of Asia: Transformation in Image and Symbol in the Art of Ancient Afghanistan and Pakistan*. Cambridge: The Ancient India and Iran Trust.

Falkenhausen, L. von 1999. The Waning of the Bronze Age: Material Culture and Social Developments, 770–481 BC, in M. Loewe and E. Shaughnessy (eds) *The Cambridge History of Ancient China: From the Origins of Civilization to 221 BC*: 450-544. Cambridge: Cambridge University Press.

Falkenhausen, L. von 2006. *Chinese Society in the Age of Confucius (1000-250 BC): The Archaeological Evidence*. Los Angeles: Cotsen Institute of Archaeology, University of California, Los Angeles.

Francfort, H.-P. 1993. La civilisation de l'Oxus : une zone marginale des civilisations du Proche-Orient ? *Grand Atlas de l'Art*: 112-113. Paris: Encyclopaedia Universalis.

Frankfort, H. 1996. *The Art and Architecture of the Ancient Orient* (Pelican History of Art) New Haven and London: Yale University Press (5th edition; 1st edition, Penguin Books Ltd., 1954).

Fujian 1990. Fujiansheng bowuguan 福建省博物馆, Xiamen daxue renlei xuexi kaogu zhuanye 廈門大学人类学係考古專業. Chongan Hancheng beigang yihao jianzhu yizhi 崇安汉城北崗一号建筑遗址. *KGXB* 1990.3: 339-369, Pl. 13-16.

Fussman, G. 1983. *Surkh Kotal: Tempel der Kushan-Zeit in Baktrien* (Materialien zur Allgemeinen und Vergleichenden Archäologie, Band 19) Munich: C. H. Beck.

Galanina, L. and N. Gratch 1987. *L'art scythe: les antiquités scythes du milieu du VIIe-IIIe siècle avant notre-ère*. Z Spetchinsky (trans.) Leningrad: Aurora.

Gansu 2002. Gansusheng wenwu kaogu yanjiusuo 甘肃省文物考古研究所, Lixian bowuguan 礼县博物馆. Lixian Yuandingshan Chunqiu Qin mu 礼县圆顶山春秋秦墓. *WW* 2002.2: 4-30, front cover.

Gansu 2008. Gansusheng wenwu kaogu yanjiusuo, Zhangjiachuan Huizu zizhixian bowuguan 张家川回族自治县博物馆. 2006-niandu Gansu Zhangjiachuan Huizu zizhixian Majiayuan Zhanguo mudi fajue jianbao: 2006年度甘肃张家川回族自治县马家塬战国墓地发掘简报. *WW* 2008.9: 4-28.

Gansu 2014. Gansusheng wenwu kaogu yanjiusuo (ed) *Xi Rong yizhen: Majiayuan Zhanguo mudi chutu wenwu* 西戎遗珍: 马家塬战国墓地出土文物. Beijing: Wenwu.

Ghirsham, R. 1962. *Persian Art: The Parthian and Sassanian Dynasties, 249 BC-A.D. 651*. S. Gilbert and J. Emmons (trans) New York: Golden Press.

Godard, A. 1950. *Le trésor de Ziwiyè (Kurdistan)*. Haarlem: Enschede en Zonen.

Greek Art 1979. *Greek Art of the Aegean Islands*. New York: The Metropolitan Museum of Art.

Green, J. 2012. Restoration of Neo-Assyrian Wall Painting from Residence K, Khorsabad, Iraq, in J. Green, E. Teeter, and J. A. Larson (eds) *Picturing the Past: Imaging and Imagining the Ancient Middle East*: 132-135, No. 20 (Oriental Institute Museum Publications 34) Chicago: The Oriental Institute.

Grenet, F. and B. I. Marshak 1998. Le mythe de Nana dans l'art de la Sogdiane. *Arts asiatiques* 53: 5-18.

Griessmaser, V. (ed.) 1936. *Sammlung Baron Eduard von der Heydt Wien*. Vienna: Krystall-Verlag.

Gruber, M., J. Il'yasov, and K. Kaniuth 2012. A Decorated Ivory Belt from Tilla Bulak, Southern Uzbekistan. *Ancient Civilizations from Scythia to Siberia* 18: 339-375.

Gryaznov, M. 1969. *The Ancient Civilization of South Siberia*. J. Hogarth (trans.) London: Barrie & Rockliff: The Cresset Press.

Guangzhou 1981. Guangzhoushi wenwu guanli weiyuanhui 廣州市文物管理委员会, Guangzhoushi bowuguan 廣州市博物館. *Guangzhou Hanmu* 廣州漢墓. 2 vols. Beijing: Wenwu.

Guangzhou 1991. Guangzhoushi wenwu guanli weiyuanhui, Zhongguo shehui kexueyuan kaogu yanjiusuo 中国社会科学院考古研究所, Guangdongsheng bowuguan 廣東省博物館. *Xi Han Nanyue wang mu* 西漢南越王墓. 2 vols. Beijing: Wenwu.

Gugong 1999. Gugong bowuyuan 故宮博物院 (ed.) *Gugong qingtongqi* 故宮青銅器/*Bronzes in the Palace Museum*. Beijing: Zijincheng.

Guo Baojun 郭寶鈞1959. *Shanbiaozhen yu Liulige* 山彪鎮與琉璃閣. Beijing: Kexue.

Guo Yong 郭勇1963. Shanxisheng Youyuxian chutude Xi Han tongqi 山西省右玉县出土的西汉铜器. *WW* 1963.11: 4-12, Pl. 1-4.

Harmatta, J. (ed.) 1996. *History of Civilizations of Central Asia*. Vol. 2: *The Development of Sedentary and Nomadic Civilizations: 700 BC to A.D. 250*. Paris: UNESCO (reprint; 1994, 1st printing).

Harper, P. O., J. Aruz, and F. Tallon (eds) 1992. *The Royal City of Susa: Ancient Near Eastern Treasures in the Louvre*. N.Y.: The Metropolitan Museum of Art.

Hebei 1962. Hebeisheng wenhuaju wenhua gongzuodui 河北省文化局文化工作队. Hebei Handan Baijia cun Zhanguo mu 河北邯鄲百家村战国墓. *KG* 1962.12: 613-634, Pl. 1-4.

Hebei 1979. Hebeisheng wenwu guanlichu 河北省文物管理处. Hebeisheng Pingshanxian Zhanguo shiqi Zhongshan guo muzang fajue jianbao 河北省平山县战国时期中山国墓葬发掘简报. *WW* 1979.1: 1-31, Pl. 1-9.

Hebei 1983. Hebeisheng wenwu yanjiusuo 河北省文物研究所. Lixian Hanmu fajue jiyao 蠡县汉墓发掘记要. *WW* 1983.6: 45-52.

Hebei 1987. Hebeisheng wenwu yanjiusuo. Hebei Pingshan Sanji gucheng diaocha yu muzang fajue 河北平山三汲古城调查与墓葬发掘. *KGXJK* 5: 157-193.

Hebei 1992. Hebeisheng wenwu yanjiusuo, Xingtai diqu wenwu guanlisuo邢台地区文物管理所. Hebei Shahe Xinggu Hanmu 河北沙河興固汉墓. *WW* 1992.9: 12-21, Pl. 3.

Hebei 1995. Hebeisheng wenwu yanjiusuo. *Cuo mu – Zhanguo Zhongshanguo guowangzhi mu* [X]墓: 战国中山国王之墓. 2 vols. Beijing: Wenwu.

Hebei 1996. Hebeisheng wenwu yanjiusuo. *Yan Xiadu* 燕下都. 2 vols. Beijing: Wenwu.

Heilongjiang 1990. Heilongjiangsheng wenwu kaogu yanjiusuo 黑龍江省文物考古研究所, Yang Zhijun 杨志军, Hao Side 郝思德, and Li Chenqi 李陳奇. *Pingyang muzang* 平洋墓葬. Beijing: Wenwu.

Henan 1960. Henansheng wenhuaju wenwu gongzuodui 河南省文化局文物工作队. Zhengzhou Nanguan 159-hao Hanmude fajue 郑州南关 159 号汉墓的发掘. *WW* 1960.8-9: 19-24.

Henan 1986. Henansheng wenwu yanjiusuo 河南省文物研究所. *Xinyang Chumu* 信阳楚墓. Beijing: Wenwu.

Henan 1990a. Henansheng bowuguan 河南省博物馆, Henansheng wenwu yanjiusuo 河南省文物研究所, Henansheng gudai jianzhu yanjiusuo 河南省古代建築研究所, Lü Pin 吕品. *Zhongyue Han san que* 中嶽汉三闕. Beijing: Wenwu.

Henan 1990b. Henansheng Nanyang diqu wenwu yanjiusuo 河南省南阳地区文物研究所. Xinye Fanji Han huaxiangzhuan mu 新野樊集汉画像磚墓. *KGXB* 1990.4: 475-509, Pl. 13-20.

Henan 1999a. Henansheng wenwu kaogu yanjiusuo 河南省文物考古研究所. Henansheng Jiyuanshi Tonghuagou Hanmu fajue jianbao 河南省濟源市桐花沟汉墓发掘简报. *WW* 1999.12: 19-24, Col. Pl. 1, front cover, inner front cover.

Henan 1999b. Henansheng wenwu kaogu yanjiusuo, Sanmenxiashi wenwu gongzuodui 三門峽市文物工作队. *Sanmenxia Guoguo mu* 三門峽虢国墓. Beijing: Wenwu.

Henan 2001. Henansheng bowuguan 河南省博物院, Taibei guoli lishi bowuguan台北国立歷史博物馆. *Xinzheng Zhenggong damu qingtongqi*新郑郑公大墓青铜器 / *Bronzes from the Prince Zheng Tomb Xinzheng*. Zhengzhou: Daxiang.

Hong Kong 2015. *Han Wu shengshi: Diguode gonggu he dui wai jiaoliu*漢武盛世:帝國的鞏固和對外交流. *The Rise of the Celestial Empire: Consolidation and Cultural Exchange during the Han Dynasty*. Hong Kong: Museum of History.

Hong Quan 2012. Archaeological Discoveries Relating to the Maritime Trade of the Kingdom of Nanyue, in Lin 2012A: 37-41.

Hsing I-tien 2005. Heracles in the East: The Diffusion and Transformation of His Image in the Arts of Central Asia, India, and Medieval China. W. G. Crowell (trans.) *Asia Major*, 3rd series, Vol. 18, No. 2: 103-154.

Huaiyin 1988. Huaiyinshi bowuguan 淮阴市博物馆. Huaiyin Gaozhuang Zhanguo mu 淮阴高庄战国墓. *KGXB* 1988.2: 189-232.

Huang Minglan 黄明兰 1986. *Luoyang Han huaxiangzhuan* 洛陽漢画像磚. Zhoukou: Henan meishu.

Hubei 1976. Hubeisheng bowuguan 湖北省博物馆. Yichang Qianping Zhanguo Liang Han mu 宜昌前坪战国兩汉墓. *KGXB* 1976.2: 115-148, Pl. 1-12.

Hubei 1981. Hubeisheng bowuguan. *Yunmeng Shuihudi Qin mu* 雲夢睡虎地. Beijing: Wenwu.

Hubei 1984. Hubeisheng Jingzhou diqu bowuguan 湖北省荊州地区博物馆. *Jiangling Yutaishan Chumu* 江陵雨台山楚墓. Beijing: Wenwu.

Hubei 1985. Hubeisheng Jingzhou diqu bowuguan. *Jiangling Mashan yihao Chumu* 江陵馬山一号楚墓. Beijing: Wenwu.

Hubei 1986. Hubeisheng bowuguan 湖北省博物馆. 1978-nian Yunmeng Qin Han mu fajue baogao, 1978年雲夢秦汉墓发掘報告. *KGXB* 1986.4: 479-525, Pl. 9-20.

Hubei 1989. Hubeisheng bowuguan. *Zeng hou Yi mu* 曾侯乙墓. 2 vols. Beijing: Wenwu.

Hubei 1991. Hubeisheng Jingsha tielu kaogudui 湖北省荊沙铁路考古队. *Baoshan Chumu* 包山楚墓. 2 vols. Beijing: Wenwu.

Hubei 1996. Hubeisheng wenwu kaogu yanjiusuo 湖北省文物考古研究所. *Jiangling Wangshan Shazhong Chumu* 江陵望山沙塚楚墓. Beijing: Wenwu.

Hubei 2017. Hubeisheng wenwu kaogu yanjiusuo 湖北省文物考古研究所, Xiangyangshi wenwu kaogu yanjiusuo 襄阳市文物考古研究所. Hubei Zaoyang Jiuliandun Chumu chutude qimunu caihua 湖北枣阳九连墩楚墓出土的漆木弩彩画. *WW* 2017.2: 38-49.

Hunan 1973. Hunansheng bowuguan 湖南省博物館, Zhongguo kexueyuan kaogu yanjiusu 中國科學院考古研究所. *Changsha Mawangdui yihao Hanmu* 長沙馬王堆一號漢墓. 2 vols. Beijing: Wenwu.

Institute of Archaeology of Shanxi Province 1996. *The Art of the Houma Foundry*. Princeton: Princeton University Press.

Jacobson, E. 1984. The Stag with Bird-Headed Antler Tines. *BMFEA* 56: 113-141, Pl. 1-39.

Jacobson, E. 1985. Mountains and Nomads: A Reconsideration of the Origins of Chinese Landscape Painting. *BMFEA* 57: 133-180.

Jacobson, E. 1988. Beyond the Frontier: A Reconsideration of Cultural Interchange between China and the Early Nomads. *Early China* 13: 201-240.

Jiang Song 江松1994. Liangzhu wenhuade guanxingqi 良渚文化的冠形器. *KG* 1994.4: 343-345, 354.

Jiangsu 1991. Jiangsu Yangzhou bowuguan江蘇扬州博物馆, Hanjiangxian tushuguan 邗江县图书馆. Jiangsu Hanjiangxian Yangshouxiang Baonüdun Xin Mang mu江蘇邗江县杨寿鄉宝女墩新莽墓. *WW* 1991.10: 39-61.

Jiangsu 1959. Jiangsusheng wenwu guanli weiyuanhui 江蘇省文物管理委员会 (ed.) *Jiangsu Xuzhou Han huaxiangshi* 江蘇徐州漢画像石. Beijing: Kexue.

Jiangxi 2015. Jiangxi Chenbao 江西晨报, Jiangxisheng wenwu kaogu yanjiusuo 江西省文物考古研究所. *Faxian Haihun hou* 发现海昏侯. Nanchang: Jiangxi jiaoyu.

Jiangxi 2016. Jiangxisheng wenwu kaogu yanjiusuo江西省文物考古研究所, Shoudu bowuguan 首都博物馆. *Wu se xuanyao: Nanchang Handai Haihun houguo kaogu chengguo*五色炫曜: 南昌汉代海昏侯国考古成果/*Splendid Finds: The Archaeological Excavations at the Royal Cemetery of Haihunhou Kingdom in Han Dynasty [sic.]*. Nanchang: Jiangxi renmin.

Jiaxing 1983. Jiaxing diqu wenguanhui 嘉兴地区文馆会, Hainingxian bowuguan 海宁县博物馆. Zhejiang Haining Dong Han huaxiangshi mu fajue jianbao 浙江海宁东汉画像石墓发掘简报. *WW* 1983.5: 1-20.

Jilin 1987. Jilinsheng wenwu kaogu yanjiusuo 吉林省文物考古研究所. *Yushu Laoheshen* 榆樹老河深. Beijing: Wenwu.

Ji'nan 2002. Ji'nanshi wenhuaju wenwuchu济南市文化文物處, Pingyinxian bowuguan 平阴县博物馆. Shandong Pingyin Mengzhuang Dong Han huaxiangshi mu 山东平阴孟庄东漢画像石墓. *WW* 2002.2: 38-52.

Jongeward, D. and J. Cribb, with P. Donovan 2014. *Kushan, Kushano-Sasanian, and Kidarite Coins: A Catalogue of Coins from the American Numismatic Society*. New York: The American Numismatic Society.

Kaifeng 2015. Kaifengshi wenwu kaogu yanjiusuo 开封市文物考古研究所. Henan Kaifeng Weixian Daxinzhuang Hanmu fajue jianbao 河南开封尉县大新庄汉墓发掘简报. *WW* 2015.8: 19-29.

Kantor, H. J. 1955. Plant Ornament, Its Origins and Development in the Ancient Near East. Unpublished book manuscript, University of Chicago (revised 1999). Chapter IV: Rosettes:127-168 <http://www-oi.uchicago.edu/OI/DEPT/RA/HJK/HJKIV.pdf>, viewed 6 April 2016; Chapter XI: The Problem of the Palmette:447-476 <http://www.oi.uchicago.edu/OI/DEPT/RA/HJK/HJKXI.pdf>, viewed 11 March 2016.

Kenk, R. 1986. *Grabfunde der Skythenzeit aus Tuva, Süd-Sibirien* (Materialien zur Allgemeinen und Vergleichenden, Archäologie b. 24) Munich: C. H. Beck.

Kong Xiangxing 孔祥星1992. *Zhongguo tongjing tudian* 中国铜镜图典. Beijing: Wenwu.

Li 2004. Lixian bowuguan 礼县博物馆, Lixian Qin Xichui wenhua yanjiusuo 礼县秦西垂文化研究所, and Zhu Zhongxi 祝中熹 (editor-in-chief). *Qin Xichui ling qu* 秦西垂陵区. Beijing: Wenwu.

Li Jaang 2011. Long-Distance Interactions as Reflected in the Earliest Chinese Bronze Mirrors, in L. von Falkenhausen (ed.) *The Lloyd Cotsen Study Collection of Chinese Bronze Mirrors* (Vol II: *Studies*): 34-49. Los Angeles: Cotsen Occasional Press, UCLA Cotsen Institute of Archaeology Press.

Li Ling 李零 2014. Lun Xixin Zhanguo mu liebanwen yin dou: jiantan woguo chutude leisi qiwu 论西辛战国墓裂瓣纹銀豆: 兼谈我国出土的类似器物. *WW* 2014.9: 58-70.

Li Meitian 李梅田 2014. Lüetan Wushan Hanmude liujin guanshi – jianji Handaide shiguan zhi fa 略谈巫山汉墓的鎏金棺饰: 兼及汉代的饰棺之法. *WW* 2014.9: 71-75.

Li Shuicheng 1999. A Discussion of Sino-Western Cultural Contacts and Exchange in the Second Millennium BC Based on Recent Archaeological Discoveries. *Sino-Platonic Papers* 97 (December 1999):1-34.

Li Yinde 李银德 and Meng Qiang 孟强1997. Shilun Xuzhou chutu Xi Han zaoqi renwu huaxiang jing 试论徐州出土西汉早期人物画像镜. *WW* 1997.2: 22-25, back cover.

Liaocheng 1989. Liaocheng diqu bowuguan 聊城地区博物馆. Shandong Yangguxian Balimiao Han huaxiangshi mu 山东阳谷县八里庙汉画像石墓. *WW* 1989.8: 48-56.

Liaoning 1985. Liaoningsheng bowuguan 辽宁省博物馆, Feng Yongqian 冯永谦, Han Baoxing 韩宝兴, Liu Zhongcheng 刘忠诚; Liaoyang bowuguan 辽阳博物馆, Zou Baoku 邹宝库, Liu Chuan 柳川, Xiao Shixing 尚世星. Liaoyang jiucheng Dongmenli Dong Han bihua mu fajue baogao 辽阳舊城东门里东汉壁画墓发掘报告. *WW* 1985.6: 25-42, Pl. 1.

Lin, J. C. S. (ed.) 2012. *The Search for Immortality: Tomb Treasures of Han China*. Cambridge: The Fitzwilliam Museum, University of Cambridge; New Haven and London: Yale University Press.

Lin, J. C. S. 2012. Protection in the Afterlife, in Lin, J. C. S. (ed.) 2012: 77-83.

Lin Meicun 林梅村 2015. Saiyima-Tu'erbinnuo (Seima-Turbino) wenhua yu shiqian sizhouzhi lu 塞伊瑪 - 图爾賓諾文化与史前丝绸之跆. *WW* 2015.10: 49-63.

Linduff, K. M. 2014. Immortals in a Foreign Land: the Kargaly Diadem. *Antiquity* 88: 160-172.

Linzi 1997. Linzishi bowuguan 临淄市博物馆. Shandong Linzi Shangwangcun yihao Zhanguo mu fajue jianbao 山东临淄商王村一号战国墓发掘简报. *WW* 1997.6: 14-26, inside back cover.

Litvinsky, B. A. 2005. Gandharan Art, *Encyclopaedia Iranica*, July 20, 2005, <http://www.iranicaonline.org/articles/gandharan-art>, viewed 28 December 2018.

Liu, C. Y., M. Loewe, Zheng Yan, L. Thompson, *et al.* 2008. *Rethinking Recarving: Ideals, Practices, and Problems of the 'Wu Family Shrines' and Han China.* New Haven: Yale University Press.

Liu, C. Y., M. Nylan, A. Barbieri-Low, *et al* 2005. *Recarving China's Past: Art, Archaeology and Architecture of the 'Wu Family Shrines.'* Princeton: Princeton University Art Museum; New Haven: Yale University Press.

Liu Dezhen 劉得禎 and Xu Junchen 許俊臣1988. Gansu Qingyang Chunqiu Zhanguo muzangde qingli 甘肃庆阳春秋战国墓葬的清理. *KG* 1988.5: 413-424.

Liu Songgen 劉松根 and Xue Wencan 薛文灿1993. *Henan Xinzheng Handai huaxiangzhuan* 河南新鄭漢代画像磚. Shanghai: Shanghai shuhua.

Liu Xingzhen and Yue Fengxia 1991. *Han Dynasty Stone Reliefs: The Wu Family Shrines in Shandong Province.* Beijing: Foreign Languages Press.

Liu Yang (ed.) 2012. *China's Terracotta Warriors: The First Emperor's Legacy*. Minneapolis: Minneapolis Institute of Arts.

Liu Yang 2013. Nomadic Influences in Qin Gold. *Orientations* Vol. 44, No. 2 (March 2013): 1-7.

Loewe, M. 1994. *Divination, Mythology and Monarchy in Han China.* Cambridge: Cambridge University Press.

Loewe, M. 2010. The Laws of 186 BCE, in M. Nylan and M. Loewe (eds) *China's Early Empires: A Reappraisal* (University of Cambridge Oriental Publications 67): 253-265. Cambridge and New York: Cambridge University Press, 2010.

L'Or 1995. *L'Or des Sarmates, entre Asie et Europe, nomades des steppes dans l'antiquité.* Finistère: Abbaye de Daoulas.

Lu Yan 盧岩 and Dan Yueying 單月英 2007. Xi Han muzang chutude dongwuwen yaoshipai 西汉蒙墓葬出土的動物纹腰饰牌. *KGYWW* 2007.4: 45-55.

Lu Liancheng 卢连成 and Hu Zhisheng 胡智生1988. *Baoji Yuguo mudi* 宝鸡 [X] 国墓地. 2 vols. Beijing: Wenwu.

Luoyang 1977. Luoyang bowuguan 洛阳博物馆. Luoyang Xi Han Bu Qianqiu bihua mu fajue jianbao 洛阳西汉卜千秋壁画墓发掘简报. *WW* 1977.6: 1-12, Pl. 1-3.

Luoyang 1985. Luoyang bowuguan. Luoyang Jinguyuan Xin Mang shiqi bihua mu 洛阳金谷園新莽时期壁画墓. *WWZLCK* 9: 163-173, Pl. 9-10.

Luoyang 1990. Luoyangshi wenwu gongzuodui yidui 洛阳市文物工作队一队, Zhang Xiang 張湘. Luoyang xin faxiande Liang Han kongxin huaxiangzhuan 洛阳新发现的兩汉空心画像磚. *WW* 1990.2: 61-66.

Luoyang 1993. Luoyangshi dier wenwu gongzuodui 洛阳市第二文物工作队. Luoyang Qianjingtou Xi Han bihua mu fajue jianbao 洛阳淺井头西汉壁画墓发掘简报. *WW* 1993.5: 1-16, Col. Pl., Pl. 1-3.

Lutz, A. (ed.) 1986. *Dian: Ein versunkenes Königreich in China.* Kunming: Yunnansheng bowuguan/ Zurich: Museum Rietberg.

Ma Jianxi 马建熙1990. Qin gongdian yizhi huaxiang zhuan shijie 秦宫殿遗址画像砖试解. *KGYWW* 1990.5: 100-101.

Marazov, I. (ed.) 1998. *Ancient Gold: Wealth of the Thracians.* N.Y.: Harry N. Abrams, Inc..

Martynov, A. I. 1991. *The Ancient Art of Northern Asia.* D. B. and E. M. Shimkin (trans and eds). Urbana/Chicago: University of Illinois Press.

Mathieu, R. 1983. *Etude sur la mythologie et l'éthnologie de la Chine ancienne : traduction annotée du* Shanhai jing. Paris: Collège de France, Institut des hautes études chinoises.

Meister, M. W., M. A. Dhaky, and K. Deva (eds) 1988. *Encyclopaedia of Indian Temple Architecture. North India: Foundations of North Indian Style, ca. 250 BC-A.D. 1100.* Princeton: Princeton University Press, American Institute of Indian Studies.

Meljukova, A. I. 1989, *Stepi evropejskoj časti SSSR v skifo-sarmatskoe vremja*. Moscow: Nauka.

Minami Rosia 1991. *Minami Rosia kiba minzoku-no ihouten: herenizuma bunmei to no deai / The Treasures of the Nomadic Tribes in South Russia*. N.p.: Asahi Shinbun.

Minjaev, S. S. 1998. *Dyrestujskij mogil'nik*. Saint-Petersburg: Asiatic Fund.

Moorey, P. R. S. 1974. *Ancient Persian Bronzes in the Adam Collection.* London: Faber and Faber.

Moorey, P. R. S. 1999. *Ancient Mesopotamian Materials and Industries: The Archaeological Evidence.* Winona Lake, Indiana (USA): Eisenbrauns.

Mukerjee, B. N. 1969. *Nana on Lion.* Calcutta: The Asiatic Society.

Muscarella, O. W. 1988. *Bronze and Iron: Ancient Near Eastern Artifacts in the Metropolitan Museum of Art.* New York: The Metropolitan Museum of Art.

Nanjing 1956. Nanjing bowuyuan 南京博物院, Shandongsheng wenwuguan wenwuchu 山东省文物館文物處. *Yi'nan gu huaxiang shi mu fajue baogao* 沂南古画像石墓发掘報告. Shanghai: Wenhuabu wenwu guanliju.

Nanjing 1973. Nanjing bowuyuan. Jiangsu Lianshui Sanlidun Xi Han mu 江蘇连水三里墩西汉墓. *KG* 1973.2: 80-87, 89, Pl. 9-12.

Nanjing 1984. Nanjing bowuyuan, Peixian wenhuaguan 沛县文化馆. Dong Han Pengcheng xiang Miao Yu mu 东汉彭城相繆宇墓. *WW* 1984.8: 22-29.

Nanjing 2013. Nanjing bowuyuan, Xuyixian wenguang xinju 盱眙县文广新局. Jiangsu Xuyi Dayunshan Jiangdu wangling erhao mu fajue jianbao 江蘇盱眙大云山江都王陵二号墓发掘简报. *WW* 2013.1: 25-66, front cover.

Nanyang 1980. Nanyang diqu wenwudui 南阳地区文物队, Nanyang bowuyuan 南阳博物院. Tanghe Han Yuping Dayin Feng Jun ruren huaxiangshi mu 唐河汉鬱平大尹冯君孺人画像石墓. *KGXB* 1980.2: 239-262.

Nanyang 1984. Nanyang diqu wenwu gongzuodui 南阳地区文物工作队, Nanyangxian wenhuaguan 南阳县文化馆. Henan Nanyangxian Yingzhuang Han huaxiangshi mu 河南南阳县英庄汉画像石墓. *WW* 1984.3: 25-37.

Nanyang 1990. Nanyang wenwu yanjiusuo 南阳文物研究所. *Nanyang Handai huaxiangzhuan* 南阳汉代画像砖. Beijing: Wenwu.

Nebelsick, L. D. 2012. Scythian Eagles with Ionic Honeysuckle – Patterns of Iconographic Acculturation in the North Pontic Steppes during the 6th and 5th Centuries BC, in P. Anreiter, E. Bánffy, L. Bartosiewicz, W. Meid, and C. Metzner-Nebelsick (eds) *Archaeological, Cultural and Linguistic Heritage: Festschrift for Erzcébet Jerem in Honor of Her 70th Birthday*: 449-473. Budapest: Archaeolingua Foundation.

Neer, R. T. 1995. The Lion's Eye: Imitation and Uncertainty in Attic Red-Figure. *Representations* 51 (summer 1995): 118-153.

Neimenggu 1991. Neimenggu wenwu kaogu yanjiusuo 内蒙古文物考古研究所, Wulanchabu meng wenwu gongzuozhan 乌兰察布盟文物工作站. Liangchengxian Beiyingzi Hanmu fajue jianbao 涼城县北營子汉墓发掘简报. *NMGWWKG* 1991.1: 25-35, 10, Pl. 2-3.

Nickel, L. 2012. The Nanyue Silver Box. *Arts of Asia* 42.3: 98-107.

Nickel, L. 2013. The First Emperor and Sculpture in China. *Bulletin of the SOAS [School of Oriental and African Studies]* 76.3: 413-447.

Nikulina, N. M. 1994. *Iskusstvo Ionii i Axemenidskogo Irana.* Moscow: Iskusstvo.

Ningxia 1978. Ningxia Guyuanxian chutu wenwu宁夏固原县出土文物. *WW* 1978.12: 86-90.

Ningxia 1988a. Ningxia wenwu kaogu yanjiusuo 宁夏文物考古研究所, Tongxinxian wenguansuo 同心县文管所. Ningxia Tongxinxian Lijiataozi Xiongnu mu qingli jianbao 宁夏同心县李家套子匈奴墓清理简报. *KGYWW* 1988.3: 17-20.

Ningxia 1988b. Ningxia wenwu kaogu yanjiusuo, Zhongguo shehui kexueyuan kaogusuo Ningxia kaoguzu 中国社会科学院考古所宁夏考古组, Tongxinxian wenwu guanlisuo 同心县文物管理所. Ningxia Tongxin Daodunzi Xiongnu mudi 宁夏同心倒墩子匈好墓地. *KGXB* 1988.3: 333-356, Pl. 9-20.

Ningxia 1993. Ningxia wenwu kaogu yanjiusuo, Ningxia Guyuan bowuguan 宁夏固原博物馆. Ningxia Guyuan Yanglang qingtong wenhua mudi 宁夏固原杨郎青铜文化墓地. *KGXB* 1993.1: 13-56, Pl. 1-6.

Olbrycht, M. J. 2009. Mithridates VI Eupator and Iran, in J. Højte (ed.) *Mithridates VI and the Pontic Kingdom*: 163-190. Aarhus: Aarhus Universitetsforlag.

Osborne, R. 1996. *Greece in the Making 1200-479 BC*. London and New York: Routledge.

Pal, P. 1986. *Indian Sculpture, Vol. 1: circa 500 BC-A.D. 700*. Los Angeles: Los Angeles County Museum of Art.

Parrot, A. 1961. *The Arts of Assyria*. S. Gilbert and J. Emmons (trans) New York: Golden Press.

Parzinger, H. *et al.* 2008. *UNESCO Preservation of the Frozen Tombs of the Altai Mountains.* Paris: UN Educational, Scientific and Cultural Organization/Flanders Funds in Trust, March 2008; <whc.unesco.org/uploads/news/documents/news-433-1.pdf>, viewed 2 January 2012.

Pfrommer, M. 1993. *Metalwork from the Hellenized East: Catalogue of the Collections*. Malibu: The J. Paul Getty Museum.

Picikjan, I. R. 1991. *Kul'tura Baktrii: Axemenidskij i Ellinističeskij periody*. Moscow: Nauka.

Pingshuo 1987. Pingshuoxian kaogudui 平朔县考古队. Shanxi Shuoxian Qin Han mu fajue jianbao 山西朔县秦汉墓发掘简报. *WW* 1987.6: 1-52, Pl. 1-6.

Pirazzoli-t'Serstevens, M. 1994. Pour une archéologie des échanges: apports étrangers en Chine – transmission, réception, assimilation. *Arts Asiatiques* 49: 21-53.

Pirazzoli-t'Serstevens, M. 2008. Inner Asia and Han China: Borrowings and Representations, in Thomas Lawton (ed.) *New Frontiers in Global Archaeology: Defining China's Ancient Traditions.* (Proceedings of the International Symposium Celebrating the Tenth Anniversary of the Arthur M. Sackler Museum of Art and Archaeology at Peking University): 1-19. Tokyo: AMS Foundation for the Arts, Sciences and Humanities.

Polos'mak, N. V. 1994. *'Stereguščie zoloto grify' (Ak-Alaxinskie kurgany).* Novosibirsk: Nauka.

Pommerening, T., E. Marinova, and S. Hendrickx. 2010. The Early Dynastic Origin of the Water-lily Motif. *Chronique d'Egypte*, LXXXV, Fasc. 169-170: 14-40.

Poster, A. G. 1986. *From Indian Earth: 4,000 Years of Terracotta Art*. New York: The Brooklyn Museum.

Powers, M. J. 1991. *Art and Political Expression in Early China*. New Haven: Yale University Press.

Průšek, J. 1971. *Chinese Statelets and the Northern Barbarians 1400-300 BC*. New York: Humanities Press and Dordrecht (Holland): D. Reidel Publishing Co.

Psarras, S.-K. 1994. Exploring the North. *Monumenta Serica* 42: 1-125.

Psarras, S.-K. 1996. Pieces of Xiongnu Art. *Central Asiatic Journal* 40.2 (December 1996): 234-259.

Psarras, S.-K. 1997. The Han Far South. *Asiatische Studien* 51.3: 757-786.

Psarras, S.-K. 1998-1999. Shared Imagery: Eastern Zhou Décors and Iconographies. *Early China* 23-24: 1-88.

Psarras, S.-K. 1999. Upper Xiajiadian. *Monumenta Serica* XLVII: 1-126.

Psarras, S.-K. 2015. *Han Material Culture: An Archaeological Analysis and Vessel Typology*. New York: Cambridge University Press.

Psarras, S.-K. forthcoming. The Xiongnu and the West. *BMFEA* 79-80.

Psarras, S.-K. in preparation. Defining 'Xiongnu.'

Pugachenkova *et al.* 1996. Pugachenkova, G. A., S. R. Dar, R. C. Sharma, M. A. Joyenda, and H. Siddiqi. Kushan Art, in Harmatta, J (ed) 1996: 323-385.

Rapin, C. 1992. *Fouilles d'Aï Khanoum*, tome VIII: *La trésorerie du palais hellénistique d'Aï Khanoum. L'apogée et la chute du royaume grec de Bactriane*. Paris: Boccard.

Rawson, J. 1989. Chu Influences on the Development of Han bronze vessels. *Arts Asiatiques* 44: 84-99.

Rawson, J. 1990. *Western Zhou Ritual Bronzes from the Arthur M. Sackler Collections* (Ancient Chinese Bronzes in the Arthur M. Sackler Collections, Vol. IIA, B) Washington, DC: The Arthur M. Sackler Foundation; Cambridge, MA: The Arthur M. Sackler Museum, Harvard University.

Rawson, J. 1999. The Eternal Palaces of the Western Han: A New View of the Universe. *Artibus Asiae* Vol. LIX, Nos 1-2: 5-58.

Rawson, J. 2006. The Chinese Hill Censer, *boshan lu*: A Note on Origins, Influences and Meanings. *Arts Asiatiques* 61: 75-86.

Rawson, J. 2012. The Han Empire and its Northern Neighbours: the Fascination of the Exotic, in Lin, J. C. S. (ed.) 2012: 23-36.

Ray, N. 1975. *Maurya and Post-Maurya Art: A Study in Social and Formal Contrasts.* New Delhi: Indian Council of Historical Research.

Reeder, E. D. (ed.) 1999. *Scythian Gold: Treasures from Ancient Ukraine.* New York: Harry N. Abrams, Inc.

Rosenfield, J. M. 1993. *The Dynastic Arts of the Kushans.* Berkeley: University of California Press, 1967; New Delhi: Munshiram Manoharlal Publishers (1st Indian edition).

Rudenko, S. I. 1953. *Kul'tura naselenija Gornogo Altaja v Skifskoe vremja.* Moscow/Leningrad: Nauka.

Rudenko, S. I. 1962. *Kul'tura Xunnov i Noinulinskie kurgany.* Moscow and Leningrad: Izdatel'stvo Akademii Nauk SSSR.

Rudenko, S. I. 1969. *Die Kultur der Hsiung-nu und die Hügelgräber von Noin Ula.* H. Pollems (trans.) Bonn: Rudolf.

Rudenko, S. I. 1970. *Frozen Tombs of Siberia: The Pazyryk Burials of Iron Age Horsemen.* M. W. Thompson (trans.) London: J. M. Dent and Sons.

Sarianidi, V. S. 1985. *L'Or de la Bactriane.* G. de Gröer (trans.) Leningrad: Aurora.

Schiltz, V. 1994. *Les Scythes et les nomades des steppes. VIIIe siècle avant J.-C.-1er siècle après J.-C.* (L'Univers des formes) Paris: Gallimard.

Schlumberger, D. 1960a. Descendants non-méditerranéens de l'art grec. *Syria* Vol. 37, Nos 1-2: 131-166.

Schlumberger, D. 1960b. Descendants non-méditerranéens de l'art grec. *Syria* Vol. 37, Nos 3-4: 253-319.

Semionov, V. 1994. Au coeur de l'Asie: nouvelles découvertes d'époque scythe. *Les Dossiers d'archéologie* (*Les Scythes*) No. 194 (June 1994): 38-43.

Shaanxi 1959. Shaanxisheng bowuguan 陕西省博物馆, Shaanxisheng wenwu guanli weiyuanhui 陕西省文物管理委員会 (eds) *Shaanbei Dong Han huaxiang shike xuanji* 陕北东漢画像石刻選集. Beijing: Wenwu.

Shaanxi 1990. Shaanxisheng kaogu yanjiusuo Peihe jijian kaogudui 陕西省考古研究所配合基建考古队. Xi'an jingshuichang Hanmu qingli jianbao 西安淨水厂汉墓清理简报. *KGYWW* 1990.6: 46-58.

Shaanxi 2003a. Shaanxisheng kaogu yanjiusuo 陕西省考古研究所. Xi'an beijiao Zhanguo zhutong gongjiang mu fajue jianbao 西安北郊战国铸铜工匠墓发掘简报. *WW* 2003.9: 4-14.

Shaanxi 2003b. Shaanxisheng wenwuju 陕西省文物局, Zhonghua shijitan yishuguan 中华世记坛艺術馆 (eds) *Shengshi jijin:Shaanxi Baoji Meixian qingtongqi jiaocang* 盛世吉金: 陕西宝鸡眉县青铜器窖藏. Beijing: Beijing.

Shaanxi 2004. Shaanxisheng kaogu yanjiusuo 陕西省考古研究所 (ed.) *Qindu Xianyang kaogu baogao* 秦都咸阳考古報告. Beijing: Kexue.

Shaanxi 2016. Shaanxisheng kaogu yanjiuyuan 陕西省考古研究院, Baojishi kaogu yanjiusuo 宝鸡市考古研究所, Baojishi Weibinqu bowuguan 宝鸡市渭濱区博物馆. Shaanxi Baoji Shigushan Shang Zhou mudi M4 fajue jianbao 陕西宝鸡石鼓山商周墓地M4发掘简报. *WW* 2016.1: 4-52, front and back covers, inside and out.

Shandong 1958. Shandong Feicheng Han huaxiangshi mu diaocha 山东肥城汉画像石墓调查. *WWCKZL* 1958.4: 34-36.

Shandong 1982. Shandongsheng bowuguan 山东省博物馆, Shandongsheng wenwu kaogu yanjiusuo 山东省文物考古研究所. *Shandong Han huaxiangshi xuanji* 山东汉画像石选集. N.p.: Qilu.

Shandong 2000. Shandongsheng wenwu kaogu yanjiusuo 山东省文物考古研究所 (ed.) *Shandongsheng Gaosu gonglu kaogu baogao ji* 山东省高速公路考古发掘报告集. Beijing: Kexue.

Shandong 1985. Shandongsheng Ziboshi bowuguan 山东省淄博市博物馆. Xi Han Qiwang mu suizang qiwu keng 西汉齐王墓随葬器物坑. *KGXB* 1985.2: 222-266, Pl. 1-20.

Shanxi 1964. Shanxisheng wenwu guanli weiyuanhui 山西省文物管理委员会, Shanxisheng kaogu yanjiusuo 山西省考古研究所. Shanxi Changzhi Fenshuiling Zhanguo mu di'erci fajue 山西长治分水岭战国墓第二次发掘. *KG* 1964.3: 111-137, Pl. 1-8.

Shanxi 1980. Shanxisheng wenwu guanli weiyuanhui, Yanbei xingzheng gongshu wenhuaju 雁北行政公署文化局, Datongshi bowuguan 大同市博物馆. Shanxi Hunyuan Bicun Xi Han muguo mu 山西渾源畢村西汉木槨墓. *WW* 1980.6: 42-51, Pl. 1, 5.

Shanxi 1987. Shanxisheng kaogu yanjiusuo Houma gongzuozhan 山西省考古研究所侯马工作站. Jinguo Shigui zuofang yizhi jianbao 晋国石圭作坊遗址简报. *WW* 1987.6: 1-15.

Shanxi 1992. Shanxisheng kaogu yanjiusuo 山西省考古研究所, Lüliang diqu wenwu gongzuoshi 吕梁地区文物工作室, Lishixian wenwu guanlisuo 离石县文物管理所. Shanxi Lishi Mamaozhuang Dong Han huaxiangshi mu 山西离石马茂庄东汉画像石墓. *WW* 1992.4: 14-40.

Shanxi 1994. Shanxisheng kaogu yanjiusuo, Yuncheng diqu wenhuaju运城地区文化局, Xiaxian wenhuaju bowuguan 夏县文化局博物馆. Shanxi Xiaxian Wangcun Dong Han bihuamu 山西夏县王村东汉壁画墓. *WW* 1994.8: 34-46.

Shanxi 1996. Shanxisheng kaogu yanjiusuo, Lüliang diqu wenwu guanlichu吕梁地区文物管理处, Lishixian wenwu guanlisuo 离石县文物管理所. Shanxi Lishi zaici faxian Dong Han huaxiangshi mu 山西离石再次发现东汉画像石墓. *WW* 1996.4: 13-27.

Shanxi 2010. Shanxisheng kaogu yanjiusuo, Shanxi bowuyuan 山西博物院, Changzhishi bowuguan 长治市博物馆, Han Binghua 韩炳华, and Li Yong 李勇. *Changzhi Fenshuiling Dong Zhou mudi* 长治分水岭东周墓地. Beijing: Wenwu.

Sichuan 1974. Sichuansheng bowuguan 四川省博物馆, Chongqingshi bowuguan 重庆市博物馆, Fulingxian wenhuaguan 涪陵县文化馆. Sichuan Fuling diqu Xiaotianxi Zhanguo tukeng mu qingli jianbao 四川涪陵地区小田溪战国土坑墓清理简报. *WW* 1974.5: 61-80, Pl. 1-2.

Sichuan 1983. Sichuansheng wenwu guanli weiyuanhui 四川省文物管理委员会, Hu Changyu 胡昌钰. Chengdu Shiyang Xi Han muguo mu 成都石羊西汉木槨墓. *KGYWW* 1983.2: 26-27, Pl. 4.

Sideris, A. 2008. Achaemenid Toreutics in the Greek Periphery, in S. M. R. Darbandi and A. Zournatzi (eds) *Ancient Greece and Ancient Iran: Cross-Cultural Encounters: 1st International Conference, Athens, 11-13 November 2006*: 339-353. Athens: National Hellenic Research Foundation, Cultural Center of the Embassy of the Islamic Republic of Iran in Athens, Hellenic National Commission for UNESCO.

Smith, W. S. 1981. (revised and expanded by W. K. Simpson) *The Art and Architecture of Ancient Egypt* (Pelican History of Art) New Haven and London: Yale University Press (2nd edition; 1958, 1st printing).

Smithsonian 1964-1965. *7000 Years of Iranian Art*. Circulated by the Smithsonian Institution (Washington, DC).

So, J. 1980. New Departures in Eastern Zhou Bronze Designs: The Springs and Autumns Period, in Wen Fong (ed.) *The Great Bronze Age of China*: 251-301. New York: The Metropolitan Museum of Art/Alfred A. Knopf.

So, J. 1995. *Eastern Zhou Ritual Bronzes from the Arthur M. Sackler Collections* (Ancient Chinese Bronzes in the Arthur M. Sackler Collections, Vol. III) New York: Harry N. Abrams.

So, J. F. and Bunker, E. C. 1995. *Traders and Raiders on China's Northern Frontier*. Washington, DC: Arthur M. Sackler Gallery.

Sun Zhixin 1993. The Liangzhu Culture: Its Discovery and Its Jades. *Early China* 18: 1-40.

Sun, Zhixin J. (ed.) 2017. *Age of Empires: Art of the Qin and Han Dynasties*. New York: The Metropolitan Museum of Art.

Teng Rensheng 滕上生1991. *Chu qiqi yanjiu* 楚漆器研究. Hong Kong: The Woods.

Terenožkin, A. I. and B. N. Mozolevskij 1988. *Melitopol'skij kurgan*. Kiev: Naukova dumka.

Thote, A. 1996. Note sur la postérité du masque de Liangzhu à l'époque des Zhou orientaux. *Arts Asiatiques* 51: 60-72.

Thote, A. 1999. De quelques conventions picturales. Le char et ses représentations aux Ve-IVe siècles avant notre ère. *Etudes chinoises* Vol. XVIII, Nos 1-2 (Spring-Fall 1999): 179-220.

Thote, A. 2001. The Archaeology of Eastern Sichuan at the End of the Bronze Age (fifth to third century BC), in Bagley , R. (ed.) 2001: 203-251.

Tian Guangjin 田广金 and Guo Suxin 郭素新1986. *E'erduosishi qingtongqi* 鄂尔多斯式青铜器. Beijing: Wenwu.

Trever, C. 1932. *Excavations in Northern Mongolia (1924-1925)* (Memoirs of the Academy of the History of Material Culture III) Leningrad: J. Fedorov.

Trofimova, A. A. (ed.) 2007. *Greeks on the Black Sea: Ancient Art from the Hermitage*. Los Angeles: J. Paul Getty Museum.

Wang, E. Y. 2011. Ascend to Heaven or Stay in the Tomb? Paintings in Mawangdui Tomb 1 and the Virtual Ritual of Revival in Second-Century BCE. China, in A. J. Olberding and P. J. Ivanhoe (eds) *Mortality in Traditional Chinese Thought*: 37-84. Albany: State University of New York.

Wang, E. Y. 2012. Jouissance of Death? Han Sarcophagi from Sichuan and the Art of Physiological Alchemy. *Res* 61/62 (Springs-Autumns 2012): 152-166.

Wang Jianzhong 王建中 and Shan Xiushan 閃修山1990. *Nanyang liang Han huaxiang shi* 南阳兩汉画像石. Beijing: Wenwu.

Wang Baoxiang 王寶祥1964. Henan Xinye chutude Handai huaxiangzhuan 河南新野出土的汉代画像磚. *KG* 1964.2: 90-93.

Wang Buyi 王步毅1993. Anhui Suxian Chulan Han huaxiangshi mu 安徽宿县褚兰汉画像石墓. *KGXB* 1993.4: 515-549, Pl. 17-20.

Wang Renxiang 王仁湘1985. Daigou gailun 帶鉤该论. *KGXB* 1985.3: 267-312.

Wang Yu 王煜 2014. Nanyang Qilingang Han huaxiangshi mu tianxiangtu ji xiangguan wenti 南阳麒麟岗汉画像石墓天象图及相关问题. *KG* 2014.10: 68-80.

Watson, W. 1962. *Ancient Chinese Bronzes*. London: Faber and Faber.

Watson, W. 1974. *Ancient China: the Discoveries of Post Liberation Archaeology*. New York: Graphic Society.

Watson, W. 1995. *The Arts of China to AD 900* (The Pelican History of Art) New Haven and London: Yale University Press.

Weber, C. D. 1966a. Chinese Pictorial Bronze Vessels of the Late Chou Period. *Artibus Asiae* Vol. 28, Nos 2-3: 107-104, Figure 1-20.

Weber, C. D. 1966b. Chinese Pictorial Bronze Vessels of the Late Chou Period. *Artibus Asiae* Vol. 28, No. 2: 271-302, Figure 21-29.

Weber, C. D. 1967. Chinese Pictorial Bronze Vessels of the Late Chou Period. *Artibus Asiae* Vol. 29, Nos 2-3: 115-174, Figure 30-50.

Weber, C. D. 1968. Chinese Pictorial Bronze Vessels of the Late Chou Period. *Artibus Asiae* Vol. 30, Nos 2-3: 145-213, Figure 51-80.

Wei Zheng 韋正2002. Dong Han, liuchaode chaofu zang 东汉，六朝的朝服葬. *WW* 2002.3: 72-78.

Weiss, H. (ed.) 1985. *Ebla to Damascus: Art and Archaeology of Ancient Syria.* Washington, DC: Smithsonian Institution Traveling Exhibition Service.

Williams, D. and J. Ogden 1994. *Greek Gold*. New York: Abrams/The Metropolitan Museum.

Wu En 烏恩1981. Woguo beifang gudai dongwu wenshi 我国北方古代動物饰. *KGXB* 1981.1: 45-61, Pl. 3-6.

Wu Guo 2009. From Western Asia to the Tianshan Mountains: On the Early Iron Artefacts Found in Xinjiang, in Mei Jianjun and T. Rehren (eds) *Metallurgy and Civilization: Eurasia and Beyond. Proceedings of the 6th International Conference on the Beginnings of the Use of Metals and Alloys (BUMA VI)*: 107-115. London: Archetype.

Wu Hung 1984. A Sanpan Shan Chariot Ornament and the Xiangrui Design in Western Han Art. *Archives of Asian Art* 37: 38-59.

Wu Hung 1986. Buddhist Elements in Early Chinese Art (2nd and 3rd century AD). *Artibus Asiae* 47.3/4: 263-347.

Wu Hung 1987. Xiwang Mu, the Queen Mother of the West. *Orientations* (April): 24-33.

Wu Hung 1989. *The Wu Liang Shrine: The Ideology of Early Chinese Pictorial Art*. Stanford: Stanford University Press.

Wu Xiaolong 2017. *Material Culture, Power, and Identity in Ancient China*. Cambridge: Cambridge University Press.

Xiangyang 1982. Xiangyang diqu bowuguan 襄阳地区博物馆. Hubei Xiangyang Leigutai yihao mu fajue jianbao 湖北襄阳擂鼓台一号墓发掘简报. *KG* 1982.2: 147-154.

Xianyang 1979. Xianyangshi bowuguan 咸阳市博物馆. Shaanxi Xianyang Maquan Xi Han mu 陕西咸阳马泉西汉墓. *KG* 1979.2: 22-28, Pl. 4-5.

Xianyang 1982. Xianyangshi wenguanhui 咸阳市文管会, Xianyangshi bowuguan 咸阳市博物馆. Xianyangshi kongxinzhuan Han mu qingli jianbao 咸阳市空心砖汉墓清理简报. *KG* 1982.3: 225-235.

Xianyang 2005. Xianyangshi wenwu kaogu yanjiusuo 咸阳市文物考古研究所. *Renjiazui Qin mu* 任家咀秦墓. Beijing: Kexue.

Xinjiang 1981. Xinjiang shehui kexueyuan kaogu yanjiusuo 新疆社会科学院考古研究所. Xinjiang Alagou shuxue muguo mu fajue jianbao 新疆阿拉沟竖穴木椁墓发掘简报. *WW* 1981.1: 18-22, Pl. 8.

Xinjiang 1999. Xinjiang wenwu kaogu yanjiusuo 新疆文物考古研究所. Xinjiang Yulixian Yingpan mudi 15-hao mu fajue jianbao 新疆尉犁县營盤墓地15号墓发掘简报. *WW* 1999.1: 4-16, Col. Pl. 1-4, front and back covers (inside and out).

Xinjiang 2001. Xinjiang Weiwuer zizhiqu bowuguan 新疆維吾爾自治区博物馆, Xinjiang wenwu kaogu yanjiusuo 新疆文物考古研究所. *Zhongguo Xinjiang Shanpula: gudai Yutian wenmingde jieshi yu yanjiu* 中国新疆山普拉：古代于闐文明的揭示與研究/*Sampula in Xinjiang of China: Revelation and Study of Ancient Khotan Civilization*. Urumqi: Xinjiang renmin.

Xu, J. (ed.) 2017. *Tomb Treasures: New Discoveries from China's Han Dynasty*. San Francisco: Asian Art Museum.

Xuzhou 1985. Xuzhoushi bowuguan 徐州市博物館. *Xuzhou Han huaxiangshi* 徐州漢畫像石. Nanjing: Jiangsu meishu.

Xuzhou 1997. Xuzhoushi bowuguan. Xuzhou Xi Han Wanquhou Liu Zhi mu 徐州西汉宛朐侯刘执墓. *WW* 1997.2: 4-21, inside front cover, back cover.

Xuzhou 1999. Xuzhoushi bowuguan. Xuzhou Dongdianzi Xi Han mu 徐州东甸子西汉墓. *WW* 1999.12: 4-18.

Yang Jianhua 楊建華 2004. *Chunqiu Zhanguo shiqi Zhongguo beifang wenhuadaide xingcheng* 春秋战国时期中国北方文化帶的形成. Beijing: Wenwu.

Yangzhou 1988. Yangzhou bowuguan 揚州博物馆. Jiangsu Hanjiang Yaozhuang 101-hao Xi Han mu 江蘇邗江姚庄101号西汉墓. *WW* 1988.2: 19-43, Pl. 4-7.

Yangzhou 1991. Yangzhou bowuguan, Hanjiangxian tushuguan 邗江县图书馆. Jiangsu Hanjiangxian Yangshouxiang Baonüdun Xin Mang mu 江蘇邗江县杨寿鄉宝女墩新莽墓. *WW* 1991.10: 39-61.

Yichang 1991. Yichang diqu bowuguan 宜昌地区博物馆, Dangyangshi bowuguan 當阳市博物馆. Hubei Dangyang Banyue Dong Han mu fajue jianbao 湖北當阳半月东汉墓发掘简报. *WW* 1991.12: 66-72.

Yikezhao 1991. Yikezhaomeng wenwu gongzuozhan 伊克昭盟文物工作站. Neimenggu Dongshengshi Nianfangqu faxian jin yin qi jiaozang 内蒙古东勝市碾房渠发现金銀器窖藏. *KG* 1991.5: 405-408, 398, Pl. 4.

Yikezhao 1992. Yikezhaomeng wenwu gongzuozhan. Yijinhuoluoqi Shihuigou faxiande E'erduosishi wenwu 伊金霍洛旗石灰沟发现的鄂尔多斯式文物. *NMGWWKG* 1992.1-2: 91-96.

Yin Zenghuai 尹增准 and Jiang Feng 江楓2010. Jiangsu Sihong Caomiao chutude Dong Han huaxiangshi 江蘇泗洪曹庙出土的东汉画像石. *WW* 2010.6: 66-74.

Young, R. S. *et al.* 1981. *The Gordion Excavations Final Reports*, Vol. 1: *Three Great Early Tumuli*. Philadelphia: The University Museum (University of Pennsylvania).

Yunnan 1962. Yunnansheng wenwu gongzuodui 云南省文物工作队. Yunnan Zhaotong Guijiayuanzi Dong Han mu fajue 云南昭通桂家院子东汉墓发掘. *KG* 1962.8: 395-399, Pl. 4.

Yunnan 1975. Yunnansheng bowuguan 云南省博物馆. Yunnan Jiangchuan Lijiashan gumuqun fajue baogao 云南江川李家山古墓群发掘報告. *KGXB* 1975.2: 97-156, Pl. 1-20.

Zhang Zhenglang 張政烺, Fu Juyou 傅舉有, and Chen Songchang 陳松報1992. *Mawangdui Han mu wenwu* 馬王堆汉墓文物/*The Cultural Relics Unearthed from the Han Tombs at Mawangdui*. Zhou Shiyi 周士一 and Chen Kefeng 陳可風(trans) Changsha: Hunan.

Zhang Weixing 张卫星2002. Qin Shihuang ling baixiyongde caihui wenshi 秦始皇陵百戲俑的彩绘纹饰. *WW* 2002.3: 65-71.

Zhejiang 1989. Zhejiangsheng wenwu kaogu yanjiusuo 浙江省文物考古研究所, Shanghai shi wenwu guanli weiyuanhui 上海市文物管理委員会, Nanjing bowoyuan 南京博物院. *Liangzhu wenhua yuqi* 良渚文化玉器. Beijing: Wenwu and Hong Kong: The Woods 兩木.

Zheng Long 郑隆1961. Neimenggu Zhalainuoer gumuqun diaochaji 内蒙古扎賚諾尔古墓群调查纪. *WW* 1961.9: 16-19.

Zhengzhou 1972. Zhengzhoushi bowuguan郑州市博物馆, Tang Xinghuang 唐杏煌. Zhengzhou Xintongqiao Handai huaxiang kongxin zhuan mu郑州新通橋汉代画像空心砖墓. *WW* 1972.10: 41-49.

Zhang Liangren 2011. Chinese Lacquerwares *(sic.)* from Begram: Date and Provenance. *International Journal of Asian Studies* Vol. 8, No. 1: 1-24.

Zhao Deyun 赵德云2016. *Xi Zhou zhi Han Jin shiqi Zhongguo wailai zhushi yanjiu* 西周至汉晋时期中国外来珠饰研究. Beijing: Kexue.

Zhong Xiaoqing 钟晓青1999. Wei Jin nanbeichao jianzhu zhuangshi yanjiu 魏晋南北朝建筑装饰研究. *WW* 1999.12: 52-65.

Zhongguo 1976. *Zhongguo gu qingtongqi xuan*中國古青銅器選. Beijing: Wenwu.

Zhongguo 1993. Zhongguo wenwu jinghua bianji weiyuanhui 中國精華編輯委員會 (ed.) *Zhongguo wenwu jinghua* 中國精華 *1993*. Beijing: Wenwu.

Zhongguo 2000. Zhongguo huaxiangshi quanji bianji weiyuanhui 中國畫像石全集編輯委員會 (ed.) *Zhongguo huaxiangshi quanji* 中國畫像石全集, Vol. 1: *Shandong Han huaxiangshi*山東漢畫像石 (Zhongguo meishu fenlei quanji中國美術分類全集) Zhengzhou: Henan meishu.

Zhongguo kexueyuan 1959. Zhongguo kexueyuan kaogu yanjiusuo 中國科学院考古研究所. *Luoyang Shaogou Han mu* 洛陽燒溝漢墓. Beijing: Kexue.

Zhongguo meishu 1988. Zhongguo meishu quanji bianji weiyuanhui 中國美術全集編輯委員會 (ed.) *Huihua* 繪畫, Vol. 18: *Huaxiangshi huaxiangzhuan* 畫像石畫像磚 (Zhongguo meishu quanji 中國美術全集) Shanghai: Shanghai renmin meishu.

Zhongguo meishu 1992. Zhongguo meishu quanji bianji weiyuanhui (ed.), Li Xueqin 李學勤, Editor-in-Chief. *Qingtongqi* 青銅器 *(xia* 下) (Zhongguo meishu quanji, Vol. 5) Beijing: Wenwu (2nd printing; 1986, 1st printing).

Zhongguo qingtongqi 1994. Zhongguo qingtongqi quanji bianji weiyuanhui 中國青銅器全集編輯委員會 (ed.) *Zhongguo qingtongqi quanji* 中國青銅器全集, Vol. 13: *Ba Shu* 巴蜀 (Zhongguo meishu fenlei quanji 中國美術分類全集) Beijing: Wenwu.

Zhongguo qingtongqi 1995. Zhongguo qingtongqi quanji bianji weiyuanhui (ed.) *Zhongguo qingtongqi quanji*, Vol. 8: *Dong Zhou* 東周, part 2 (Zhongguo meishu fenlei quanji) Beijing: Wenwu.

Zhongguo qingtongqi 1998. Zhongguo qingtongqi bianji weiyuanhui (ed.) *Zhongguo qingtongqi quanji*, Vol. 12: *Qin-Han* 秦漢 (Zhongguo meishu fenlei quanji) Beijing: Wenwu.

Zhongguo shehui kexueyuan 1980. Zhongguo shehui kexueyuan kaogu yanjiusuo 中国社会科学院考古研究所, Hebeisheng wenwu guanlichu 河北省文物管理处. *Mancheng Han mu fajue baogao* 满城汉墓发掘報告. 2 vols. Beijing: Wenwu.

Zhongguo shehui kexueyuan 1981. Zhongguo shehui kexueyuan kaogu yanjiusuo dongbei gongzuodui 中国社会科学院考古研究所东北工作队. Neimenggu Ningchengxian Nanshan'gen 102-hao shiguo mu 内蒙古宁城县102号石椁墓. *KG* 1981.4: 304-308, Pl. 7.

Zhongguo taoci 2000. Zhongguo taoci quanji bianji weiyuanhui 中國陶瓷全集編輯委員會, ed. *Zhongguo taoci quanji* 中國陶瓷全集*/ The Complete Works of Chinese Ceramics*. Vol. 3: *Qin Han* 秦漢 (*Zhongguo meishu fenlei quanji* 中國美術分類全集) Shanghai: Shanghai renmin meishu.

Zhonghua 1973. Zhonghua renmin gongheguo chutu wenwu zhanlan gongzuo weiyuanhui 中華人民共和國出土文物展覽工作委員會, (ed.) *Zhonghua renmin gongheguo chutu wenwu zhanlan zhanpin xuanji*中華人民共和國出土文物展覽展品選集. Beijing: Wenwu.

Zhongshan 1984. *Zhongshan: tombes des rois oubliés*. Paris: Ministère des relations extérieures, Association Française d'Action Artistique.

Zhou Dao 周到, Lü Pin 吕品, and Tang Wenxing汤文兴 1985. *Henan Handai huaxiangzhuan* 河南汉代画像砖. Shanghai: Shanghai renmin meishu.

Zhu Jieyuan 朱捷元 and Li Yuzheng 李域铮1983. Xi'an dongjiao Sandiancun Xi Han mu 西安东郊三店村西汉墓. *KGYWW* 1938.2: 22-25, Pl. 5-7.

Zhu Xilu 朱锡禄1992. *Jiaxiang Han huaxiangshi* 嘉祥漢畫像石. Ji'nan: Shandong meishu.

Zoucheng 1994. Zoucheng shi wenwu guanlisuo 枣城市文物管理所. Shandong Zoucheng Gaolicun Handai huaxiangshi mu 山东枣城高李村汉代画像石墓. *WW* 1994.6: 24-40.

Index

acanthus, 66

Achaemenid, ix, 6, 13, 26, 32, 34–35, 48, 57–60, 67, 69–70, 76

Aegean, 57, 61, 67

Afghanistan, 6, 18, 26, 30

Aï Khanoum, 26, 30, 70

Alexander the Great, *see also Hellenistic*, 6, 76

Altai, 6, 16, 57–60, 67–68

Aluchaideng, 46, 50, 58, 100, 103, 107

anguiped, 25–27

animal combat, 25, 27–28, 33, 45–48, 51

animal master, 5–6, 14–15, 17–30, 37–42, 45–48, 50, 57, 75–76

animal predation, 4–6, 14, 18–19, 22, 45–53, 57–58, 75–76

 dead prey, 45, 49–50

 live prey, 14, 45–51, 58

 multiple-predator, 51

 predator, 4, 14, 29, 45–53

 prey retaliates, 45

animal sacrifice, 18

animal throne, 23–24, 40

animal-headed, 21, 25

animal-human/-humanoid, 20, 25

antlers, 16, 21, 40, 52, 60, 72–73

Api, 27

Apollo, 48

Archaic period, 33

architectonic tombs, 3–4, 11

aristocratic residences, 3

Artemis, 24, 30

Aržan, 68

Ashur, 38–39

Atchana, 43

Atlas, 40

Attic, 33

attributes, 4, 19, 21

Bactria (Bactrian), 6, 23–24, 26, 31–32, 35, 41, 57–59, 65, 68, 75–76

bas reliefs, 2, 15, 20–23, 25–28, 31–32, 37–40, 42–43, 49, 51, 53, 58–59, 71–72, 86–91, 94, 97, 99, 102, 105, 108–109, 111, 118

battle scenes, 33, 44

bear, 16, 34, 70, 76

bird, 15–16, 18, 20–21, 23–24, 39, 45–48, 51–53, 60, 65, 72

 antlered birds, 52

 crested bird, 52

bird heads, 16, 52–53, 60

black-glazed ware, 33

blossoms, 66, 73

boar, 32, 35, 50

boshanlu, 5, 19, 42, 84

braid, *see also rope*, 12–13

Buddhism, 2, 5–6, 23, 26, 30–31, 37, 40–41, 75–76

bull, 18, 26, 37, 43, 45

Burjatija, 45, 51, 62

Central Asia, 6, 14, 26, 44, 46, 75–76

chimaera, 58

Chu, 19, 21, 52, 65

Classical, ix, 32, 57, 61

 Classical period, 32

clouds, 1, 15–16, 20, 43

'cloud' pattern, *see meander*, 1

Commagene, 62

coneflower, 71

constellations, 43

cost, 3, 7

Cretan, 66, 110

Cycladic, 62
deer, 32, 37–38, 40, 45–48, 50, 52, 59, 72–73
deities, *see also immortals*, 1, 4–5, 14, 17, 21–23, 25–31, 30, 37, 41, 59
 primordial deities, 23
Delphi, 48
double twist, 39
double-headed horse, 59
dragon, 14, 23–24, 26–27, 38, 40, 47, 50, 70
eagle, 27, 45, 57–58, 110
Eastern Zhou, vii, 1–2, 4–5, 7, 11–23, 26, 28–29, 31, 37, 39, 41–43, 46, 48, 50, 61, 64–66, 69–70, 75–76
egg-and-dart, 17
Egypt, viii, 5–6, 25, 31–32, 48, 57, 61, 63, 67, 71, 76
embossed, 69
embroidery, 42, 68
enthroned, 22–23, 26, 29, 47
entwined, 23–24, 49–51, 72
 entwined branches, 72
 entwined necks, 49
Etruscan, 33
fantastic, 7, 15, 21, 57–60
 fantastic animals, 15, 21
feline, 4–5, 18, 23, 28–29, 45–49, 51–52, 58–59
figural, 2–4, 7, 11, 14–17, 34, 51, 62
figured, 29, 110
flames, *see also kavaem khvareno*, 31, 41
fleur-de-lis, 66–67, 69
floral, 4–5, 11, 51, 64–70, 73, 75–76
 floral frieze, 51
flowering tree, 37
flowers, 63, 66, 71
 buds, 66
 cinqfoil, 64
 daisy, 70–71, 73
 peony, 71
 trefoils, 66
 tulip, 66
 water lily, 71
flying gallop, 31–32
foliage, 63, 71–72
full frontal, 28, 34–35
full rear, 35
Fuxi, 23–26
Gandhara, 26
Gaozhuang, 18–21, 29–30, 34, 38, 41–42, 83, 85
garlic, 69
genii, 5, 20
geometric, ix, 3, 11–12, 14, 51, 63, 65
goat, 4, 37–39
godroon, 69–70
Gondla, 35
Greco-Persian, 64
Greece, ix, 6, 13–14, 24, 26–28, 30, 32–35, 40, 44, 48, 57, 61, 63–65, 67, 70–72, 75–76, 93, 106, 110, 119
griffin, 33, 45, 57–59, 69
halo, *see also kavaem khvareno,* 30–31
Han Far South, 43
Hatra, 62
heart, *see also ivy*, 61, 63
Hellenic, 58, 68
Hellenism, 65, 76
Hellenistic, ix, 5, 13, 26, 30, 44, 57, 59, 61–62, 64–66, 68–71, 73, 75–76
Hellenized, 26, 35, 37, 41, 68, 70
heraldic, 24, 30, 38
hero, 27, 37
Hindu, 26
hollow bricks, 12, 39–40, 51
hoofed animal, 4–5, 32
horse, 4, 24, 29–35, 40, 45–46, 49, 51, 58–60
 unhitched horse, 40
human-animal, 19, 21
human-headed lion, 57

humanoid, 4–5, 16–21, 25, 40–42
hunt, 18, 22–23, 29, 32
hunting, 4, 17–19, 21–22, 27–35, 37, 42–44, 46
hybrids, 11, 18–21, 23–26, 41, 47, 59
 primordial hybrid, 23
immortals, *see also deities, xian*, 19, 21, 31, 39, 41–42
India, 6, 13–14, 23, 25, 35, 37, 62, 64–65, 68, 70, 75–76
Inner Mongolia, 6, 18, 46, 50, 58, 95, 100, 103, 107
interlace, 26, 39, 51, 65–66
inverted hindquarters, 60
Ionian, 34, 119
Iran, 6, 17, 20, 30, 43, 82, 98
Iraq, 6, 20, 24, 26, 37–38, 40, 45, 62
Islamic, 30
Issyk, 72
ivy, *see also heart*, 61–64
kavaem khvareno ('flaming shoulders,' flaming halo), *see also flames*, 30–31, 41
Kazakhstan, 20, 73
Khaltchayan, 32
kidneys, *see also tear*, 66, 68–70
King Father of the East, 5, 22, 25, 29, 31, 41
King of Nanyue, 16, 33, 68
Kushan, 23, 26, 30, 59, 71–72
landscape, 21, 23, 29, 37, 42–43
leaf, 12, 30, 39, 41, 61–63, 66–67 , 70, 73
 weeping leaves, 39, 41
Lijialou, 21, 39, 43, 47
lion, 18, 23–24, 37, 45, 57–59, 69
Liulige, 20, 27, 29–30, 38–39, 46–47, 52, 87, 95
Liulihe, 65
Liyu, 18, 47
lizard, 23, 27
lotus, 41, 61, 66–67, 71–72
lozenge, 12
Luristan, 49
Macedonian, 76
man-animal combat, 25, 27–28, 33
Mancheng, 5, 16, 19, 21, 39, 41–42, 52, 70, 84, 95, 105
Mari, 72
Marquis of Haihun, 24, 42, 50
Marquis Yi of Zeng, 19, 21
Mashan, 4, 65–66, 68–70, 73, 115–117
Mathura, 40
Mawangdui, 3–5, 15, 17, 19–21, 43, 81
meander, *see also vines*, 1, 5, 14–16, 20–23,26, 31, 33, 39, 42–43, 51, 73
Mede, 32
Mediterranean, 5, 77
Mesopotamia, ix, 6, 72
Minoan, 31–32
Mitanni, 43, 72
money trees, 5, 31, 71
Mongolia, 6, 18, 42–43, 46, 50, 58, 62, 64, 73, 95, 97, 100, 103, 107, 112
moon, 24
mountains, 5, 15, 29, 37–39, 41–44, 51
 scale-form, 37, 43
multiple heads, 53
murals, 2–4, 11–12, 15–16, 33–34
mushroom, 41
Mycenaean, 66
Nana/Nanaia, 24
Nanyue, 16, 33, 68
narrative, 2–4, 11–12, 17, 30, 33–34, 37
naturalism, 57, 72, 75–76
Near East, 5, 12–14, 17, 20, 23, 26, 28–32, 37, 40, 43–46, 57, 59, 61, 67, 71, 75–77, 113
Neo-Assyrian, ix, 20, 23, 37–38, 62, 66–69, 71, 86
Nineveh, 38
Ningxia, 28, 35, 48, 60, 91, 109
Nippur, 40
nomad, 32–34

non-Chinese, 14, 20, 28–29, 31, 33, 47, 49, 62, 65, 67, 75
Noyon Uul, 42–43, 62, 64, 73, 97, 112
Nüwa, 23–26
Nuzi painted pottery, 43
Oxus, 44, 48, 58–59, 69
paintings, 2–3, 16, 19, 25, 31–32, 34, 43, 71, 117
Pakistan, 13, 26, 48, 64
palmette, 66–67
papyrus, 61, 66–67, 71
paradise, 3, 5, 7, 11, 14, 17, 22, 25, 28, 30–31, 33, 39, 42–43, 57, 61, 73, 75
Parthian, 31–32, 37, 48, 62, 70–71, 113
  Parthian shot, 31–32
Pazyryk, 6, 16, 32, 50, 58–60, 67, 107–108
Persia, viii, 6, 13, 26, 28, 57, 63–65, 67, 69, 76, 113
perspective, 34–35
Phrygian bonnet, 33
plant, 5, 19, 21, 39, 41, 57, 61, 73
priest, 27
Pu-abi, 37–39, 42–43
Punjab, 35
putti, 42
Qin, vii, 1, 3–4, 7, 11–12, 19–20, 34, 39, 69–70
  Qin palaces, 3–4, 12, 19–20, 34, 39
Qinglongshan, 32–33, 42–44, 97
quatrefoil, *see also rosettes*, 61–63, 66, 69, 75
  cruciform quatrefoil, 69
  Zhou quatrefoil, 61–62, 66, 69, 75
Queen Mother of the West, 5, 22–26, 29–31, 40–42, 47
rabbit, 21, 24, 32
ram, 46
red figure ware, 33
rhomboids, *see also lozenge, zigzag*, 12, 62
ritual, 1–2, 4, 11, 17, 30, 76
  ritual activities, 4
  ritual vessel, 1–2, 11
rope, *see also braid*, 12–14, 17–18
rosettes, 42, 61–64, 67–68, 70–71
  quatrefoil rosette, 61, 63, 66
sacred, 17–18, 21–23, 29–30
Sanci, 37, 72
Sarmatian, 28, 38, 51, 68, 80
Sasanian, 44
Scylla, 26–27
Scythian, 13, 27–28, 33, 35, 45, 52, 59, 65, 70, 80
secular, 28–30, 43
serpent, 26–27, 41, 50
  sea serpent, 27
Shang, vii, 12, 15
Shaogou, 50, 101
Shuihudi, 34, 49, 99
Shunga, 70–71
Siberia, 6, 14, 32, 58, 62, 72
  south Siberia, *see also Burjatija*, 6, 62
silk, 3–4, 19, 21, 115–117
snake, *see also serpent*, 15, 20–21, 23–27, 39, 41, 46, 48
  snake-bodied, 21, 25
Sogdiana, 24
sphinx, 26, 53, 57–59
Springs and Autumns, vii, 12, 14, 16, 19, 21, 38, 46–47, 52, 61, 63–64, 66, 75–76
stamped brick, 2–3, 12, 14, 23–24, 28–29, 32–33, 39, 41, 44, 51, 58, 70–71, 85, 90, 112
stars, 66
steppe, 4–6, 13–14, 16, 20, 27–28, 32, 34–35, 37–38, 43–48, 50–52, 57–58, 60, 65–70, 72–73, 75–76
Suide, 15, 21–23, 41, 88–89, 91
sun, 24
Susa, 69
Syria, 6, 20, 32, 43, 72
Tajikistan, 6, 24, 44, 48

Taxila, 48
tear, *see also kidney*, 66, 68–70
tendrils, 1, 31
three quarter view, 33–35
throne, 23–24, 40–41
    lion throne, 23
    mushroom thrones, 41
    lotus throne, 41
    plant throne, 41
    tree-like thrones, 41
thunderbolts, 4
tiger, 23, 27–28, 33–34, 38, 40, 45–49, 50–51, 58
Tillia-tepe, 18, 24, 28, 50–51, 62, 64, 66–68
traceries, 16, 64–65
tree, 5–6, 14, 20, 28–29, 31, 37–46, 48, 50–52, 57, 63, 71–73, 75
    twisted tree, 72
    volute tree, 72
tree of life, 5–6, 14, 20, 37–42, 44–46, 48, 50–52, 57, 75
Turkey, 43, 62
Tutankhamun, 71
Tuva, 60, 68
twisted helix, 46
umbrellas, 72
Ur, ix, 26, 37
Uruk, 24
Uzbekistan, 6, 32
vegetal, *see also plant*, 5, 15, 23, 31, 38–39, 73
vine, *see also meanders*, 15–16, 42, 63
Wang Deyuan, 21
Warring States, vii, 1, 12, 14, 16, 18–19, 30, 34, 41, 47–48, 50, 52, 58, 60–61, 63–71, 75–76, 114
warrior, 28, 32, 34
Western, vii–viii, 3, 5–7, 14–15, 19–20, 25, 28, 31, 33, 45–46, 48, 57, 61, 63–68, 75–76, 98
Western Regions, 6
Western Zhou, vii, 46, 63, 65
wheel, 40
winged animals, 57
Wu family shrines, 16, 25–26, 40, 52, 59, 71–73, 108
Wuhuan, 34
xian, see also immortals, 19–24, 27–28, 31, 33, 41, 46–47
Xianbei, 18, 34, 38, 40, 58, 67, 72–73, 95
Xichagou, 28, 34–35, 72–73, 94
Xinjiang, 6, 37, 60, 68, 71
Xinzhuangtou, 50
Xiongnu, 6, 16, 28–29, 33–35, 38, 40, 46, 48–50, 52, 58, 67, 72–73, 91, 94, 99–100, 103, 107
Yi'nan, 15, 59
Yuezhi, 32
Zeus-Mithra, 30
Zhongshan, 47, 58–59, 64
zigzag, *see also lozenge*, 62–63